Youth in Postwar
Guatemala

D1713373

The Rutgers Series in Childhood Studies

The Rutgers Series in Childhood Studies is dedicated to increasing our understanding of children and childhoods throughout the world, reflecting a perspective that highlights cultural dimensions of the human experience. The books in this series are intended for students, scholars, practitioners, and those who formulate policies that affect children's everyday lives and futures.

Edited by
Jill E. Korbin, Associate Dean, College of Arts and Sciences; Professor, Department of Anthropology; Director, Schubert Center for Child Studies; Co-Director, Childhood Studies Program, Case Western Reserve University

Elisa (EJ) Sobo, Professor of Anthropology, San Diego State University

Editorial Board
Mara Buchbinder, Assistant Professor, Department of Social Medicine, University of North Carolina, Chapel Hill

Meghan Halley, Assistant Scientist, Palo Alto Medical Foundation

David Lancy, Emeritus Professor of Anthropology, Utah State University

Heather Montgomery, Reader, Anthropology of Childhood, Open University (UK)

David Rosen, Professor of Anthropology & Sociology, Fairleigh Dickinson University

Rachael Stryker, Assistant Professor of Department of Human Development & Women's Studies, California State University, East Bay

Tom Weisner, Professor of Anthropology, University of California, Los Angeles

Founding Editor: Myra Bluebond-Langner, UCL-Institute of Child Health

For a list of all the titles in the series, please see the last page of the book.

Youth in Postwar Guatemala

Education and Civic Identity in Transition

MICHELLE J. BELLINO

Rutgers University Press

New Brunswick, Camden, and Newark, New Jersey, and London

978-0-8135-8799-8 (paper)
978-0-8135-8800-1 (hardcover)
978-0-8135-8801-8 (e-book (epub))
978-0-8135-8802-5 (e-book (web pdf))
978-0-8135-9089-9 (e-book (mobi))

Cataloguing-in-Publication data is available from the Library of Congress.

A British Cataloging-in-Publication record for this book is available from the British Library.

Copyright © 2017 by Michelle J. Bellino
All rights reserved
No part of this book may be reproduced or utilized in any form or by any means, electronic
or mechanical, or by any information storage and retrieval system, without written permission from the publisher. Please contact Rutgers University Press, 106 Somerset Street, New
Brunswick, NJ 08901. The only exception to this prohibition is "fair use" as defined by U.S.
copyright law.

∞ The paper used in this publication meets the requirements of the American National Stan-
dard for Information Sciences—Permanence of Paper for Printed Library Materials, ANSI
Z39.48-1992.

www.rutgersuniversitypress.org

Manufactured in the United States of America

Contents

Youth in Postwar Guatemala

1

Citizen, Interrupted

Carlos was the first *guerrillero* I met.[1] I stared at his small body from across the room with a mixture of awe and fear before working up the nerve to talk to him. His nephew Marco, who was too young to be a guerrillero during the war, beamed as he introduced us. He presented me as a student and Carlos as an ex-guerrillero, an identity I had assumed was to be kept secret. Carlos was quick to remind me that there was no such thing as an ex-guerrillero. They were guerrillas for life. Carlos said I could ask him anything, but it took time before it felt right to tread into his past. I told him about what I was doing in Guatemala, explaining my interest in education and the ways that young people were learning about the civil war. This was usually enough to show that I knew something about Guatemala's history and cared about its future. We soon dipped into the sardonic space of contemporary "postwar" Guatemala, which invited bitter declarations from around the room that life was more insecure now than during the war. It was different, but the same. Clumsily curling my fingers into quotes around "postwar" often earned me the added respect that I knew something about Guatemala's present. I initially saw this gesture as overtly political and somewhat risky, but soon came to realize that everyone was dissatisfied by the postwar. No matter who they were, and no matter what this history meant to them, the war's aftermath held everyone captive.

After the peace process, Carlos moved to Villa Nueva, one of the most dangerous neighborhoods in Guatemala City today. It took him almost a decade to return to his family home in Quiché. At first no one there remembered him. They looked straight into his eyes but still needed to hear his family lineage before placing him in the community. He laughed and explained that many of them remarked, "We thought you were dead." Not being remembered was one thing. It had been a long time, he reasoned, and he had grown up, looked different from the boy from the *pueblo* they once knew. But what really got him about going home was coming face-to-face with what he had lost in exchange for what his people had gained. He explained, "When I return to my village, I see what I fought for. I fought for roads for my people. I fought for schools for my children. I fought for the voice of the humble people. . . . [Today] they have put in roads, but the roads lead nowhere. They have put in schools, but there are no teachers and no books. There are community spaces but no community." When I asked Carlos if he would one day let his young children join the *lucha* (struggle), he made a long, drawn-out *noooo*. He told me that to struggle was hard, lonely work. He was cold and wet and hungry all the time. He shivered and said something about suffering alone even though the struggle was bigger than he was. Several times he said, "I struggled so my children would not have to." Over the years Carlos has continued to wrestle with his desire to grant his children a peaceful future even if it means filing away the past and his open recognition that little has changed, that there remains much left to fight for.

By evening that first night we met in the Highlands, the men began drinking and Carlos's wife, Tania, nudged me into a small bedroom, where the children were watching television. She explained, "When they drink, the stories come." The stories were war memories, flashes of "things they did" and "things that had been done to them." It was better this way, she said. Better to let them drink and remember the pain than to stay silent. In the morning it would be like it never happened. "You will see," she said. And I did.

Praise and Critique in the Postwar

Transitional justice processes are regularly shaped by and for those who survive mass violence, but it is often postwar generations that expose the strengths and weaknesses of particular forms of reckoning and the decisions made in pursuit of the better postwar future (E. Cole, 2007a; Jelin, 2003; Murphy, in press).[2] As Carlos explained, wars are often fought in pursuit of future opportunities, struggles taken on so that the next generation will not have to. But the flawed realities that postgenerations encounter may radically undermine the hope that survivor generations invested in the better future. These flaws also speak to the intergenerational nature of historical injustice and the fiction constructed around peace as a "single line in time" (Lederach, 2005, p. 43).

From 1960 to 1996 Guatemala experienced one of the most brutal civil wars in Latin America's history, called the Conflicto Armado, the "Armed Conflict."[3] Though the principal actors featured in history books are the state military and several guerrilla groups, various sectors of civil society became willful or unwitting perpetrators or targets of violence that at times appeared selective and other times gave way to indiscriminate repression. Nevertheless, the vast majority of victims of torture, rape, kidnapping, disappearance, displacement, and death were indigenous civilians, unaffiliated with either the state or the guerrilla movement (Comisión para el Esclarecimiento Histórico [CEH], 1999). The truth commission that investigated the conflict determined that atrocities committed by state forces included ethnic genocide in their intentional targeting of indigenous peoples. During the course of thirty-six years of conflict, over one million Guatemalans fled to Mexico and other Central American countries, seeking refugee status. Thousands of others hid in the mountains and starved to death.

Nearly two decades after peace negotiations, Guatemala's postwar society is hardly at peace. The country ranks as one of the most dangerous places in the world, exhibiting homicide rates four times greater than what the World Health Organization considers "epidemic."[4] A majority of young people endure both poverty and existential insecurity, while facing a profound lack of opportunities to be educated, to find work in the formal sector, and to sustain—let alone surpass—their family's current socioeconomic conditions, often already located on the fringes (United Nations Development Programme [UNDP], 2012). For many, desires to bring about change sit uneasily alongside hopelessness abided by history. What should survivors like Carlos tell their children about the ways that violence, terror, and loss so profoundly shaped the trajectories of their lives, when so little seems to have changed? This is a story about postwar youth in Guatemala, but I begin with Carlos to remind us that young people are relationally embedded in generational politics and are subject to hopes and anxieties that are stitched into postwar transitions.

Amid a host of postwar challenges, today's Guatemala is experiencing a severe "youth problem" (Burrell, 2009, p. 97; 2013, p. 20).[5] Reflective of the global "youth bulge," nearly 40 percent of Guatemalans are younger than age fifteen (Urdal, 2012). It is not the high proportion of youth alone that is worrisome, but the large number of young people in "social limbo" (Reimers & Cardenas, 2010, p. 144)—out of school, unemployed, or underemployed. These "school-to-work linkages" influence youth civic development in significant ways (Youniss et al., 2002, p. 135), risking social exclusion and political distrust when states cannot fulfill the promises of egalitarianism, inclusion, and meritocracy conveyed to young people as they invest in their education.

In the particular context of Guatemala, growing numbers of criminal youth and climbing rates of youth homicides have provoked, and been provoked by, the grim reality that "young people [are] locked into a dead end future" (Adams, 2011, p. 45). Traditionally a symbol of hope, Guatemalan youth, once imagined as the "vanguard of modernity" (Levenson, 2013a, p. 13), have been "turned upside down to signify the radically dangerous present, chaos and death, an obstacle to the future instead of its herald" (p. 2). On a societal level, many adults have come to fear and pity young people rather than support and empower them.

Given the scale of postwar violence and entrenched structural inequality in Guatemala, one might wonder whether the history of war is worth remembering at all. In 2009, after I presented on social memory and postwar violence in Guatemala at an international human rights conference, a member of the audience directed me to the literature in the field of transitional justice that showcases the sometimes necessary and desired work of forgetting. How better to institutionalize forgetting than through a curriculum that treats decades of violence as incidental to the country's democratization? Although I am sensitive to the ways in which survivors might opt to express their agency not through narrative but through silence and selective forgetting (see Husseyn, 2005; Jelin, 2003; Theidon, 2013), I was troubled by the suggestion that the rise in Guatemala's youth gang violence necessitated silencing decades of armed conflict, brought on by centuries of structural inequality and institutionalized racism, and whose consequences remained agonizingly visible. The comment evoked the discourses of power operating in Guatemala, which make a persuasive case for ahistorical compartmentalizing of injustice, presuming that looking forward requires not looking back. Even if the war could be erased from public memory, legacies of violence and division would continue to mark society and structure power inequities in the present. Moreover, who gets to decide that it is better to actively *dis*remember violence, when erasing the past so clearly benefits those who committed atrocities and marginalizes those who were targets of violence and repression? In part, this book is my response to claims that postwar problems demand postwar solutions such as historical silence.

In making this argument, I do not discount the scale of violence afflicting Guatemalan and Central American youth. I do, however, believe that a complex set of historical circumstances accounts for this rise in violence, so that the *postwar* cannot be so easily disentangled from the history of war from which it emerged. I could not have come to this realization without the guidance of young people, who presented savvy critiques of their social conditions, attentiveness to the legacies of colonialism compounded by civil war, and the enduring unequal and exploitative relations that organize their society. It was young people who helped me see that Guatemalan adolescents are the perpetrators and the victims, the killer gang members and the disaffected youth sorting through the city trash for food scraps—and that both of these paths were born from the history of extreme terror and violence that forever marked the lives of their parents during the Conflicto Armado. Though today's youth did not live the violence, they inherited its legacies and the failed dreams of the popular movement—in material ways such as lost family members, underresourced schools built atop clandestine graves, and roads that "lead nowhere," as Carlos notes. They also inherited the symbolic remnants of the conflict in the purposeful silence and unanswered questions about the past, lingering fears about collective action, and the uncertainty about whether and when the future might get better.

Many scholars regard Guatemala's contemporary violence as a once-preventable outgrowth of the civil war (Grandin, 2004; Isaacs, 2010a; Manz, 2008; Sanford, 2008), but the state recounts a different story. The consistent denial by state officials that genocide happened, that war trials would restore trust in democratic institutions, and that today's popular movements remain targets of political repression dovetail with public claims that postwar peace was achieved, only to be violently ruptured by the influx of transnational, "apolitical" gangs (Levenson, 2013a, p. 8) and criminal networks (see Benson, Thomas, & Fischer, 2011). On the contrary, today's "land problem" (Palma Murga, 2011, p. 454) and "indigenous problem," a term used to signal the challenges of multilingualism and pluralism, are not new forms of exclusion and marginalization but rather unresolved political issues, rooted in a history of conflict and inequality. While the scale of today's "youth problem" (Burrell, 2009, p. 97; 2013, p. 20) manifests as a distinctly postwar phenomenon, its roots too spring from the past. Political and criminal violence have been described as "two sides of the same coin" (Stanley, 2001, p. 535). In this sense, efforts to disarticulate postwar, "apolitical" crime from the history of "political" violence serve distinct purposes in the present (Cruz, 2011; Isaacs, 2010a, 2010b; Levenson, 2013a, 2013b; Moodie, 2010). Downplaying long-term consequences of the Conflicto Armado evokes a hierarchy of suffering between past and present, while transferring accountability from the state to criminal youth.

Under these conditions, educating postwar generations about historical injustice is often dismissed as irrelevant and potentially harmful to stability, national unity, and postwar peace (Bellino, 2014a, 2015b). Whether citizens should cultivate critical historical consciousness of injustice has repolarized debates among educators and the public about what good citizenship entails in a fragile, postwar state.[6] As we will see, historical injustice plays a key role in young people's civic identity formation and their sense of agency to participate in the civic life of a democracy in transition.

Historical Consciousness and Leaps of Civic Faith

Throughout the text I pursue two complementary aims: to illustrate the varied ways that youth learn about historical injustice in formal and informal educational spaces as a component of citizenship education and to explore how urban and rural adolescents draw on their construction of the violent past in shaping their evolving sense of themselves as civic actors and as members of a postwar, postauthoritarian democracy. Through ethnographic accounts in four communities, I examine how postwar political processes and global discourses of peace, democracy, and transitional justice influence educational reform and everyday opportunities in and outside of schools to narrate, commemorate, and contest injustice.

Long heralded as society's primary citizen-making institution, education has recently been recognized as an ideal, albeit underutilized, civic space that can be honed as a mechanism of transitional justice in the context of everyday life (Bellino, 2016; E. Cole, 2007b; Cole & Murphy, 2009; Davies, in press a; Paulson, 2009). Education as a sector is far-reaching and multigenerational, and the messages, relationships, and practices that young people are exposed to in schools profoundly influence their civic identity development, sense of belonging, and connectedness to fellow citizens and the state (Flanagan, Stoppa, Syvertsen, & Stout, 2010; Murphy, in press). In particular, history education is envisioned as a model space for aligning civic knowledge, skills, and attitudes with the societal needs of transitioning democracies. Teaching about historical injustice in the aftermath of mass violence has been conceived as a collective obligation to clarify the historical record, reestablish moral frameworks, promote reconciliation, and acknowledge past atrocity for future generations (E. Cole, 2007a; Minow, 1998; Weinstein, Freedman, & Hughson, 2007), all of which are regarded as essential means of reckoning for the transitional citizen. In line with other transitional mechanisms, education can cultivate a "two-way gaze" (Davies, in press a, in press b) among learners, acknowledging past conflict while aspiring toward a shared vision of future transformation.

Teaching the past in any context is susceptible to politicization and public contest, particularly on subjects of violence and injustice (e.g., Barton and Levstik, 2004). What underpins these debates is often a deeper question about the purposes of teaching history and its civic implications, which take on particular significance in settings undergoing democratic transitions. But because of history's potential divisiveness, it is more often silenced in curriculum and classroom discussions, orienting youth to their civic roles as shapers of the postwar future (see Paulson, 2015), while granting young people little interpretive agency to question and critique past events. As in many postconflict contexts, the "two-way gaze" (Davies, in press b) often gives way to historical silence and idealistic projections of postwar peace and harmony (Paulson, 2009). In the process, schools convey postwar citizenship as conditional on particular engagements with historical injustice. But memories circulate in the private sphere, even under conditions of public censure. The construction of the past is therefore not confined to schools or textual resources, suggesting that young learners make meaning of the past through various educational exchanges, some formal and others informal, while embedded in broader sociocultural contexts (Ahonen, 2005; Angvik & von Borries, 1997; Seixas, 2004). Yet, as this book illustrates, youth do not simply inherit memories of violence and visions of peace from their parents and teachers; they actively interpret, reconstruct, and place themselves within these narratives, even when they are intentionally silenced. Through this process, young learners construct the role and relevance of the past in their present lives. That is, they construct historical consciousness, organizing the meaning of the past around what they deem "'worthy of remembering'" (Funkenstein, 1993, p. 17). In doing so, they build temporal and agentic connections between themselves and the past, present, and future (Murphy & Gallagher, 2009; Murphy, Sleeper, & Stern Strom, 2011).

In and outside of schools, young people have daily experiences with civic agents and institutions, which shape their understanding of the social contract, fairness and justice, and individual and collective roles within a democratic society (Flanagan, 2004; B. Levinson, 2007; M. Levinson, 2012; Rubin, 2007, 2012). Young people in all societies come to understand democracy and the civil contract through experiences with their weaknesses and "disjunctures," as well as their strengths and "convergence" with democratic ideals (Abu El-Haj, 2007; Dyrness, 2012; Rubin, 2007, 2012). Particularly in transitional democracies, the deficiencies and exclusions evoked through "democratic disjuncture" (Holston & Caldeira, 1998) powerfully resonate with historical injustice and the illusory promises of the better future. For many Guatemalans living the violent aftermath of war, these breaches have come to mean more than the failures of an "anorexic" postwar state (Inter-American Dialogue and Organization of American States, 2007, p. 16). Gaps in the civil contract evoke the deception and corruption embedded in the promises made to transform Guatemalan society. They signify unresolved historical legacies and the elusiveness of the postwar peace, freedom, and equality future generations were promised. They signify that Guatemala is *not yet* a democracy.

I argue that democratic disjunctures are entangled with authoritarian legacies, remnants of the authoritarian past that "lie in the fissures between formally democratic institutions and the institutionalization of undemocratic practices" (Cesarini & Hite, 2004, p. 5). Failings of the democratic system, then, are not merely reflections of today's flawed political arrangements; they simultaneously encompass the history and politics of transition rooted in those arrangements. Young people experience these disjunctures in their daily lives, and they too imbue them with historical significance. In the exploration of young people's lives that follows, I illustrate how adolescents' construction of the unresolved past, the unstable present, and the unfulfilled future mediate their development as civic actors, influencing everyday decisions about whether to engage with, trust, question, or challenge fellow citizens and the institutional structures that organize their society. Importantly, young people's construction of the violent past influences their expectations of self and others, including their sense of agency to shape a better future. Wars leave their marks visibly on wounded bodies and landscapes, but also in less visible ways, in shaping the subjectivity of future generations. This is one of the currents on which war legacies travel.

Guatemala is not alone in its uneven transition from war to war's violent aftermath, with postwar generations caught in between. South Africa's Truth and Reconciliation Commission has been considered one of the prototypical models for restorative justice, although the majority of the "born free" generation faces ongoing racism, inequality, segregation, and a lack of opportunities for social advancement. Set against the optimism for inclusion in the postapartheid "Rainbow Nation," disenfranchised youth have constructed alternative future paths through delinquency (Stanley, 2001; Swartz, Hamilton Harding, & De Lannoy, 2012). Postgenocide Rwanda has similarly been praised for its embrace of grassroots and ostensibly culturally relevant Gacaca courts (justice among the grass) and increased spending on social services, yet Rwandan youth today contend with a society so restrictive that they are prohibited from criticizing the government or speaking openly about ethnicity (Sommers, 2012). In postwar El Salvador, where contemporary youth violence is on par with neighboring Guatemala, citizens have come to understand peace as "worse than war" (Moodie, 2010). This trope similarly plays a significant role in understandings of Guatemala's postwar violence: as Guatemalan activist Amílcar Méndez has said, Guatemala's contemporary dysfunction has converted victims of the war into "victims of the peace."[7] Timothy Smith (2009) encourages scholars to move beyond accounting for postwar politics to investigate "what comes from failure" (p. 17) and how citizens make meaning of democracy when it fails to transform society. In the chapters that follow, I explore what young people expect of their democracy and how they view themselves as civic actors when their peace is routinely cast as "worse than war."

Wait Citizenship and the No-Future Generation

Guatemala's "youth problem" is a significant challenge for civil society and the long-term stability of an already fragile democracy. Civic engagement is considered a near-universal dimension of youth development and an essential element of resilient democracies (Flanagan & Levine, 2010; Kassimir & Flanagan, 2010; Youniss et al., 2002), a particular concern in transitional states where democracy lacks a record of stability. Additionally, transitional justice and peace building depend on active and authentic civic engagement (Davies, 2004a; Lederach, 2005). According to some, transforming civil society toward an active stance should be the "new normality," the foundation on which all "post" life is imagined (Davies, 2004b, p. 243). Because civic attitudes and values are "rooted in social relations" (Flanagan, 2004, p. 724), this study begins with the everyday lives of youth in schools, homes, and communities, examining how postwar-generation adolescents make meaning of historical injustice, while developing their civic identities in a struggling democracy.

In war-torn and postwar contexts, the lack of opportunities available to youth has contributed to "waithood" (Honwana, 2013) or "wait adulthood" (Sommers, 2012, p. 3), where youth are "stuck" in "arrested liminality" (p. 5) as they struggle to meet cultural expectations that facilitate their transition to social adulthood. Alcinda Honwana (2013) conceives of waithood as a consequence of international aid regimes and their failed neoliberal policies, coupled with global political, social, and economic crises. Others identify similar states of waithood and stalled youth transitions, arguing that globalization has fundamentally shifted the life course. Jennifer Cole's (2005) work on in urban Madagascar illustrates that youth transitions in some cases are postponed indefinitely: "For some people in the third world, 'youth' is a stage they cannot escape" (p. 892).

In Guatemala, democratic instability and high rates of violence coexist with the contradictions of modernity and globalization, creating additional disjunctures. Postwar generations are structurally positioned in a "liminal" wait stage (Turner, 1967), anticipating the transformation embedded in authentic democratic citizenship. The democratic transition contains a liminal condition between *Guatemala at war* and *Guatemala after war*, though all citizens appear to be entrapped by the violent present, "no longer" at war and "not yet" at peace (p. 96). Along with the adults in their lives, Guatemalan youth are instructed to *wait*—for peace, stability, opportunity, voice, inclusion; to wait for the changed nation they were promised at the end of the conflict; to "wait . . . for returns on their investments of hope" (Burrell, 2013, p. 165), even as they question whether that future is attainable. Youth civic development is thus impeded by legacies of the past and their undercurrents in the present. In effect, the legacy of the loyal, "apolitical" citizen who strategically survived the war through willful noninvolvement intersects with the transitional state's call for patient citizens who acquiesce to positions of waithood during times of uncertainty. Together these conditions contribute to young people's structural inability "to become social adults and full-fledged citizens" (Honwana, 2013, p. 4).

Active citizenship depends on a sense of faith that one's actions will make a difference, however small the scale and however broad the timeline for change, as well as a predictable logic that actions lead to consequences, however that effectiveness is measured. But neither stance prevails in postwar societies, where individuals often learn, through the experience of injustice and its legacy, not to see themselves as the protagonists of their past, present, and future (Lederach, 2005) but instead to look to intangible forces such as a "culture of violence" as accountable agents (Oglesby, 2007a, 2007b). The future, like the violent past and the transitional justice process that followed, is plainly out of the hands of ordinary citizens. In this book, I argue that youth are relegated to positions of *wait citizenship*, where they conceive of their private autonomy over their own moral development but see little capacity to impact the broader social, political, and economic reality that they share with morally corrupt others. Young people are expected to adapt to structural conditions shaped by the actions of previous generations rather than foster a sense of civic agency to change those conditions. Powerlessness to affect the course of one's life not only leads to individual withdrawal but also risks becoming a driver of violence (Dryden-Peterson, Bellino, & Chopra, 2015; Sommers, 2012). Real and perceived lack of agency to shape individual and public affairs explains why large numbers of Guatemalan youth turn to criminal pathways, even when doing so grants them agency only over their violent deaths (Levenson, 2013a).

As youth cope with insecurity and uncertainty in their everyday lives, risk settings can also become "generative contexts" (Edberg & Bourgois, 2013, pp. 190–195) so that delinquency and disengagement from the public sphere shift from traditionally conceptualized risk factors to adaptive strategies. Large numbers of youth have found protective value in strategic withdrawal from collective action and community spaces. Young people's "calculus of risk" (p. 190) fundamentally alters where they invest effort. It is not that Guatemalan youth are naively skeptical of democracy; rather, their daily experiences confirm that their society is *not yet* a democracy. Nonparticipation can signify a lack of civic knowledge or empowerment, but it also speaks to impressions of deeply flawed and untrustworthy institutions. In exploring youth civic development in the violent aftermath of war, this book argues that many young Guatemalans are conditioned to avoid risk and stay vigilant, instructed that good citizens wait for, rather than actively shape, the better future. In this way, young people's emerging sense of themselves as civic actors revolves around the need to embrace or avoid risk, in part informed by their encounters with historical injustice in their everyday lives and the messages about justice and citizenship conveyed in schools (see also Bellino, 2015b).

While wait citizenship structurally positions youth as compliant and patient in the face of unfulfilled promises, young people are not passively waiting for peace to arrive, nor do they unanimously view themselves as victims of the past or the present. They make decisions about when to act and when to withdraw, when to project hope and when to relinquish hope, and who to hold accountable—even if only in the private space of their thoughts—for the challenges they face. And some walk bravely into the streets of their oppressors in search of a better future, even when they are uncertain that they will survive to see the changes their actions might bring. Young people's assessment of the risk structure they inhabit thus figures importantly into the ways they enact their agency as wait citizens in a fragile, postwar state.

A Multisited, "Vertical" Ethnographic Design

Comprising a multisited ethnography (Marcus, 1998, 1999), this book explores the ways that postwar-generation adolescents at four schools, embedded in distinct urban and rural communities, make meaning of their country's history of authoritarianism, while developing their civic identities in a struggling democracy. The social and political context of Guatemala's democratic transition is central to these aims. For this reason, the text is organized as a "vertical case study" (Bartlett & Vavrus, 2014; Vavrus & Bartlett, 2006), in that I examine the national history curriculum and postwar education reforms across vertical, horizontal, and transversal axes, linking youth experience to macrolevel sociopolitical shifts. These multiple axes facilitate analysis within and across urban and rural family, community, and school settings, while illuminating a more complex ecology of youth civic culture in postwar Guatemala. In tracking the vertical flow of ideas from state-led transitional justice processes to the educational sector, I examine how recommendations for educational reform have been implemented by policy makers, enacted and reinterpreted by educators, reinforced and challenged by families and communities, and experienced by young people, for whom they were designed. Within each context, I trace youth experiences horizontally from schools to their homes and communities to demonstrate how knowledge and attitudes toward historical injustice travel—often contentiously—across public and private spaces, as well as between generations. Throughout, I explore the ways that young people's stances toward democracy and human rights are influenced by, and at times develop in resistance to, global frameworks. In this way, I make the case that not only are schools significant outlets *for* transitional justice, but their role in shaping youth civic pathways functions as a mechanism *of* transitional justice, even decades after the war's end.

While this design facilitates comparisons across urban and rural learning contexts, it simultaneously enables comparisons within each of these geographically and historically distinct spaces. Differences within localities are routinely masked by marked distinctions across spaces and the assumptions that culture is inherently anchored in space (Gupta & Ferguson, 1992). Recognizing varied experiences and interpretations of historical injustice, citizenship, and youth aspirations within community spaces complicates our understanding of the reproductive tendencies of educational institutions (Bourdieu & Passerson, 1990) and the implied reproduction of war legacies embedded in these institutions. Analytically, this design allows for the pursuit of connections across sites rather than merely juxtaposition, while also accounting for the flow of ideas and practices between these disparate contexts, where indigenous and nonindigenous Guatemalans live and learn, often separately from one another. Organized in this way, the book allows for exploration of what is at stake for youth situated in particular communities, before moving toward "contextual comparison" (Steiner-Khamsi, 2010, p. 327) across communities.

This study is based on fourteen months of ethnographic fieldwork, carried out from 2009 to 2012 in Guatemala City and the rural province of Izabal, though earlier fieldwork in Chimaltenango, Quetzaltenango, Sololá, and Sacatapequez dating back to 2004 also informs this work. During this latter span of time, I selected four distinct school and community sites and spent six to twelve weeks attending classes in each community, participating in formal and informal activities throughout school days, weekends, and holidays. In an effort to immerse myself in young peoples' social worlds, I arrived at and departed from school classes and events with students, abiding by the rules that organize students' time and govern their movement. Though I did not take exams, I sat at a student desk, attended class regularly, and participated in routine class activities. If the students rose to greet their teachers, I also rose from my desk. If they passed notes under the table, I too passed notes. There are clear limits on the capacity for adult researchers to become participant observers in secondary school classrooms, and I tried not to pretend that these differences did not exist (e.g., differences in age, income, educational experience, exposure to different cultures of teaching and learning). Despite the power that my cultural and institutional home carried into the field, the young people I interacted with often took on parenting and guiding roles with me. I actively positioned them as experts of their worlds, and they actively taught me, protected me from danger, and included me in intimate social gatherings.

My social and civic identity affected the nature of my engagement with Guatemalan youth and their communities. Despite my occasional ability to "pass" as Guatemalan, in some indigenous regions my light brown hair earned me the nickname *blondie*. I believe that my whiteness further influenced the relationships I was able to build and the exchanges I had with participants, who varied in their initial distrust of an outsider who had come to attend school and ask questions not of adults but of young people who teachers and parents feared did not know Guatemala's "true story." Beliefs about U.S. citizenship comingled with white privilege and prevailing assumptions that I came to Guatemala with money, a political agenda, and ready answers to resolve local challenges. Moreover, my questions about civic identity and participation evinced the uneasy reality that my own citizenship rested on a historically unequal relationship between the United States and Latin America. Young people, as well as adults, evoked these patterns of external domination as challenges to our potential for mutual understanding, referencing U.S. involvement in Guatemala's civil war as well as linkages to contemporary violence through drug consumption, rigid immigration policies, forced deportation of gang members, and support for megadevelopment projects. Despite our countries' historical legacies, however, we actively built relationships around our mutual concern for young people's trajectories in the postwar era. Additionally, I often explained to young people that my own learning about U.S. involvement in Latin America became my call to action to carry out this research. In this sense, my researcher reflexivity merged with my own sense of historical injustice and civic obligation—the very relationship I was exploring in Guatemala.

Semistructured and unstructured interviews with teachers, parents, and students supplement observational data, highlighting how young people make meaning of their educational encounters with injustice and particularly how they understand the role and relevance of historical injustice in their postwar lives. Ellen Moodie (2010) writes of having to "'learn to ask' [about violence] in culturally appropriate ways" (p. 14). I too struggled to ask respectfully and sensitively about (often violent) experiences with state institutions and historical injustice. Conducting anthropological research in contexts afflicted with violence, past and present, involves one's own entanglement in "fields of power," which we may not perceive (Theidon, 2013, p. 16). When I began my fieldwork, I intended to explore the educational encounters young people had with the state-generated history curriculum. Over time, young people persuasively demonstrated to me that legacies of the past did not exist in isolation—they intersected with, eclipsed, and accentuated the scope of current violence. Young people's daily struggles coming of age as civic actors in a high-risk setting resituated the driving research questions of this study.

I designed this study mindful of calls from researchers to consider how youth understand citizenship, rooted in their daily experiences with the civil contract within and outside of schools, rather than rely on pre-existing theoretical constructs or adult-constructed projections of what young people *should* know (Ríos-Rojas, 2011; Rubin, 2007). Ethnographic approaches are unique in their capacity to unearth "vernacular notions of citizenship" (Rosaldo, 1999, p. 260) and probe everyday meaning-making processes, even when they do not conform to traditional conceptions of civic and political engagement (see also B. Levinson, 2011). In addition to these sources of data, I analyze written texts such as policy documents, curricular resources, and student assignments. In pulling together these various sources, this book accounts for the ways that education interacts with both macrolevel strategies to reconcile legacies of the violent past and local

Table 1. Overview of Four School Cases

	International Academy	Paulo Freire Institute	Sun and Moon	Tzolok Ochoch
Location	Guatemala City	Guatemala City	Rural village in Izabal	Rural village in Izabal
Student composition*	100% mestizo; 90% multiple nationalities	99% mestizo; 1% indigenous	100% Q'eqchi' Maya	90% indigenous (Kaqchikel, Q'eqchi', K'iche') 9% mestizo 1% Garifuna
Teacher composition	80% U.S. American; 20% mestizo	90% mestizo; 10% indigenous	100% indigenous	100% indigenous

*Statistics reported here on the student composition of each school were recorded through conversations with school leaders. In some cases, administrators had not formally collected data but made estimates based on their knowledge of where students were born, their home language, and whether students' parents wear traje. International Academy students' multiple nationalities, indicated by their possession of multiple passports, were confirmed in conversations with students.

approaches to grappling with historical injustice, while shaping young people's civic identity and sense of efficacy.

This work is intentionally grounded in formal and informal educational contexts, encompassing participant observation in eleventh- and twelfth-grade social studies classrooms, as well as observations collected during extracurricular activities, over family dinner tables, and at community events. The four schools included in this study adhere to the national curriculum, though they are all private institutions, reflecting the national (and global) trend toward private postprimary education (see UNDP, 2012).[8] In selecting schools as principal field sites, I considered dimensions that would facilitate comparison across several units of analysis: location (urban or rural), demographics (ratio of indigenous to nonindigenous students), socioeconomic factors (inclusion of private schools catering to the urban elite and working class as well as the rural poor), and local experiences with different scales of violence, past and present.

School selection was also guided, in part, by my existing social networks with urban and rural human rights advocates. These prior connections facilitated rapport and my capacity to access students' families and their social worlds outside of school. Building sufficient trust to stay with families in their homes was an important aspect of this design, one that enriches its findings but also limited the possibilities of where and how I could carry out this work. The location of secondary schools that offered *bachillerato* (college preparatory) diplomas was an added challenge in rural communities. Many villages simply do not have secondary schools or the only postprimary institutions feature vocational training with no social studies or history classes at the upper grades. The two rural schools included in this study are privately run within communities, established with local indigenous leadership and maintained with varying degrees of community engagement. Nevertheless, these cases are not prototypical or representative of the regions from which they are selected. Table 1 presents an overview of student and teacher demographics in the four school sites.

Outside of school, the nature of my community interaction varied in each context. During my immersion at the International Academy, I lived with one student, Alejandro, and his family for the entirety of my field-work in his school. While attending the Paulo Freire Institute, I stayed for a brief time with two different students' families (Paulina and Xila). While studying at Sun and Moon, I lived with a family with six children who were pursuing educational opportunities at different stages and institutions, though most of Sun and Moon's students were our neighbors. At Tzolok Ochoch, I boarded with the female students in the senior class, sharing a spare bunk bed in their dormitory. "Shadowing" students provided an important guide for my fieldwork in and outside of school contexts, in that I followed the choices that young people made about how to spend their free time, exploring when opportunities emerged as civic in nature or in young people's interpretation of them (whether they participated or contested these opportunities). In this sense, I sought to connect the experiences of young people within and outside classrooms, developing an ecological account of their civic development.

Each time I transitioned from one site to the next, I was cautioned about the community I was entering and the kind of people I would encounter there. These warnings were intended as protective, instructing me how my social identity would be reconfigured among peoples with particular experiences with the Guatemalan state and the Western world, particularly the United States. Simultaneously, they oriented me to the divisions that persist between and within urban and rural; indigenous and nonindigenous; elite, working class, and poor; and dominant images of how "those people" understand justice and the realm of civic responsibility.

At the International Academy, the art teacher encouraged students to collect materials from spaces they encountered in their everyday lives, such as the cardboard placemats from a popular coffee shop. Weeks later I stood with Paulo Freire students outside that same café, watching the cook fold crepes from the window until a waiter asked us to move along, knowing we would not order anything. Inside, eating at the tile countertop might have been the families of International Academy students, who had cast Paulo Freire as a community of delinquent youth who would rob people like them if given the chance. Despite mutual awareness of this social divide, girls at Paulo Freire asked if I could find them rich boyfriends at the elite school, scanning through my phone for attractive faces while remarking on the abundance of materials in the school's classrooms. On my last day at Paulo Freire, I told the teachers and students about the villages I would be visiting, and one after the other they warned me, "They do justice differently there," referencing the rise in community vigilantism. They advised me to be careful so many times that I began to reconsider my plans. Once settled at Sun and Moon, I learned that students there viewed urban areas as distinctly violent, unlike the violence afflicting their communities, which was aimed at social justice and inclusion. Though they distanced themselves from "people's justice," they maintained that their violence contained a social message, whereas what was happening in urban areas could be understood only as chaos. Meanwhile, their ambivalence toward social movements contesting the megadevelopment projects affecting their livelihoods and future prospects offered a counternarrative to the movements that Alejandro's family vigorously organized across the country and which students at the International Academy dismissed as disruptive to democratic and economic stability. As Sun and Moon students conjured fearful images of *capitalistas*, they also saw in urban spaces opportunities for employment and higher education and for the modernity that their teacher framed as constructive exits from a stagnant rural life. At Tzolok Ochoch, rural solidarity was forged in opposition to those outside who spoke about indigenous revitalization but made no efforts at redistribution, repair, or inclusion. One student bragged that she had survived middle school in the most dangerous zone in the capital but was relieved to be away from urban insecurity. When an outspoken teacher and alumni of the school was targeted for her efforts at community organizing, her brother sought safety in the capital, just as others had sought safety in the school's isolation. In the spirit of multisited ethnography, the four sites serve not only as divergent cases but also as relational compositions situated within a more complex whole (Marcus, 1998, 1999). The text intentionally highlights moments where individuals, ideas, and movements traverse implicit racial, class, and political borders. In doing so, I demonstrate how marginality is "constructed spatially" (Auyero, 2013, p. 94), as well as reproduced and resisted through educational spaces.

Over the course of my fieldwork, I attended and participated in community and youth group meetings and projects, protests organized by various sectors of civil society, public commemorations and marches, community theater, religious groups, school-led volunteer projects, and political gatherings, in both urban and rural areas. I was in the field during two presidential elections (2007 and 2011). I was also present when families discussed whether their children should become involved in public events such as protests, as parents mediated news coverage about pressing issues unfolding in the country, considered migrating, and contemplated postsecondary opportunities and as students discussed among themselves the value of civic participation and the meaning of human rights in Guatemala. Taking place in the private sphere, these moments reveal insight into the civic development process that I would have missed if I had limited my fieldwork to public spaces and expressions. Throughout my research, my intention has been to share in educational interactions, as well as expressions of civic participation, in both private and public spaces. Whenever possible, I recorded these interactions in audio or video files, narrative field notes, and memos. Like all ethnographic research, however, much has been left out.

Finally, I draw on the methodological tradition of portraiture (Lawrence-Lightfoot & Hoffman Davis, 1997) as a recasting of ethnography that places value on the finding, naming, and deep exploration of "goodness." The "search for goodness" (p. 9) is not a call for gratuitous praise but a reminder of the power of researching and representing human lives and the responsibility to document complex realities without slipping into critiques that highlight what is flawed, broken, or damaged at the expense of what is healthy and strong. Research that seeks to understand the lives of oppressed groups requires confronting, describing, and critiquing injustice, even when it implicates the researcher herself in an unjust reality. Researching injustice also entails the need to carefully balance representations of human agency, not overstating the narrow openings for vulnerable groups to express their agency, but not discounting how even the most marginalized choose to enact their agency (Fine & Weis, 2010). Like other ethnographers working in contexts of violence and social suffering (e.g., Nordstrom, 2004; Sanford, 2003a; Theidon, 2013), I have struggled to represent the legitimate harms of social and political violence and exclusion, alongside the innovation and resilience of those who endure. In the chapters that follow, I confront these challenges and make explicit the search for goodness that I undertook with the support of young people who invited me into their lives.

Organization of the Text

The following chapter, "Education and Conflict in Guatemala," maps the trajectory of Guatemala's history of conflict, democratic transition, and the postwar context. Moving chronologically, I trace the vertical movement from state-led transitional justice processes to national educational reforms intended to change opportunity structures for marginalized populations and forge a new citizenry. Through an analysis of the social studies curriculum, I examine the ways in which the official conflict narrative has shaped enduring discourses around historical memory, a culture of peace, and democratic citizenship. Visions of future peace and democracy permeate the curriculum, positioning postwar generation youth as ambassadors of the peaceful future, even as this imagined future began to collapse amid escalating postwar violence.

The core of the text is composed of four ethnographic cases, documenting the experience of youth in school, family, and community spaces as they learn about the Conflicto Armado and reflect on the legacy of injustice in their country, while considering the civic choices they face as members of the postgeneration. Chapter 3, "International Academy: The No-Blame Generation and the Post-Postwar," centers on Alejandro, an outlier at his elite international school in the capital city, as he struggles to reconcile his family's radical political stance and the conservative beliefs circulating at school. I argue that despite his parents' strong counternarrative and modeling of engaged citizenship, Alejandro becomes increasingly constrained by his own fatalism and a persistent desire for a "normal" life outside of Guatemala. Chapter 4, "Paulo Freire Institute: The All-or-Nothing Generation and the Spiral of the Ongoing Past" illustrates the experience of urban working-class youth attending a self-described "liberal" school. The narrative centers on a group of students who navigate everyday struggles to survive in a city where their socioeconomic status easily renders them criminal delinquents who fall outside the civic space. I argue that young people's perceptions of Guatemala's democratic failures hinge on their impressions of ongoing injustice and an unresolved past. Chapter 5, "Sun and Moon: The No-Future Generation and the Struggle to Escape" portrays the experience of Q'eqchi' Maya students completing their education at their village's sole secondary institution. As students reflect on adults' messages encouraging their escape from rural poverty, they apply the lessons of the past to the challenges they face in their community today, ranging from megadevelopment projects, dispossession of ancestral land, escalation of street violence and vigilantism, and fears of state military intervention. Chapter 6, "Tzolok Ochoch: The Lucha Generation and the Struggle to Overcome" serves as a significant contrast to the previous three cases. The chapter revolves around the experience of students at a rural, indigenous boarding school with a mission of community empowerment. I argue that students at this school draw on the history of collective struggle in shaping their role as civic actors at the margins, integral to their identity and empowerment as a historically oppressed group. In doing so, they respond to the positioning of wait citizenship by willfully embracing the risks of public and collective action.

In each case, schools are situated as important sites of civic development, while adults' representations of the violent past illustrate how historical interpretations—often distilled into a set of bullet points—manifest as civic intentions for today's youth. Though there is no homogeneous youth experience in any one of these sites, each chapter highlights a particular dimension of the relationship between youth historical consciousness and the development of civic stances, while demonstrating the ways that national and local educational spaces shape young people's evolving sense of themselves as civic actors, in part through their structuring of encounters with historical injustice. In each chapter, I profile several young people and explore in depth their attitudes and actions in authentic everyday contexts, limiting my analytic interruptions to privilege the unfolding of story. The style of "narrative ethnography" (Stoller, 1989, pp. 154–155) and my decision to employ the ethnographic present, despite its risks of locating "the Other outside of time" (Fabian, 1983, p. xli), allows for an emphasis on the escalation of worry in everyday interactions, the momentum gained by social movements as they traverse rural and urban spaces, and the contextualized development of youth civic agency as a process of formal and informal educational encounters.

The final chapters embrace a comparative discussion of youth civic development within and across the four school communities. In chapter 7, "What Stands in the Way," I discuss the ways that young people's historical consciousness, constructed through formal and informal educational interactions, functions as a mediator in their civic development in Guatemala's postwar present. In accounting for the preservation of divisive memory communities, divergent strategies for interpreting injustice, and varied perceptions of Guatemala's legitimacy as a democracy, I analyze how the history of war alternates as a call to action or a bid for compliance, depending on one's social location and vulnerability within the postwar period. Chapter 8, "The Hopes and Risks of Waiting," centers on how young people conceive of their agency as wait citizens. I argue that young people in each community approach decisions about participating in civic issues as a risk calculus, in which they take into consideration the risks and benefits of both participation and nonparticipation, as well as their obligation to abstain or join communities in struggle. The construction of the past is a decisive factor in how youth perceive risk and responsibility. In this way, young people's emerging sense of themselves as civic actors revolves around the need to embrace or avoid risk, in part informed by their encounters with historical injustice in their everyday lives. I close by analyzing the ways that schools, family narratives, and community practices knowingly and unwittingly contribute to nonparticipation as an alternative to risk and a vital dimension of wait citizenship.

Across the ethnographic portraits that follow, young people struggle to reconcile their desires for positive national identity with the reality of violence and limited opportunities for structural inclusion, made more challenging by adult pressures to perform, develop, and transform, all while under the gaze of the outside world. This global scrutiny penetrates even the most privileged urban youth, who share the rural poor's yearning for a better Guatemala. Adults solemnly observe, searching for an answer to the question, *what future will these young people create?* This question permeates society, even while many young people come to believe that they do not have the capacity to shape their lives. In their withdrawal and waiting, they ask, *what future will shape who we become?*

2

Education and Conflict
in Guatemala

Today Guatemala's pluricultural, multiethnic, and multilingual features are officially sources of national pride, yet this diversity has also played a decisive role in a long history of violence and ongoing inequality. For centuries Guatemala's majority indigenous population has been marginalized by the state, whose policies have ranged from political exclusion and social discrimination to overt repression and violence, including acts of genocide (Grandin, 2005; Ibarra, 2011; Manz, 2004; Sanford, 2003a). As Kimberly Theidon (2013) reminds us, "Wars are fought. They are also told" (p. 6). Narrating war is an essential component of postwar life, linked to the reclamation of agency and power exercised in public forms of truth telling (Jackson, 2006). Schools play a critical role in constructing the past, institutionalizing particular knowledge and sanctioning omissions (Apple, 1995). Exploring the ways in which young people today learn about historical injustice necessitates an understanding of how the civil war came to be narrated in curricular texts, exposing educational choices made in the context of particular transitional moments.

Because "school history" and "academic history" rarely narratively correspond without political intention (Carretero, 2011), this chapter recounts this history from the perspective of historians and human rights investigators before examining curricular representations. In setting school interactions alongside these accounts deemed official through their inclusion in transitional justice mechanisms, I aim to show how schools both strengthen and undermine messages of reconciliation and justice embedded in the peace process and democratic transition. There are three aspects of the transitional justice process relevant to the story I want to tell. I first consider the evolution of transitional justice mechanisms and the way they constructed the historical narrative of injustice. Second, I highlight the way the education sector was conceived—albeit subtly—as an important instrument of transitional justice with the potential to redress centuries of racial inequality. Again the dissonance between how these recommendations were articulated during the transition and the reforms implemented demonstrate the ways in which narrating the past became a particular challenge for the postwar state. Last, in situating the armed conflict as a significant historical event worthy of educational attention in today's postwar context, I illuminate the reproductive tendencies of violence and the ordinary, "socially permitted" nature of violence to uphold order (Scheper-Hughes & Bourgois, 2004, p. 5). The escalation of postwar violence confounds the risk structure that citizen youth inhabit, while shaping their construction of the past and present, as well as their relationship to patterns of historical injustice.

Knowing and Not Knowing

In July 2007 I visited Comalapa for the first time and was struck by the location of the town's middle school. A metal gate wound around the yellow structure, located on a main road at the village entrance, where buses lined up for trips to the cities, engines rumbling and black smoke curling toward the school steps. More striking was the overgrown cemetery directly across from the school. It was a strategic decision to build the school across from the cemetery, to keep young people close to their ancestors. Visibly linking the cemetery, school, and village entrance is a well-known community mural painted by the Comalapa Youth Group, stretching nearly two hundred feet across a narrow pedestrian walkway and the main road. The mural serves as a visual history of the Maya, depicting ancient and colonial times alongside spiritual imagery resonant with the sacred text of the *Popul*

Vuh. Its central frames encompass the armed conflict, captured in images of men in military fatigues wielding machetes and pointing rifles at villagers and bodies of men and women lying face down in small pools of blood or kneeling and crying, their hands covering their faces, while others flee in the background of burning houses and *milpa* (cornfields). One image depicts the frightening searches on public buses, with soldiers lining men against the bus for inspection. The army and guerrilla figures are not easily distinguishable, though a careful analysis reveals a different shade of fatigue green, distinct hats, and red kerchiefs for guerrillas. The mural concludes with images of contemporary Maya, men and women conjuring futures as literate professionals engaging with technology and interacting with the global community. Comalapa is famous for its artists, and the mural draws tourists from around the world.

No one minded the tourists snapping photos at the entrance, as their visits brought money into the community and often supported local artists. But the purpose of the mural, Marta and Edelberto explained, was expressly "not tourism." Marta and Edelberto helped paint the mural and remained active in the youth group. Nearly in their thirties, they continued to refer to themselves as *jóvenes* (youth). The mural was also more than a commemoration of the past for public consumption. Many villages had murals and community memory projects, but this was expansive in its size and scope of time. In the views of the youth group, the mural was distinctly educational. As Edelberto said, "It is about reclaiming our memory." In addition to displaying significant historical events in the life of the Maya, one of its educational purposes was a form of identity "buffering" to protect against indigenous internalization of racial inferiority. Although the mural incorporated painful episodes of violent subordination, Edelberto explained that it also showed how "the Maya have continually resisted hegemony." Marta noted, "Many people come here to find a more dynamic way to talk to their kids about the past." Passing the mural, I was inspired by the critical historical consciousness expressed in the village walls and prepared for my first classroom visit, imagining that this would be a village where young people actively identified themselves as Guatemala's postwar generation.

Inside the school gate, the two-story building was fairly open, with a large gymnasium at the center. Classrooms lined the upstairs balcony, which overlooked the basketball courts. On the first floor, doorless administrative offices lined the courts and bleachers. With boys' soccer practice underway, the principal, Gustavo, introduced himself and noted that it was remarkable that the school supported so many young students in the community. More remarkable, they had an all-indigenous teaching staff, educators from the village who understood the students' struggles to locate themselves as indigenous youth in a modern world and as a historically oppressed group in a postwar democratic state. Only a generation ago Gustavo's own education was assimilationist "schooling" aimed to strip indigenous peoples of their cultural identity. His teachers were nonindigenous, and his parents, who only spoke Kaqchikel Maya, had no common language through which to communicate with them. By his late elementary years, his learning was interrupted by the civil war. He let out a sigh and explained that education was so important to Guatemala's future, although not everyone saw it that way.

In this first meeting with a school official, I noted several tropes that would resurface in the near dozen schools I visited thereafter. First, Gustavo explained that although teaching about historical injustice was important to Guatemala's future—"even critical"—I would not find what I was looking for by visiting schools. If I wanted to know *the truth* about the violence, I should consult books and talk to adults who "lived the war." Young people simply did not know their past. There were many reasons cited for this, ranging from adult decisions to protect their children from painful memories to beliefs that the war was not relevant to contemporary society and the challenges youth would face in their lives. Over and over I heard from teachers and school leaders insistence that "we don't talk about that here." Some lamented that schools did not have resources with which to teach the violent past, because it was not included in the national curriculum, while others worried about the charged nature of teaching a past that continued to divide people on national and local levels.

Institutional silence frequently transitioned into broad claims about contemporary youth and youth culture. "Today's youth," adults would begin, shaking their heads, before launching into a litany of complaints about young people's uninterest in public affairs, whether past or present; youth corruption and moral degradation; preoccupation with modernization and material consumption; and their obvious lack of interest in history and Maya culture. Moreover, school actors often legitimated and reproduced boundaries around who had the power and civic responsibility to retell these events. In my visits to schools situated in both urban, ladino-majority and rural, indigenous communities, educators frequently reinforced beliefs that historical injustice was "not my [their] story" to tell, justifying a lack of ownership on the basis of their age (i.e., they were too young to have firsthand knowledge), location (i.e., they lived in urban areas or a rural region that was relatively secure during the violence), or ethnicity (i.e., they self-identified as ladino or as a member of a Maya population that was not targeted with the same cruelty as other Maya groups) (Bellino, 2014b). Despite the insistence of many teachers that the history of ethnic and political violence needed to be publicly remembered, school actors participated in the silencing of these events by conveying that only certain populations had authentic access to these narratives.

Perceived youth uninterest in the historical details of their parents' generation also played a role in institutional silencing, in that teachers simultaneously argued for the significance of knowing the past while questioning its relevance to young people. Although the perception that young people do not care about history is a potentially global phenomenon cloaked in adult nostalgia, the hazards of not knowing are perceived as higher in a postwar state. At stake is more than adult pride in times passed or a set of objective facts to be memorized for school exams. Had I not met several youth who wanted nothing to do with school, principals like Gustavo asked; had I not seen the young boys loitering on the streets during the day, doing who-knows-what with their time? I had indeed noticed these young people, mostly males, gathering at park benches and street corners. Despite estimates that as much as 50 percent of youth in Guatemala were out of school, in a place like Comalapa it was difficult to tell. There were flexible evening school programs for children and youth who worked the *milpa* during the day or sold in the market with their families. But even here in a village people considered "safe" and "apart from the urban violence," one boy, walking with his horse, casually told me of his plans to drop out of school by the end of the year. Speaking hypothetically, he explained that joining a local gang—a *pandilla*, not a *mara*—would be more profitable than anything he could become on his own by studying.[1] I stood there stunned, immediately upholding the value of education despite my awareness of the lack of jobs available to him in the formal economy. He laughed, and we continued walking to the dusty center as I tried to think up more persuasive things to say. When the path ended, I was relieved to find myself in the crowded market. I never saw the boy again.

Gustavo pointed me to a room on the second floor of the school. I climbed the stairs to Gladis's social studies classroom, where at least forty students rose from their desk chairs to greet me in unison. During this first class visit, I displayed several photographs depicting historical and current events in Guatemala, including one image from the mural painted along the walls of their school. Students came to the blackboard and held the images in their small hands, one by one. As I anticipated, they instinctively focused their attention on what the images were meant to represent rather than the personal meanings the images held for them. I invited them to share what they thought rather than worry about what they knew and did not know. Slowly, students began sharing their views on violence and the historical details they recognized, declaring "Rigoberta Menchú was *muy guerrillero*" and pointing to an image of the Peace Accords, shouting "That's the 1996 Peace Accords!" One student believed that war happened during a time when Guatemalans were "more violent." Another explained that it was the state that was better "back then," not the people who had changed.

Gladis grew frustrated, as if her students' lack of historical knowledge reflected poorly on her teaching abilities. She noted that they were being especially quiet today and there was no need to be shy. She reminded them that they had to know something about the armed conflict, perhaps from stories their parents told at home. The room was quiet for what felt like minutes. Eventually, a small boy in the back raised his hand and asked, "What is the Conflicto Armado?" A few students giggled at the absurdity of his question, but I am certain there were others who were relieved at his honest admission that he had no idea what we had been discussing for the past thirty minutes. I wrote in my field notes, "How could young people know so little about something so big?" I wondered about what Marta and Edelberto had told me, that the mural was an educative force in the community, a counternarrative expressed so visibly that it could not be ignored. Were they idealizing their own impact on the community? Was Gustavo right that students in the room walked by the mural every day without a thought as to what it meant? Or had they never asked—or had they asked and no one answered? Or was this an intentional display of silence to protect against the uncertain intentions of an outsider, to guard the privacy of their parents' suffering, to avoid controversy through not-knowing? In distinguishing between knowledge and acknowledgement, Stanley Cohen (2001) explains that *not-knowing*, as a form of denial, is not always a personal choice but rather might be "built into the ideological façade of the state" (p. 11).

The Conflicto Armado

Guatemala is composed of four pueblos, twenty-two linguistically distinct indigenous Maya groups, as well as Xinca, Garifuna, and mestizo populations. But many nonindigenous Guatemalans actively self-identify as ladino rather than mestizo, a remnant of the colonial social hierarchy and its blood distinction between *mestizaje* and European ancestry. Colonial divisions, notably between indigenous and nonindigenous groups, have persisted, in part because they have been cemented by state policy, violence, and their frequent and lethal convergence. Poor, rural, and indigenous populations— social identities that often converge—have been routinely subordinated by state structures. But one period in Guatemala's past stands out as a "symbol of a lost alternate history for the country" (Rothenberg, 2012b, p. xxvii), one that might have stripped ladino elites of their power and redistributed resources to the poor majority—and, in the process, prevented a devastating civil war. In the period from 1944 to 1954, known as the "Eternal Spring" or "Democratic Spring," two popularly elected social-democratic presidents (Juan José Arévalo and Jacobo Árbenz) aimed to address Guatemala's colonial legacies of racism and structural inequality by introducing a minimum wage, an improved education system, and eventually a program of agrarian reform in which the state would purchase land from foreign companies and the country's elite *finqueros* (plantation owners) and redistribute it to the majority landless population. At this time the United States Fruit Company was Guatemala's largest landowner and stood to lose its monopoly on the country's banana industry (Schlesinger & Kinzer, 2005). Capitalism and Cold War fears merged as the company requested U.S. aid to protect their business investment against growing "communist" sentiment. Mired in Cold War fears that communism would gain influence across the region, but also highly motivated to protect U.S. economic interests in Latin America, the U.S. Central Intelligence Agency conspired an intricate plan to remove President Árbenz from power (Cullather, 1999). U.S. involvement was designed to support elites and mitigate the growing popular interest in expanding social and economic rights to Guatemala's poor. This coup is considered a "watershed" moment in Guatemala's history (Grandin, 2000, p. 309; Oglesby, 2007a, p. 89), directly leading to "decades of military rule, fraudulent and restrictive elections, and the systematic use of repression to protect empowered interests" (Rothenberg, 2012b, p. xx).[2]

With an abrupt end to the Democratic Spring, various popular movements emerged in frustration at the diminishing space for political expression: student movements supported by teachers and urban intellectuals, labor unions working for fair compensation and the right to organize, community and campesino groups struggling for access to land and a political voice, catechists and members of the Catholic Church adopting liberation theology and speaking out on behalf of grave inequalities. In the eyes of the state, these movements for social justice became increasingly threatening to state authority, so that virtually any popular movement or vocalization of dissent was viewed as a subversive threat and, accordingly, was met with state violence justifiable on claims of national security (CEH, 1999). The earliest years of the war were characterized by popular uprising continually met with state violence until any gesture to organize became "tantamount to a death sentence" (Grandin, Levenson, & Oglesby, 2011a, p. 361). Death squads, acting as covert arteries of the military, routinely kidnapped and disappeared activists, union leaders, and intellectuals. In this sense, political violence became a "direct expression of structural violence," in that the state utilized mechanisms of repression to maintain the status quo (CEH, 1999, p. 18). In the context of an increasingly authoritarian state, a guerrilla movement began to organize, arguing for armed struggle as the only means of social and political transformation in the current climate. Though it turned to illicit means, the guerrilla movement "had its base in the democratic struggles of that era" (Sandoval & Ramírez, 2011, p. 252). As activism and popular organizing became criminalized, the use of state violence against dissenters became increasingly legitimized in a distorted logic that victims "deserved their fate" (Rothenberg, 2012b, p. xxiii).

The army's counterinsurgency campaign, devised to eliminate the guerrilla threat, eventually expanded its target to encompass the indigenous peasant as the "internal enemy" (CEH, 1999, p. 20). In the rural Highlands the military launched a "scorched-earth" campaign in which soldiers actively targeted indigenous civilian populations as potential guerrilla actors, supporters, and sympathizers. Soldiers set fire to homes, schools, and churches; razed crops; slayed livestock; stole possessions; killed the elderly; sold or killed children, including the murder of unborn children; raped women; tortured men; and desecrated cultural symbols. Violence intentionally targeted Maya community and spiritual leaders, as well as cultural markers central to indigenous identity, making public displays of their desecration (CEH, 1999; Grandin, 2005). During this time, the army massacres destroyed more than six hundred villages. Meanwhile, the counterinsurgency project diverged into two strategies: a continued effort to destroy the indigenous, whom the state perceived as the guerrillas' "natural ally," and an effort to help indigenous victims by placing them in "model villages," where they received food, clothing, and aid.[3] In an effort to disrupt potential popular support, the military forced indigenous males ranging from ages twelve to seventy to participate in the Patrullas de Autodefensa Civil (PAC; Civil Defense Patrols), local "volunteer" paramilitary forces that both militarized and divided communities (CEH, 1999). The PAC became an extreme instrument for settling personal vendettas and committing petty crime. Villagers were under intense surveillance, from both occupying soldiers and PAC members, further eroding solidarity and community trust, as well as "binding the perpetrators in a blood ritual to the state" (Grandin et al., 2011a, p. 363).

The guerrilla rebel movement organized across ethnic lines in the name of the country's poor and excluded, though popular support for their cause varied over time and across urban and rural regions. Some individuals joined or supported guerrilla groups with genuine revolutionary sentiments and alignment with their objectives for radical reform, while others joined out of despair, having witnessed extreme suffering at the hands of the military and viewing the guerrillas as their only recourse for action (Menchú & Burgos-Debray, 1984). In other cases, popular support for the guerrillas was calculated according to pragmatic criteria such as existential security. Although guerrilla groups intended to protect people from military attacks, they were ultimately ill equipped to match the scale of the state military in numbers, weapons, and military intelligence. The notion that guerrilla presence in a village "invited" military attacks or used indigenous as pawns in a political scheme became grounds for a widespread fear of associating with either militant group, as well as the conviction that innocent people were forcibly positioned "between two armies" (Stoll, 1994). This trope constitutes a central organizing frame in curricular depictions of the civil war.

What the People Lost

On July 5, 2007, I traveled with my research partner, Ixkat, to the Chimaltenango Programa Nacional de Resarcimiento (National Reparations Program) office. We made our way through a long stretch of highway to the ambiguous address, an estimated number of kilometers off a bus route. By the time we arrived, I had blisters on my feet, and my hair was damp with sweat. The small building was swarming with people who evidently had no trouble locating the office. The line curved through the building and out the door, rows of mostly Maya women from across the department, babies swaddled across their chests. Several children ran around in the dirt, their giggling out of sync with a place I was told was frequented by spirits of ancestors killed in the war. Ixkat explained that the women were here to tell their stories and to see if they could be compensated in some way for their loss. It was already a decade after the peace process had formally ended the war, and so many stories remained untold, losses unregistered.

In the back office we met Rodolfo, a small man with neatly combed dark hair, an embroidered top, and dress slacks. He rose from the table smelling like salt and lime. He closed the office door and explained that these walls have heard many difficult stories the people lived. His comment spoke to the need for strategic distancing, as if the losses accumulated in the room rather than under his skin. He and Ixkat exchanged words in Kaqchikel. Later she told me Rodolfo was worried that the office would be closed before they could finish their work. "As you can see," he said to me with a smile, gesturing to the line of women outside, "there are many victims who have suffered. The Maya people lost so much. Some lost everything. . . . There is little we can do to compensate for their loss."

At one point, the office had a budget to grant reparations, but it was now only a place to register complaints. One could no longer leave with the assurance of any material compensation. Still every day hundreds of people traveled to put on paper what they lost during the war. Perhaps they believed that reparation would eventually come, or perhaps they were searching for recognition and the chance to (re)claim agency, as Michael Jackson (2006) theorizes, through the narrative telling of their lives. Sometimes they waited in line for days before the chance to sit down with Rodolfo or another officer. It took time to listen. By the time they arrived in Rodolfo's office, they had waited a long time to tell their story. "I take the time to listen, and this is why the process goes slowly." Rodolfo believed in the power of solidarity and storytelling, explaining that the women in line found solace in knowing they were not alone. His own mother waited in this line once to be heard, and this is what she told him, so this is how he knows. "It is good to know you are not alone in your suffering." He clasped his hands over the thin pages of a massive book, where his notes were handwritten in script, each word as small as the fleas jumping into the folds of my socks. I thought of a document I once saw appended in the Comisión para el Esclarecimiento Histórico (CEH; Commission for Historical Clarification) report, a list of things one man reported as "lost" during the war. I thought how difficult it was to list the things, massive to minuscule, that make a life.

On the bus ride back to Comalapa, we passed a sign with a village name in big letters, followed by the declaration "Language: Español." Ixkat said it was a "ladino town." "They don't use this," she said, folding her skirt between her fingers. In a few hairpin turns, we were back in Comalapa, where everyone wore *traje* (traditional dress) and where everyone had lost something to the war—but exactly what they lost, I was beginning to discover, depended on who they were. When we returned, her sister asked where we had been. I was about to recount our day, when Ixkat hooked her arm around me and explained that I needed to find some books at an office in Chimaltenango. It was not until weeks later that I put together some of the political divisions operating within Ixkat's family. Ixkat had wanted to join the guerrillas, but her sister's husband was a state soldier. Ixkat saw the conflict as a clear case of state aggression toward indigenous communities, while her sister believed it was a problem of rebel organizing and "political involvement," disturbances that provoked the state to respond with force. Years later Ixkat continues to regard Efraín Ríos Montt, a former military general and a chief architect of the genocide, as a criminal that the country needs to bring to justice. Her sister contends that his leadership "did a lot of good for Guatemala" and that trials against state soldiers necessitate bringing the guerrillas to the courts too. I never heard Ixkat and her sister openly debate these questions of state accountability, but alone my conversations with them unfolded, with their children hovering around us. Ixkat's niece, Debi, listened to her mother's descriptions of highways that Ríos Montt built, which strengthened Guatemala's economy, and assertions that his power ensured "security and order." When I asked Debi what she thought, she used her mother's words exactly, telling me, "Lots of people think badly of Ríos Montt, but he did a lot of good for Guatemala."

Education for Peace and Democracy

The Peace Accords culminated in 1996, officially ending the Conflicto Armado. Encompassing cultural rights and social development, the Peace Accords acknowledged the role of the educational sector in perpetuating racism in Guatemalan society through unequal access to schools, poor treatment of indigenous students, and the deficiency and discriminatory representations of indigenous culture in the curriculum. The accords outlined a number of steps toward making education a more equitable system and thereby contributing to long-term peace, ranging from increased access to schools, bilingual instruction, government investment, community involvement, and institutional decentralization in addition to curricular reform. It was imagined that, through schools, postwar citizens would shape a new national identity and democratic citizenship based on their understanding that "respect for and the exercise of the political, cultural, economic and spiritual rights of all Guatemalans is the foundation for a new coexistence" (Peace Accords, 1996, p. 39, app. 2). This shared civic identity would aim to unite a previously divided nation, a quintessential goal of postwar educational reform (Freedman, Weinstein, Murphy, & Longman, 2008; Tawil & Harley, 2004).

Guatemala's Peace Accords also created the truth commission, charged with investigating the causes of war and the extent of violations committed by various actors. In their report, *Memory of Silence*, the CEH (1999) attributed 93 percent of the human rights violations committed during the war to the state military, paramilitary, and police forces, leaving the guerrilla forces responsible for 3 percent, while 4 percent remained undetermined. Further, the commission determined that state forces committed acts of genocide toward select Maya groups. The report stretched into the prewar past to explore the roots of racism in Guatemala and the political mechanisms that maintained difference, revealing a recurrent clash between the state and the sector of civil society that sought to change the social and political order. Given the historical patterns, the commission concluded that the Guatemalan state's strategic use of terror was not confined to the context of war but instead was a fundamental "component of state formation" (Grandin, 2005, p. 50). Rather than cast the Conflicto Armado as a historical "parenthesis" (Booth, 1999, p. 250) or a "state of exception" (Agamben, 1998), the report made clear that violence and terror served as a routine state instrument of stabilization aimed at controlling uprising and dissention. These patterns of human rights violations characterized and defined the relationship between the state and civil society—not their "exception." Collectively, they composed a "continuum of violence" (Manz, 2008) or "ellipses" of ongoing historical injustice (Booth, 1999, p. 250), in which the Conflicto Armado needed to be inscribed.

Though education is not highlighted through an explicit narrative of harm in the report, the commission, perhaps inadvertently, documented the role of the education system in legitimizing a racial hierarchy that fueled the conflict, thus acknowledging the ways that educational inequity functioned as a contributor to indigenous exclusion and as a space where intergroup divisions were legitimized and reproduced. Through their collection of thousands of *testimonios*, investigators uncovered stories of indigenous children who were systematically denied access to schools, endured habitual humiliation in classrooms, and were subsequently endangered in school spaces during the war. Although these testimonies were collected with the intention of understanding the extent of violence committed by various actors, the stories detailed the circumstances of children forced to abandon school during the conflict for security reasons or who could not attend school because their teachers were killed or endangered or because their schools became targets of aggression. Their testimonies centered on the loss of childhood, such as one survivor who shared, "We could not go to school. We grew up with the machete, with fear, terror, pain, and poverty, rather than growing up in peace with education" (CEH, 1999). But schools were not only sites where the conflict spilled over into the everyday lives of citizens. These testimonies lent credence to claims that the "Guatemalan educational system was designed as an instrument for ethnocide" (Cojtí Cuxil, as cited in Maxwell, 2009, p. 93; see also Jiménez Estrada, 2012). Assimilationist curriculum and the systematic denial of educational access had a cumulative effect, leading to the purposeful exclusion and alienation of indigenous peoples from nonindigenous citizens and the state. In essence, schools were spaces where structural, symbolic, and eventually physical violence was reproduced.[4]

While education's role in the conflict composed a subtle thread in the CEH report, education was integral to the commission's recommendations that all Guatemalan citizens learn the historical truth, asserting that truth would lead to democratization and peace. Authors advocated that "curricula of primary, secondary, and university level education" include "the teaching of the causes, development, and the consequences of the armed conflict" (1999, p. 55). Members of the commission hoped for explicit integration in the national curriculum so that the CEH report would be a primary historical document accessible to future generations (Rothenberg, 2012a).

In addition to the United Nations–sanctioned truth commission, the Oficina de Derechos Humanos del Arzobispado de Guatemala (Human Rights Office of the Guatemalan Catholic Archdiocese) organized a parallel commission, the Recuperación de la Memoria Histórico (REMHI; Recovery of Historical Memory Project), culminating in a report called *Guatemala: Nunca más* (*Never again*). The findings of the REMHI report (1999), led by Bishop Juan Gerardi Condera, corroborate many of the repressive historical patterns documented in the CEH report. REMHI authors similarly pointed to the importance of educational reform. In their recommendations section, they argued that educational policy makers have a particular responsibility to "carry out curricular reforms and incorporate into textbooks relevant historical and official documents that provide an accurate account of what happened during the armed conflict" (p. 315). The report similarly encourages the inclusion of the CEH and REMHI reports in the curriculum as primary historical resources. Two days after presenting the REMHI report, Bishop Gerardi was found bludgeoned to death. Though an obvious political assassination to many, this crime was spun by police authorities as either an attack by a wild dog or a crime of passion (Goldman, 2007). Gerardi's vicious killing and subsequent cover-up sent a clear and chilling message about the limits of what could be discussed in public. The war was over, but its narrative—linked to calls for accountability—would remain deeply fraught.

Curricular Reform and the Two Devils

Following the peace process, there were high hopes that educational reform would lead to significant changes in schools and society, undoing centuries of racial inequality reinforced through a monolingual and monocultural education system. In the postwar era indigenous populations would have equal access to schools, be treated fairly in educational institutions, learn in their mother tongues, and recognize themselves in the national curriculum as both equal to, and culturally distinct from, nonindigenous citizens. Yet many of these reforms have been critiqued as "cosmetic," in their attempts to "improve the State's image in the eyes of international organizations, but not to change indigenous conditions nor their place in the country's ethnic structuration" (Bastos, 2012, p. 167). Guatemala's Ministry of Education implemented a program of Educación Intercultural Bilingüe (EIB; Intercultural Bilingual Education), though coverage is low even in indigenous regions, and little has been done to integrate these reforms at the postprimary level (L. López, 2014). Though there is continued support for implementing EIB, it remains a hotly contested issue, debated within and outside of indigenous communities, as well as at the ministry level (Bastos, 2012; Jiménez Estrada, 2012). In line with (pre-2015) global education trends and the Education for All development agenda, policy makers have devoted significant attention to educational access in the postwar years, though again these reforms have been directed principally at the primary school level. Educational access for young people has improved dramatically in recent decades, however—as alluded to by Gustavo, the principal of the Comalapa school—nearly half of Guatemala's youth remain out of school (UNDP, 2012). Meanwhile, Guatemala's educational system continues to rank as one of the region's most unequal (Poppema, 2009; UNDP, 2012). Inequitable access and variable quality of educational opportunities remain critical issues for youth development and key drivers of inequality, at times contributing to conflict (Buckland, 2005; Burde, 2014).

For many states in transition, the primary educational concern is increasing access to safe schools rather than curricular reform or professional training. In these cases inequitable conditions rooted in the institutional structure of schooling can prevent policy makers from thinking beyond them. For example, there is a frequent assumption that addressing educational access in postconflict societies must precede attempts to focus on quality (Buckland, 2005). Accordingly, it can seem impractical to study the quality of educational exchanges in Guatemala, a place where deep structural inequality persists. Yet access alone does little for the life trajectories of youth from the margins when the quality of education remains poor, and the curriculum is sharply disconnected from their lived realities (Dryden-Peterson et al., 2015). Without attention to curricular reform and professional learning, educators in postwar societies are often left on their own to grapple with questions about how to make education relevant to young people's lives, when they are born into conditions of protracted violence and the harm and division of war's legacies (Freedman et al., 2008).

Guatemala's Ministry of Education began the process of curricular reform as most ministries in the aftermath of identity-based conflict do—by vetting the national curriculum to remove discriminatory representations of indigenous peoples and culture (Bush & Saltarelli, 2000). Reforms have noticeably gravitated toward teaching respect for Guatemala's diversity, as well as cultivating pride in the state's pluricultural, multilingual, and multiethnic national identity (e.g., Ministry of Education, 2010). Meanwhile, curricular adjustments have focused attention on the human rights of children and women and the cultural rights of indigenous groups, positioning rights awareness as essential civic knowledge (Instituto Interamericano de Derechos Humanos, 2007). Theoretically, schools devote one day per week to civic rituals such as singing the national anthem, seeking to foster a sense of national "unity among diversity" (Ministry of Education, 2010, p. 4; see also Maxwell, 2009; Rothenberg, 2012b).[5] The curriculum includes extensive coverage of Guatemala's need to foster a "culture of peace" (Oglesby, 2007a, 2007b), a peace education framework adopted from the United Nations Educational, Scientific, and Cultural Organization, emphasizing that citizen responsibilities include abstaining from drugs and violence, while promoting peaceful solutions to conflicts (e.g., Ministry of Education, 2001, 2003). Emphasizing the peace process has proved central to the dissemination of these civic skills and values; yet like many postwar societies, Guatemala's narrative of past violence remains a fraught subject for policy makers and educators (Bellino, 2016).

Originally servicing the nation-state, history education was designed to shape citizens and their affinity to the nation, romanticizing and essentializing national identity (Anderson, 1983; Carretero, 2011; Heater, 2004). Often grounded in "master narratives" intended for students to memorize, internalize, and reproduce (Carretero & Bermudez, 2012, p. 632), traditional approaches to teaching the past have in recent years been critiqued as imparting "collective memory" rather than emphasizing the critical skills that underpin the discipline of history. In contrast, disciplinary approaches advocate for historical thinking and historical understanding as central pedagogical goals rather than transmitting particular narratives of the past (Wineburg, 2001). Although there is emerging evidence that disciplinary approaches stand to benefit postconflict societies in their capacity to strengthen critical reasoning, apply evidence, and adopt multiple perspectives (McCully, 2012), educational policy makers frequently opt to silence past conflict in order to tell a "best story" (Seixas, 2000, p. 20) about a nation, even when doing so leaves notable gaps. Shaping the history curriculum around a nation's "best story" captures the ongoing fascination with the "usable past," a "hallmark of collective memory," in that a particular historical narrative is conceived as "usable" toward nation building (Wertsch, 2002, p. 70). Usable pasts hinge on the assumption that the "right national narrative would lead to common civic and political outcomes" (M. Levinson, 2012, p. 113), a relationship that presupposes a single narrative will appeal to diverse populations whose civic identities have been shaped by distinctly unequal experiences with the state over time.

Across various sectors in Guatemala, there has been moral concern and outrage over the lack of curricular engagement with the Conflicto Armado, as well as dissatisfaction over the nature of its representation when schools do address it. Critiques expressed by civil-society organizations, as well as academics and policy institutions, fault politicians and policy makers for inadequately commemorating the past (e.g., Rothenberg, 2012a) and poorly distinguishing between democratic and authoritarian governments (Schultz, Ainley, Friedman, & Lietz, 2011); blame teachers and parents for ignoring the past or transmitting biased interpretations (Giracca, 2009); and critique youth for not knowing, not caring, and not understanding the violent past's implications for their current lives (Sandoval, 2011). In this sense, public contest over Guatemala's history curriculum resembles curricular debates and culture wars in many parts of the world (e.g., Nash, Crabtree, & Dunn, 2000). Yet, more particular to Guatemala, concerns over representations of historical injustice seem to pendulum from claims of absence and invisibility to allegedly biased inclusion (Bellino, 2014b). How is it possible that educational policy, schools, and families are simultaneously silencing the past and politicizing it through biased representations?

Understanding this widespread dissatisfaction, as well as disputes over what constitutes historical silence, requires an exploration of (at least) three enduring and widely available narratives of the Conflicto Armado. The Guatemalan military, transitional state, and conservative Right maintain that the Conflicto Armado involved the (heroic) army, who protected civilians from the (radical, communist) guerrillas; international human rights organizations and development agencies tend to support the testimony of Nobel Peace Prize winner Rigoberta Menchú and the CEH findings that the conflict took the form of the (oppressive) army versus the (innocent) people, despite the goals of the (liberating) guerrillas. And anthropologist David Stoll (1994) has complicated these polarizing narratives with one that runs counter to both. Stoll argues that many did not view themselves as political agents in the struggle but rather felt trapped between two rival groups, experiencing the Conflicto Armado as the (oppressive) army versus the (manipulative and incompetent) guerrillas versus the (innocent) people. To be sure, these are simple renderings of complex narratives for everyone involved, and at times they appear mutually constitutive of one another rather than mutually exclusive.

While there is arguably a distinct level of "historical silence" on the part of schools (Bellino, 2014b; see also Rubin, 2016a, 2016b), "no national project to address the teaching of historical memory" (Oglesby, 2007a, p. 83), a social studies curriculum with more emphasis on civic values and little history after the 1960s (Oglesby, 2007a, 2007b), and "only cursory mention" of the extent of the war's brutality (Rothenberg, 2012a, p. 224), elements of these narratives feature heavily in curricular accounts of the violent past that are endorsed by the state and frequently used in schools. Given the politics of transition, one might expect the national curriculum to uphold the state's account of the brave and loyal military rescuing the state from an impending fall into communism. Although there are glimmers of this heroic past in Guatemalan school texts, this narrative upheld by the transitional government appears to have been tempered by recognition of state repression by the international community and subsequently imagined through the lens of a compromise narrative that diffuses accountability evenly across fighting parties.

A number of curricular texts depict the Conflicto Armado as having taken place between "two devils," the state and the guerrilla armies (Bellino, 2014b; Oglesby, 2007a). The two-devils trope has been coined and critiqued in the context of other Latin American conflicts, for its omission of asymmetrical power dynamics and the allusion that violence exclusively involved two parties, thereby criminalizing nonstate actors who took up arms and removing political agency from civilians ostensibly caught in the middle (Jelin, 2003; Kaiser, 2005). By extension, this narrative conveys a message that all actors who took up arms are equally responsible for the harm and destruction that ensued. Despite that state forces were found to have committed 93 percent of the rights violations during the conflict, including genocide—statistics almost always omitted from curricular resources—state accountability is nullified when set against the radical (and illegal) violence of guerrilla forces. In the process, the notion that *everyone* is accountable becomes (mis)taken for the notion that *no one* can be held accountable (Barkan, 2009).

Yet these narrative tendencies to reduce war to a cast of criminal perpetrators and apolitical victims do little to help us understand how members of the postwar generation make meaning of war while developing as citizens in its aftermath. Are these narratives, as anticipated, "usable" for youth in shaping the peaceful, multicultural, and democratic citizenry envisioned by curriculum reformers and transitional actors? Are their identities and experiences reflected and included in these "orderly" narratives of mass violence (Nordstrom, 2004, p. 33)? How do young people draw on these official narratives to construct their own understandings of the past and its relationship to their identity and social location in society? History is often conceived as a window or lens through which students view themselves and their current choices in context. This lens, however, is not a perfect window or mirror but rather a "prism" through which present concerns and past situations illuminate and coinform each other (Shaw, 2002, p. 265). According to Jörn Rüsen (2004), the construction of the past serves a particular purpose toward present actions: it "aid[s] us in comprehending past actuality in order to grasp present actuality" (p. 66). This implies a reciprocal relationship between past and present, in that we construct the past in line with our present belief systems, and, when necessary, we reinterpret the past based on our present choices.

Despite the presumed goals of usable pasts imparting a sense of national pride and requiring that young learners see positive aspects of their identity that they can "use" in the present, I argue that all pasts—no matter how harmfully depicted—become "usable" toward some civic outcome. To argue otherwise removes interpretive agency from young people, who interpret, critique, and deploy history "as a basis for creatively comprehending their present situation and making informed choices about how it [history] is to be addressed and lived" (Jackson, 2007, p. 83). In the chapters that follow, it becomes clear that the two-devils narrative contains several usable entry points for divergent historical interpretations. But this narrative depiction of mass violence, interpreted in a time of ongoing violence, fails to disrupt enduring cultural beliefs that civic participation constitutes criminal involvement. One of the most salient lessons of the two-devils trope is the high value it places on neutrality, linking a stance of conflict aversion and disengagement to perceptions of good citizenship. As youth come of age in a high-risk postwar setting, this narrowly "usable past" becomes increasingly relevant to their sense of security, efficacy, and civic purpose.

Legacies of Transition and Historical Injustice

On paper Guatemala seems to have demonstrated an exemplary transitional justice process. The state engaged in many of the formal mechanisms that cross-cultural research and policy experience have deemed valuable, including a comprehensive peace process, a third-party truth commission, and a national reparations program. Even during peace negotiations, democratic elections were instituted, with a growing number of political positions supported by a multiparty system. Human rights organizations grew exponentially after the ceasefire, reflecting the state's pledge to change its human rights record. In addition, the state made efforts to revise national identity to be more inclusive of indigenous groups.

The transition, however, was essentially brokered by the military, as they had "won" the war on the battlefield and did not need to concede power to the Left (Cruz, 2011; Oglesby & Ross, 2009). Furthermore, the military viewed themselves as "the stabilizing institution of this transition ... the institution that strengthens democracy" (Guatemalan Army High Command, 2011). In this sense, the peace negotiations, and especially the truth commission and reparations programs, were not compromises per se but rather concessions to the Left and "demonstrat[ions] that the army had won the war" (Grandin et al., 2011b, p. 441). The state reluctantly tolerated the CEH and did little to support its work, intentionally withholding internal security documents (Doyle, 2012; Weld, 2014). State actors openly denounced CEH findings, clinging to the explanation that guerrillas threatened the nation (Grandin, 2005; Oglesby, 2007b). Denial of genocide continues at the highest state levels, a debate intensified by the former head of state Ríos Montt's recent genocide trial. Meanwhile, though the CEH report is technically publicly accessible, its length (exceeding four thousand pages in twelve volumes) and legal language remain obstacles to public readership. Needless to say, neither the CEH nor the REMHI report has been formally integrated into the national curriculum with any historical authority, though there have been some individual, faith-, and community-based efforts to construct counternarratives in line with these sources.

Disputes over which voices and institutions have legitimate claims to the historical narrative are common in the aftermath of conflict. Narrative contests are one of the defining features of societies in transition (Jackson, 2006; Jelin, 2003). But in Guatemala the ongoing work of human rights advocates, lawyers, judges, activists, journalists, forensic scientists, and community leaders seeking truth, justice, and reparations for the past has generated a new wave of repressive and violent responses aimed at discrediting the activist voice and the act of organizing as a mechanism of social change. In other words, Guatemala's violent history is not past, but present "in the form of new victims" (Grandin, 2004, p. 171). Today Guatemala is not only one of the most violent countries in the world (United Nations Office on Drugs and Crime [UNODC], 2010) but one of the most dangerous environments for political activism and collective movements (Unidad de Protección a Defensoras y Defensores de Derechos Humanos de Guatemala, 2011), even in cases where contemporary justice struggles are not tied to the past, such as indigenous cultural movements. Political crime is often concealed by a complex web of actors engaged in a range of violent pursuits: drug trafficking, organized crime, femicide, social cleansing, gang activity, and community vigilantism. Many of these actors rely on "hidden power" networks (Peacock & Beltrán, 2003) through active and retired military officers, as well as transnational criminal networks, at times functioning in "parallel" to state powers (Adams, 2011, pp. 40–41) and other times operating as the state by proxy (see Sanford, 2008, 2003b). In either case, these networks thrive in what Carolyn Nordstrom (2004) has called the "shadows," in that they traverse categories of licit and illicit, political and criminal, functioning with some level of state complicity. Under these conditions, the incomplete transitional justice process at once signals permission to "outsource" justice to the private sphere, in which citizens are expected to narrate and commemorate—or silence—the past, thus "reconciling themselves" (H. Mack, 2011, p. 450), and to terrorize, stigmatize, and criminalize those who seek historical justice in public spaces (Bellino, 2015a).

High rates of impunity underpin this landscape of violence, with a virtual guarantee that perpetrators will not be apprehended for violent crimes. Together, violence and impunity have earned Guatemala a reputation as a "killer's paradise" (O'Connor & Portenier, 2007). At the policy level there are two leading explanations for Guatemala's impunity: the lack of political will and skill to bring perpetrators to justice (Alston, 2007; Sanford, 2008). Corruption and extortion have crippled already underresourced state institutions, in part because of the linkages between government officials and organized crime groups, including powerful drug cartels. Rather than overthrow the government, the goal of these groups is to weaken and infiltrate the state to "neutralize [state] interference with their businesses" (Heymann, 2012, p. 2). Nevertheless, the state is not simply *subject to* these forces but complicit in them, at least to some extent. Even as homicide rates grow, the state has done little to effectively increase public security and transform the justice system, conveying that it "has very limited responsibilities to society, and that it is wholly appropriate for even security and justice to be private rather than public goods" (Alston, 2007, pp. 21–22). Private security forces in Guatemala, for example, have outnumbered police officers by four or five to one (Adams, 2011), though these trends have shifted as Guatemala has remilitarized. Most recently, the scale of political corruption rose to the former president himself, who resigned amid extreme civilian pressure and accusations of his involvement in a multimillion-dollar fraud case.

Given the reality that postwar Guatemala is not, in many ways, *post*, there are different theories about how contemporary violence relates to the history of the Conflicto Armado and to what extent it is a natural outgrowth of protracted civil war or a deliberate extension. Contemporary violence is at once indiscriminate and selective, at once disruptive and stabilizing, and at once exceptional and emblematic. The multiplicity and convergence of violent actors and structures complicate the linkages between past and present actors and mechanisms of repression, suggesting that it is at once old and new, at once connected to the history of violence and independent of it.[6] Underlying these questions lies more than a historical tension between continuity and change; there is a deep uncertainty as to whether Guatemala actually experienced a postwar transition at all or undertook an elaborate process of "restoration" or "instauration" (Torres-Rivas, 1999, p. 294).

Anxiety over claims to the past, then, is not confined to the space of history books or the school walls. Rather, valorizing one's account of the past as historically significant and relevant in the postwar era contributes to the relationship that all citizens forge with the state through civic identification, trust, and action. Accordingly, young people's impressions of historical connections between past and present justice issues are not merely measures of disciplinary thinking but critical—and highly contested—sites for civic identity development. The way young people orient themselves within their construction of past-present-future, that is, their historical consciousness, functions as a significant mediator in their civic development, particularly when the injuries of war have been left untreated.

3

International Academy

The No-Blame Generation and
the Post-Postwar

A State of Emergency and the Drums of War

Alejandro leans forward on the couch until the blanket wrapped around his legs falls to the floor. "This is how it happened." He corrects himself, "Well, this is how we think it happened." Flipping his long brown hair out of his eyes, he explains, "The hydroelectric company has been repressing people, and when a man turned up dead—a community leader, and I think some others were injured too—the people were angry, because it was the security guards for the hydroelectric company [who did it]. They grabbed their guns, so now they were armed and angry, and then the government said, 'Okay, we are going to establish a state of siege here in Santa Cruz Barillas because you people are all violent *narcos*.' So now there is a curfew, and you can't leave your home. Now the military is there, *to keep people safe*." His voice dips into melodramatic sarcasm when he says the part about empty streets and armed soldiers implying safety. Though people of all ages make dark jokes about the everyday nature of Guatemala's violence, moments like these make it clear that Alejandro is only seventeen. Adults' sarcasm comes off as much more subtle.

From across the room, his mother listens to him describe why the government instituted martial law. Anastela nods as Alejandro speaks and seems generally satisfied with his account despite its circular moments, though she adds some clarification: "But the point is that they are not narcos; they are humble people who are trying to survive under the repressive presence of this corporation." I nod gravely, conjuring familiar images of Guatemala's rural poor. "And the historical roots here are important, because this is not new. It has been going on for years that the corporations repress the indigenous people, even though the indigenous rejected the proposal to build on their land. . . ." She trails off when the news program returns. I lean in to hear the newscaster over the sound of Alejandro trimming his fingernails with a chef's knife. Anastela scolds him with her eyes, and he places the knife on the plate of mango skins. Looking at the screen, Anastela touches my elbow, "This show is really right wing. This guy here, he is really promilitary. The other news channel we watch is more left, it gives space to the [indigenous] communities and will cover human rights violations." This background is for my benefit, so that I understand why they would listen to a man insist that the "events in Barillas" have nothing to do with the hydroelectric company. To Alejandro she says, "You see, I think he has to be connected to the hydroelectric [corporation]." He murmurs and nods slightly without turning his head.

When the segment ends, Anastela stands and flattens her traje. She is Greek, born in Greece—not Guatemalan, nor indigenous. But she has lived here since her midtwenties, married a Guatemalan, and, once they separated, chose to raise her only son, Alejandro, just outside the capital city. Her second husband, Rodolfo, is Kaqchikel Maya, and her traje carries the distinct patterns and thread colors from his home village of Comalapa. Clearing the table, she continues to explain, "This is an international business thing now—because people don't want the corporations. First they repress the people, they force them to sell their land. . . . Then if the people say no, the corporations go to the military."

Alejandro finishes her thought, "and the state protects the interests of the corporations. . . . Did you know that human rights are for corporations, not for people?" "And now . . . the streets are filled with soldiers and the people are hiding in the mountains, afraid they will take them away . . . because they think it is going to be the Conflicto Armado all over again." The deeply political nature of this conversation is a nightly ritual in this house. Anastela has participated in indigenous rights movements for decades, even attending protests when Alejandro was a baby, secured in a blanket across her chest. Alejandro was a "baby revolutionary," and Anastela always imagined he would be by her side in the lucha, even as she hoped there would be less to fight for by the time he was old enough to decide for himself.

Anastela holds her hand out for Alejandro to pass the knife, which has found its way back onto his lap. She then excuses herself and moves into the kitchen to prepare sandwiches for the small neighborhood shop at the back of their home. When the sound of the kitchen knives on the counter-top is louder than her sandals clicking on the floor, Alejandro turns to me. "Tell me about that thick raincoat of yours. Is it Kevlar?"

I hold my fingers apart to show him how thick the rubber is, that I will be properly prepared for the Guatemalan rainy season.

"Yeah, but is it bulletproof?"

"I think it could handle a hurricane," I joke. The last time I stayed with Alejandro's family, the Volcano Pacaya erupted, followed by Hurricane Agatha. It rained, hailed, and then black ash fell from the sky for three days, as city streets collapsed and swallowed people, cars, and multistory buildings.

He stares at me with a serious face, and it hits me then that he is talking about real bullets. "Because you might want to think about investing in one of those. It's that bad here now." In English he says, "You can hear the war drums." When he says these words I realize that part of me expected to hear them sooner, several years ago when I met Alejandro during the 2007 presidential election. Former military general Otto Pérez Molina, now president of Guatemala, was close to winning his first presidential race. Alejandro and I were both spectating, fascinated by the young people his age who were latching hands in long rows on both sides of Pérez Molina, their faces glowing at being close to the potential next president, one who promised to make Guatemala a safer place to live. Four years later the first military officer since the Conflicto Armado to hold the position of president won the majority vote based on his *mano dura* (iron fist) platform. Since he became president, the National Civil Police and military have both grown in size and heightened their presence across the country, notably in Guatemala City but also in rural areas such as Barillas, responding to signs of civil unrest or popular violence, as well as drug and gang-related massacres.

"Is that what they say, that there could be a war any second?"

"No, that's what *I* say. My parents think that any conflict will be diplomatically resolved this time. . . . They think people here have learned from the Conflicto Armado." In recent years Guatemala's postwar violence is increasingly set against the thirty-six-year civil war, as a consequence, a continuation, or a contrast. Once silenced, the war is suddenly on the tip of everyone's tongue. "I think it's gotten too bad to fix. These guys running things, they are *bad guys*. These *militares*."

I begin to apologize for the way things are, adding an unpersuasive assurance, "But you'll be safe." As soon as I promise that Alejandro will be safe, I know I have made a mistake. In the seven years that I have been visiting Guatemala, no one has made me a promise that they were not sure they could keep. But there is something in his voice that sounds more scared than angry tonight, a side of Alejandro usually hidden by his teenage bravado, and I struggle to protect him with my words. "You are moving on to different things. You will be safe in the U.S." Alejandro's acceptance at a university in the Midwest gave his family some peace of mind, though they mention more than once a day that they don't know what they will do without him.

To this he says, "You have to leave the country if you want to survive."

Leaving Past Mistakes Behind

Before seven in the morning we are outside with wet hair and containers of warm potatoes, waiting at the bus stop. Anastela waits with us under a small ledge protecting us from the rain. Alejandro cranes his neck to check around the corner, muttering, "stupid bus." He wears an oversized leather jacket that belonged to his father and pulls his scarf up over his chin. "What are you, a Zapatista?" his mother says. I laugh, but he gives her a stinging look. Softening his face, Alejandro asks for money to make photocopies, explaining that he printed the "Open Letter to the President" and plans to show it to his friends at school. The letter demands that they lift the state of siege in Barillas, investigate the circumstances of the recent murder, free all townspeople who have been captured, suspend corporate activity, and resume democratic dialogue between the indigenous pueblo and the businesses. Anastela's face widens into a smile. She kisses Alejandro on the top of his head and squeezes her arms around him, telling him how proud he has made her. Patting her apron pockets, she empties a pile of change into his hand, calculating that he can make at least five copies of the four-page letter.

A full-size yellow school bus pulls up, and we are the first ones on. I follow Alejandro to the last seat. At each stop, the older boys head to the back. The boys wear their school uniform polos with the collars popped, khakis, and skater sneakers. The girls wear school sweatshirts that hang past their waists. Some shake hands, then drop into a seat and pull on their headphones. The little ones sit three across in the front seats, little blond boys from the United States, the Honduran girl, the twins from India. We ride through *colonias* (private neighborhoods) with elaborate glassed-in security booths and guards in uniform who operate mechanical gates to let the bus pass. Alejandro once told me he was glad to be picked up first, and now I see why. We pass through the most elite colonias in Guatemala City, houses with ornate doors, three-car garages, jet skis and motorboats parked alongside Range Rovers. The neighborhood is filled with workers, skinny indigenous men in knee-high boots washing car windows and trimming hedges.

Alejandro sings softly to himself and tucks his mouth into his coat collar. His family struggles to send him to the International Academy, one of the most expensive private schools in Guatemala City. Though they barely make ends meet with their shop, they are convinced it is Alejandro's only opportunity for high-quality education. The International Academy is designed to reflect the U.S. private school model, with an institutional hierarchy that stems from the superintendent to principals and vice principals, as well as a private school board made up of parents in the school community. Most teachers are from the United States, teach classes in English, and are not fluent in Spanish. (Exceptions are Spanish language, Spanish literature, and social studies classes, which are taught in Spanish.) Inside school walls, students are encouraged to socialize with one another in English as well as Spanish. The International Academy advertises itself as one of Guatemala's highest quality educational experiences, promising bilingual mastery, strong moral values, and high acceptance rates at national and foreign universities. The school mission emphasizes the "professional" development of students, many of whom will become Guatemala's future business leaders. The school caters to children of business owners, government officials, high-ranking military officers, and foreign diplomats. Since elementary school Alejandro has shared classes with the very elite that his parents struggle against. The irony is not lost on him, though over the years I have watched Alejandro shift between disdain and distrust of his classmates to apologetic affection.

The bus pulls into the parking lot, past the security gates and the cluster of men in suits, whom Alejandro identifies as his classmates' bodyguards. Most of the "men in black" wait in the school parking lot throughout the day, playing games on their cell phones, but prepared for the "anything" that can happen "because Guatemala is Guatemala," as I have been told over and over by young people frustrated with the unpredictability of Guatemala's violence. Nearly one third of the academy's students have permanent bodyguards, though there is some disagreement among students about whether guards "make a show" that prevents violence or attracts it. While Isabella is accompanied by armed security to protect against narcos only when she travels to the Guatemala-Mexico border, Nicolás jokes that he has had four guards since birth who had even surveilled the hospital nursery for kidnappers, a legitimate threat in his powerful family. Yet in spite of this never-safe reality and the constant accompaniment of armed guards, most of Alejandro's friends do not subjectively feel at risk. They travel in private cars to malls, social clubs, and one another's colonias or by helicopter to the interior of the country to their family's second home or to Miami to visit relatives and possibly a third home. Their freedom is not Alejandro's freedom. For him, the prohibitions and restraints on his physical movement are "oppressive" and akin to "living in a chicken coop."

The school grounds resemble a small university campus—long meandering buildings enclosed by lush plants, an open stadium, painted basketball courts, a cafeteria with a full staff and a daily lunch menu, a well-lit library with shelves of hardcover books and large windows, a music room with a variety of instruments, an art studio with thick paper and rows of supplies, a lawn with trimmed grass and stout trees, a central office with well-dressed receptionists seated outside a row of glass-paneled administrative offices. Each teacher has his or her own classroom, furnished with a computer and Internet access, printer, blackboards with boxes of extra chalk, bulletin boards, bookshelves with class sets of glossy new textbooks, and a large Guatemalan flag hanging from the wall.

Alejandro takes a seat in the back of Profe Castillo's class, the sleeves of his leather jacket dangling past his wrists. He drops his woven bag on the floor, placing nothing on his desk but his folded arms. Students pile in, some sipping to-go mugs of coffee. They line their backpacks and lunch cases on the floor. Girls place cloth pencil cases on their desks. Several students move to the perimeter of the room to charge their cell phones and tablets. Though it is not prescribed, the boys sit on one half of the room near the windows and girls on the opposite side near the hallway.

Profe Castillo, a middle-aged, self-described mestizo, has been teaching social studies for nearly ten years. He has sharp, clean-shaven cheekbones, serious gray eyes, and enough gel in his hair that it looks wet from morning to evening. When the bell rings, Profe Castillo folds up today's newspaper and looks out at the room. Students are still fumbling with their cell phones or digging into their backpacks for juice boxes. A girl in the front tears off a piece of sweet bread and passes it to a row of girls to share.

Profe begins by describing the global context of the "Red Scare," then moves swiftly into the subject of the Conflicto Armado. "There were two parties. Who were they?" Students continue to chat and text on their phones. Alejandro looks coolly toward the front of the room. Profe continues, "The Guatemalan side, the state. And the guerrillas. Every one of us has our own version of the Conflicto Armado." He pauses and asks a question I have heard many teachers pose, presumably on my behalf and to validate their claims that the younger generation does not care about the past, "Now, who had never heard of the Conflicto Armado before we learned about it here in school; who never knew there was a civil war?" Six students timidly raise their hands, giggling and a little embarrassed when they see how few of them there are. Two of them are newly immigrated Korean students. The other four are from families who have lived in Guatemala for generations. Profe Castillo does a quick calculation and announces that about 25 percent of the class had "no idea" there was a civil war. "And this is sad, because this is part of the country that we live in, so we don't know our history, right? And it's important that we develop and conserve what we are going to call our historical memory." He adds, "The term *historical memory*, in my opinion, has been somewhat defamed. . . . What do you all think of this term, what does it mean, what does it sound like?"

"Not to forget the past."

"Not to forget what happened."

Profe nods and transitions into a careful positioning of the uses and abuses of historical memory. While he makes it clear that "we need to remember our history," he also warns that historical memory has been a source of ongoing division and conflict. He says, "In some sectors of the population, they have used historical memory as an instrument of reproach, to blame, and to continue acts of revenge that are not sufficiently justified." The USB cord he wears swings around his neck as he moves from one corner of the room to the other. "Personally—and this is my personal reflection—I don't say, let's not remember the past, let's forget history, because history is part of us, we are a consequence of this history that our predecessors have lived." By now, most of the students have settled in their desks, and the boys nod visibly. "But we can't use this history to hold us down, to create rancor, or to continue developing practices that only . . . guarantee the delay of Guatemala's development or that guarantee discord, you understand?"

Profe goes on to describe starkly oppositional accounts of the Conflicto Armado, depending on the author's perspective, then asks, "Now, which of these is right?" A handful of students answer together, "the first one," referring to historical accounts written from the perspective of the state military. In the back of the room, Alejandro glares at his classmates. Profe Castillo waits just long enough for the students to begin to doubt their answer, but several of them repeat, "the first one, the army."

Though I don't hear a single student say "both," Profe Castillo confers with the class, "both?" as if confirming a consensus. Several students continue to shake their head no, but Profe does not acknowledge their disagreement. "If we can see both sides, we can analyze and *objectively* critique—this is the objective, to critique objectively. And from there, we make our own conclusions. . . . The idea of historical memory should be . . ." His voice goes staccato, "Not. To commit . . ." Instinctively, students chime in, "the same mistakes of the past." Profe grins at their spontaneous participation and affirms that Guatemalans needs to "resolve" the mistakes of the past to ensure that they do not repeat them. There is hardly a pause before Profe transitions into the present day, justifying Otto Pérez Molina's right to be president. "We've heard, Guatemala is going to have a military president; he's an assassin; he's this, he's that. He *was* a military officer, but right now he's a civilian. And as a civilian, he has every right to be president."

In recent years Guatemala's security agenda has essentially supplanted the postwar peace agenda, and the most recent presidential election brought the unresolved tension between these issues and their linkages to past and present violence into sharp relief. Current president Otto Pérez Molina ran on a platform of mano dura. Indigenous communities vocalized their opposition based on Pérez Molina's alleged involvement in human rights violations during the conflict, as well as fears of electing the first *militar* (military) head of state since the return to democratic elections. The issue revealed the intense polarization in civil society between justice for the past and security for the present. As president, Pérez Molina has since delivered on his promises through a substantial remilitarization campaign and requests for foreign aid to augment the military budget, justifying military expansion as the primary security mechanism in the state's antidrug agenda. Pressures of contemporary crime have led to the restoration of authoritarian security approaches such as mano dura, contributing to the reproduction of violence, as well as the blurring of state and extrastate violence (Holston & Caldeira, 1998). Currently, there is a strong discourse around whether President Pérez Molina is a civilian or a *militar* and whether the state now has a "military government."

Profe goes on to lament that today's "situation" is "worse than during the Conflicto Armado, because during the Conflicto Armado there was a 'justification' to kidnap and disappear people. Today there isn't." He gestures quotes with his hands. "Today we're living supposedly in times of 'peace.'" Profe's voice rises to a level of anger, but the students laugh, as they often do when confronting the subject of Guatemala's extreme violence. "It's ironic, what we are living, that this is our peace. . . . It's chaos . . . a real chaos."

Guillermo, a skinny boy who has been eagerly waiting for an opening, says emphatically, "It's a disorder." Negative attitudes toward democracy have led to an increased sense of the state as the "enemy" (Adams, 2011, pp. 28–30) and a paradoxical "longing" for increased state presence (Bocarejo, 2013), often accompanied by nostalgia for the protection of former authoritarian regimes. Studies have revealed a direct and negative relationship between surges in violence (and perceived insecurity as its corollary) and civil society's support for democracy, indicating that democratic systems experiencing high levels of violence are perceived as untrustworthy and ineffective at providing citizens with basic security needs (Cruz, 2008). Contemporary concerns among Guatemalans fall in line with this trend, among both adults and young people.[1] In a multinational survey administered by the International Association for the Evaluation of Educational Achievement, Guatemalan youth reported significantly lower trust in their national government, political parties, courts of justice, police, and "people in general" than their peers in other Latin American countries (Schultz et al., 2011, pp. 42–43). On measures of democratic attitudes, a large majority of Guatemalan adolescents revealed support for dictatorships and authoritarian governments (believing these political arrangements could be "justified") when they stood to bring about "order and safety" and "economic benefits" (p. 45).

Profe looks around the room at the few faces, mostly boys, who are listening. "Anyway, the only thing we can do is analyze and interpret the past so that we don't commit the same mistakes. Because the political power is going to be in your hands in fifteen, twenty years." The room falls quiet, but there are still distractions. The girl in front of me tags photos on Facebook. Another shops online for a prom dress. "And if you don't know how to interpret the history of Guatemala, you're going to be exactly the same. . . ." Profe folds his hands. "The promise is big. The promise is big."

Progress and Its Resisters

After class, Alejandro gathers the photocopies and assembles copies of the "Open Letter." Guillermo grabs one from the stack. "Is this it? I want to know about the shit you're interested in."

"Take one then. Show them to our classmates—let's see if they can learn something about their country." David overhears and grabs the letter from Guillermo, teasing that this is Alejandro's secret campaign to run for political office. He pretends to tear the paper in half. Alejandro chastises David for not knowing about the state of siege in Barillas, "Do you know that the number one issue in Guatemala is the unequal distribution of land and wealth?" Alejandro could continue, but over the years he has learned to hold back, that his peers take him more seriously when he says less. David laughs and replaces the letter on Alejandro's pile.

At lunch we sit under the "seniors only" tree and Alejandro shares the letter with Isabella, a girl he once loved. She notes the header, where it says Santa Cruz Barillas. "I went there. I was just there," she says excitedly. "I worked as a translator. Well, sort of a nurse and a translator."

Laura stretches her legs on the lawn. "You speak Mayan?"

"No, I was translating English, stupid. Like I speak Mayan!" The students at International Academy are adamant that there is "no racism" in their school, which they believe sets them apart from other elite institutions. Yet moments like these, it seems there is a shared impression that "race talk" counts only when directed *at* someone rather than about them.

Alejandro audibly clears his throat. "They speak Mam there. There is no such thing as 'speaking Mayan.'" Alejandro is one of the only students at the school with a connection to Maya culture, originally through his mother's activism but eventually through his Kaqchikel stepfather and extended stepfamily.

"Sorry," Isabella jokes, unfazed by Alejandro's mocking tone. Isabella explains that she volunteered with a traveling health organization so that she could learn about nursing. When I ask how she was able to access the area during the state of siege, she insists that she had nothing to fear. "There are so many soldiers there, and we were in the military base, so we were safe." As she speaks, I hear my assumption that she would be alarmed at the number of armed soldiers in the streets, the strict evening curfew, and the rules about not congregating in groups. Instead, she saw these emergency measures as protections against the unruly townspeople. In contrast to Alejandro's story of a military that disguises repression as national security, Isabella is able to "think like a state" in need of "progress," ideas that permeate Profe Castillo's social studies classes. Who feels threatened and who feels protected by the state's army is an indicator of the deep lines that have taken root between the rich and the poor, the urban and the rural, and the Right and the Left.

Isabella returns to the photocopied letter and reads aloud, "Open Letter to the President of Guatemala Otto Pérez Molina, regarding the events in Santa Cruz Barillas and the state of siege." Before reading on, she turns the page to see almost four sheets of text and groans about how long it is. She tells Alejandro that she has never heard the names in the letter, not the community leaders, the development project title, or the sacred river. She reads another phrase from the middle of a page, "And when the population responds, the authorities forget the previous causes and outcomes and accuse and criminalize them as 'villains,' using all the public force of the law." She flips to the last page, the numbered list of demands. The last line of the letter calls for the state to "fulfill its obligation to defend its citizens and not the businesses." Isabella folds the letter and places it next to Alejandro's leg. The lines on her face reveal a combination of affront and apology. Her parents own a finca (estate) nearby, and the president is a family friend. She says gently, "Alejandro, I don't understand."

On other occasions Laura and Isabella have shared their tentative critiques about the country's social service structure, which they believe teaches people to receive rather than "learn how to take care of themselves." Indigenous people in particular accept these "donations" but cannot escape poverty because they do not send their children to school and because they continue to have more children to receive additional services. Many of

Alejandro's classmates crave "improvement" and modernization, viewing megadevelopment projects in rural areas as the key to Guatemala's future. The development projects, in their view, offer a pathway out of poverty for individuals and a chance at global competitiveness, but, as Isabella explains, "It is unfortunate that they [indigenous] do not want development and modernization in our country. . . . They want their culture to be separate."

This exchange encapsulates Charles Hale's (2002) critique of "neoliberal multiculturalism" in Guatemala, in that the neoliberal project conceives a "limited version of indigenous cultural rights" (p. 487), "*so long as it does not go too far*" (p. 490). Maya demands for self-determination are viewed as counterproductive to Guatemala's need to establish a unified national identity, as well as become a developed country. Accordingly, enacting citizenship is expected to be "non-ethnic" (Bastos, 2012, p. 164).

Alejandro's hands remain folded over his legs, and he says nothing until they agree to swap lunches, his homemade sandwich for Isabella's cafeteria pizza. Laura dips chips in a container of cream cheese and says to Isabella, "I want to do what you did. I want to be a nurse, too."

Provocation and Power

At dinner Anastela asks Alejandro about the letter: how many copies did he make, who did he show them to, did anyone say anything? She tells him she is happy to see that he has taken an interest in educating his friends and raising their consciousness about injustice in Guatemala. "If you don't do it, who will?" She is genuinely excited, but there is something uneasy in her voice. Rodolfo ladles a portion of hot *caldo* (soup) into each of our bowls. There is always exactly enough to fill everyone's plate, but no more.

"I don't know. I gave it to Mr. M., and Guillermo wanted to show some people."

She suggests Alejandro uses the copies as talking points with his friends rather than hand out the letters for people to take home only to lose or ignore. Alejandro keeps his head bowed toward his soup, but I believe he knows what his mother is cautioning—that those letters might be dangerous if they fall into the wrong hands.

To no one in particular, Rodolfo asks, "Have you seen the way they are talking about Barillas in the press? They describe it as an angry mob attacking the military base. You would never know there was provocation and a history of repression on behalf of the company. You would never know the people were consulted about whether the corporation could work in their region, and the people said *NO*, and the corporation said yes and the state said yes, and so the answer was *YES*."

In a steady voice Anastela agrees that the state is "covering up for the corporations," and they want the public to believe the village people are "crazy with violence." To me, she adds, "This is why our work is so important, because there is so much to clarify." Anastela asks Alejandro about his physics homework, noting that he has been putting it off for several days. They go back and forth about whether he will complete his university assignments without her there to remind him but drop the subject when Rodolfo announces that he and Anastela will be going to Barillas for a protest the next day. To arrive in time they will sleep only a few hours and leave at three in the morning. They tell Alejandro that if he didn't have school, they would love to have him join them.

"Well, I wouldn't love to be there," he says. Though he often turns down their offers to join their activism—with mixed success—I am surprised to hear that he does not want to join them to protest an issue that he obviously cares about. As his parents have become further committed to the lucha, Alejandro has become more skeptical of the capacity for collective action to change the course of Guatemala's future.

When I first met Rodolfo, he was working at the Chimaltenango National Reparations Program office, listening daily to testimonies of widows and orphaned children who had lost their families, homes, and all of their possessions to the Conflicto Armado. Since the office closed nearly three years prior, he and Anastela began an online network for justice-related issues. In its early stages the network centered on engaging indigenous youth around long-term consequences of the conflict, though recently the network has begun to organize around issues of protecting indigenous autonomy over their land and resources in the face of encroaching multinational corporations. The network continues to be a forum for intergenerational engagement but increasingly has become an alternative news outlet for issues that do not receive national press and a medium to garner transnational support for rights issues. Often Rodolfo calls himself a "young elder" because of the mentoring role he takes on with the younger generation, in his words, "to teach them about civic action and responsibility" so that they "learn the laws and their rights, not just how to resist."

Alejandro describes how Rodolfo's personality has shifted over the years since he came to live with them: the dramatic ups and downs, the periodic addiction to alcohol, the depression and debilitating nightmares, and more recently his increasingly withdrawn and secretive behavior. Both Alejandro and Anastela attribute these habits to his having survived such terrible violence during the Conflicto Armado but also to his work with the reparations office, where he had to carry the memories of other survivors, along with his own. These memories live among them, walking the house at night like ghosts.

Alejandro disputes the impact that a protest march might have on national decisions. Rodolfo insists that the people need to demonstrate their dissatisfaction and simultaneously their support for the people who are suffering, but Alejandro believes that marches are easy for the state to ignore. He has yet to see evidence that they are effective and pushes his parents to "leave it" and live a "normal life," which I take as his call to unburden themselves of this ongoing struggle. Anastela asks him to recall Gandhi's peaceful protests, to which Alejandro snaps, "Gandhi did not have to live in Guatemala." Things get heated when he says that, and there is a look of hurt in Anastela's eyes. "What would you have us do instead?"

When Alejandro does not respond, Rodolfo says gently, "You know, Alejandro, we do [this] because we like it." In a drawn-out voice, Alejandro says, "I know. I don't." He holds his bowl to his mouth, drinks the broth, then promptly leaves the room. Anastela stacks the plates, and Rodolfo quietly returns to his laptop to update the network webpage with details about tomorrow's march.

In the kitchen Anastela hands me warm dishes to dry. She whispers, "Do you know who he gave that letter to?" Sensing my discomfort, she explains that she was so proud of Alejandro's interest in the lucha that she shared the news with her friend. He warned her to be careful, not to let Alejandro share the letter. Shaking her head, she admits to naively disregarding a strict rule of caution by which she and Rodolfo live, namely the idea that they never know who they are talking to. There are stories about the people who betrayed them during the war, trusted people, "good people," who they thought were their friends but who turned against them. The *orejas* (ears) do not belong to the past but live among them as spies in an environment of deep civic distrust. Not long ago, they received an unannounced visit from state officials at their home, urging that Anastela stop "riling up" people about issues she "knows nothing about" and that she ought to be a better model citizen, especially since she is a foreigner.

Usually Anastela is candid with Alejandro about the current state of affairs, even if it means being brutally honest. But tonight I see worry in her eyes. "I know they are watching us. They think we are terrorists." In the years since the war, beliefs about good citizens and destructive citizens have merged with wartime interpretations of guerrilla "involvement." Today's social-justice movements confront public claims that they are so disruptive to national order that their actions are akin to terrorism, a discourse that lends itself to extreme national security measures. Consequently, advocates who continue the struggle in spite of these challenges are forced to connect the dots between past and present patterns of repression, while subverting claims that they are terrorizing the state. Meanwhile, the orejas are always listening.

We Are All Together

Before classes start Guillermo finds Alejandro and gestures for him to meet at his locker. Guillermo shuffles through a few notebooks and finds Alejandro's letter, creased from being pressed between books. Just for a moment, I see Alejandro's face sink, but he replaces it quickly with a blithe, know-it-all grin and holds out his hand. Guillermo frees the letter from his clutter and shrugs his narrow shoulders. "I tried to show it to people, but they didn't care. Sorry, buddy, nobody wants this."

Alejandro waits a long time before he says something. Girls rush by with warm cups of coffee from the teachers' lounge. María Jiménez stops just long enough to greet each of us with a kiss on the cheek, then resumes flipping through photos on her camera. Guillermo looks at his watch. Finally Alejandro says, without a trace of self-pity, "I don't know why I tried."

Days earlier Alejandro kept the pages of every copy straight and clean, but now he shoves the letter into his backpack. A part of me is relieved that one less copy is floating around, thinking about Anastela's concerns. I chase after him, asking what it means that no one "wants this."

"Does it matter? They read it and say, 'I don't care about this.' . . . Or they don't read it. . . . They look at it and they're like, 'This has nothing to do with me. I don't care about this. I don't care about these people, or this issue.' They are all passive. It's a problem of passivity. They don't care, because they care only about their petty lives."

Other times Alejandro interprets his classmates' "closed eyes" as a form of self-preservation: "They know everything is going to hell. They just choose not to acknowledge it. They don't watch the news or read the newspaper—not because they don't want to read, but . . . because they know the country is going to hell." Ellen Moodie (2010), writing about postwar El Salvador, considers the ways in which "*knowing* and *not-knowing* implicate each other" (p. 173). Drawing on Slavoj Žižek, she explains the ways in which citizens actively "unknow" the structures of power that order their social and political world. Alejandro's private life makes it impossible to *unknow* anything, but his classmates can choose to close their eyes to the ongoing struggle unfolding around them. And yet, he reminds me, the message of "KONY 2012" had traction in these same school walls.[2] During art class students busily made signs to raise awareness and, with the permission of school leadership, hung posters in the halls. The prospect of child soldiers and ongoing war outraged them—this was a story they wanted to *know*. But their contemporary lives depended on *unknowing* the struggles that might incriminate their parents or undermine their elite status.

We continue along the hallway and pause under a handmade sign that says *dona*, with the letters tucked inside the curve of a doughnut. It is a play on words, since *dona* means both *doughnut* and *donate*. Daily, teachers have been reminding students in their morning announcements that the school is organizing its annual donation of clothing, shoes, notebooks, and lunchboxes. Alejandro points to the sign and says it is a shame that the community service club is "all donations, instead of actually doing something productive and useful." The principal himself is aware of the limitations on the kind of civic participation that the school can promote, noting that parents view civic action as "something . . . rebels do, not something you want your nice kids getting involved in." Here the legacies of the armed conflict exert themselves in paradoxical ways—the discourse of civic participation is socially desirable in textbook segments describing democracy and the responsibilities of citizens, but enacting citizenship is confined to service activities that cannot be misconstrued as "involvement."

Alejandro admits that distributing the letter at school was "more of an experiment . . . to see how little people know about their country" than an effort to educate them about the conflicts over resources in which many of their families' companies are likely implicated. This idea of his friends' limited view on the Guatemalan reality is one of Alejandro's most persistent frustrations at school. It is as if he could excuse their privilege if they made an effort to understand the unequal system that their elite status relies on.

I offer to help Alejandro make signs to display in the school hallways. He believes the principal would approve posters about Barillas if it took the form of an information campaign and not a call to action and "as long as I didn't put up any names, so as not to offend anyone." He adds, "Names of individuals, but also names of corporations, because we have to be very diplomatic about this at our school." He explains that he could be putting up the name of someone's family company and that would "cause problems," not only for the school but for his family. In the end, Alejandro reasons that making posters would be a waste of time and resources, because students would have the same "who cares" reaction that they had to his letter. "Maybe they will stop and read it the first time they see it. But then it will become part of the wall and they will just walk by it and not see a thing . . . like that one." He points to a poster about cleaning Lake Atitlán, one of Guatemala's premier tourist attractions. "That poster has been up for years. I don't even know if the lake is clean or still polluted."

It is late when Anastela and Rodolfo return from the protest in Barillas. Alejandro carries a warm pot of rice and vegetables to the table in front of the television, where his parents flip through news channels, looking for coverage of the protest. They each sit with laptops on their knees, unable to pull themselves away from the TV and Internet to see how long will it take before there is national news and how the president will respond. This is one of their rituals following the protests, listening for how it will be talked about and then participating in the dialogue through the anonymous space of the network's website. Part of Alejandro's civic education is maneuvering the intentional dialectic between official and unofficial knowledge. He teases that the word *hegemony* was already in his vocabulary while his friends were still learning to hold a spoon.

During commercials Anastela and Rodolfo tell stories about the march: how many thousands of people were there from all over the country, all over the world; how everyone was assigned different tasks and Rodolfo was granted "press" status to snap photos for the network; how they formed a thick line and filled the streets like a swarm of bees; how they carried painted banners on cotton sheets that read, "we are not terrorists"; how the police looked on at the edges of the road, unable to stop them even if they tried; how the people spontaneously and then deliberately chanted,

"We are all Barillas." Rodolfo explains what it meant to vocalize this explicit message of solidarity, that "repression in one pueblo is repression for all pueblos.... resistance in one pueblo is resistance for all pueblos." He describes how he yelled at drivers to be patient and how he couldn't help but pound their cars and say confrontational things like, "Listen, you wait here for ten minutes while we march. It will take only ten minutes, and if you don't wait, well, we're going to march all over your car and turn it into dust." Anastela, who was assigned the task of shepherding the march-ers and protecting them from other vehicles by driving at the back of the line, was surprised to find her husband's palms slapping her window, telling her to get back, get back. At that, Alejandro laughs like it is the funniest thing he has ever heard. They flip through images, recounting the variety of protest signs and how it felt marching alongside strangers, but Alejandro looks away, having heard stories about protests his whole life and witness-ing what little effect they seem to have. When the news ends with no cover-age of the protest, Alejandro believes his point has been made, but Rodolfo and Anastela view this silence as an invitation to speak louder. Rodolfo quickly types a statement about the lack of coverage proving that the pro-test got under the skin of the right people.

Later Rodolfo says that if the government does not lift the state of siege, they will organize people to "paint," meaning they will spray politi-cal graffiti on the mountains and cement walls that line the highways just outside the capital. He assures us that graffiti is legal if it is protesting a violation of human rights. They will write something about stealing the land, how the land belongs to the pueblo, so that people driving by can understand the struggle. Wistfully, Rodolfo adds, "I haven't painted since I was seven or eight years old, during the Conflicto Armado." His face has the same glimmer of nostalgia as when he describes learning to make two kinds of smoke bombs during the student movement, one to protect against police attacks and another to send messages out to fel-low rebels. Alejandro seems mildly convinced that graffiti could prompt greater awareness, but like the posters at school, he worries that they will too easily be ignored or removed. To my surprise, no one worries that graffiti might be dismissed as a marker of delinquency, adding fuel to the fire that activists are criminals. Before the night is over, Rodolfo and Anastela upload photos from the protest to the network webpage. Mean-while, they boast, nothing about the march has come out on the televi-sion news or the newspaper websites.

Balancing the Scales

Profe Castillo begins class with a review of the counterrevolution that followed the revolutionary presidents and how both were followed by a series of coups and the Conflicto Armado, "which ended with the Peace Accords, signed by whom?"

Several students shout, "Otto Pérez," bringing on a collective burst of laughter.

As students settle, their concerns begin to surface. Right away, they want to know who was right, which period was better, and who were Guatemala's best and worst presidents. Profe seems hesitant to offer more of his personal opinions, as he has done throughout the unit. After a long pause, he says, "This depends on the side you're on. . . ."

Nicolás shouts, "The military side! Of course." He holds out his hand in a salute and lets it drop to the desk with a slap.

Alejandro comments that all of Guatemala's presidents have been narcos, "thugs," and criminals, with numerous transgressions and unequal capacities to cover up their deviance. To Alejandro's amusement, Profe shoots a warning look in his direction.

Julia raises her hand. "Profe, how many presidents and military coups were there during the Conflicto Armado?" The teacher looks to Guillermo, who begins naming presidents and the years of coups in chronological order. The looming exam has amped up the anxiety and participation in the room, and several girls complain that Guillermo listed the names too quickly, so Profe asks him to write the list on the board. Guillermo skips to the front of the room and begins chronicling Guatemala's presidential history with years and names. The girls turn to me and giggle, "Guillermo knows everything, everything about Guatemala."

Juan Carlos asks, "Profe, were the Peace Accords good for Guatemala? I mean, I'm not sure if it would have been better if we never signed them. I think maybe Guatemala would be better today."

Profe answers, "Well, again, it depends on what side you are on, right? Because if I take the side of the state, I think . . . we could have resolved everything ourselves, and then we wouldn't have those *infamous* Peace Accords that are causing so many problems in the country today. Why? Because you have all the indigenous claiming, arguing, *demanding* that we respect the accords, when the government doesn't have any obligation to respect them." As he speaks, it becomes unclear whether he is still exhibiting an exercise in perspective taking or whether the state's point of view gives way to a generic fact of life in Guatemala: that the Peace Accords hold a set of problematic promises about respecting indigenous rights. In line with his earlier warnings that historical memory produces rancor and division, Profe again emphasizes the limits of applying historical knowledge to the present day. This interpretation is distinct from the position promoted in their textbook, which they have largely ignored throughout this unit. Their book states that, although many of the promises made in the Peace Accords have yet to be fully realized, "the time that has passed since the signing does not diminish their validity. The Peace Accords will be in effect until they are fulfilled; and this compliance depends on, in large part, Guatemala's progress as a democracy, economic development, and social justice" (Ruiz Cabrera et al., 2009, p. 111).

Juan Carlos appears satisfied with this answer. He then asks, "Profe, what do you think of Ríos Montt?" Juan Carlos looks at his friends and holds back a smirk, likely posing the question to get a rise out of his teacher. Efraín Ríos Montt was one of the most brutal military dictators during the war, one of the authors of the scorched-earth campaign to massacre indigenous villagers, burn their land, and force them into the mountains, where hundreds of thousands of people hid, fled, and starved to death.[3] Though their textbook offers limited details about the Conflicto Armado in the one-page synopsis, authors note that the early 1980s were the "most violent" period of the war and link Ríos Montt's regime to the formation of the paramilitary, the scorched-earth campaign, and "massacres and genocides in the country's interior" (Ruiz Cabrera et al., 2009, p. 101).

Profe places his hand over his mouth, nodding. "That is a tough one. If we tally up which presidents have the most murders, he would be one of the winners." He turns to the board, but Guillermo has not yet arrived at 1982, when Ríos Montt came to power through a military coup. "But again, it depends on which side you are on. And it is complex, very complex, because there are indigenous people who love Ríos Montt." A proponent of the carrot-and-stick method, as Ríos Montt led devastating genocidal campaigns in the Maya Highlands, he also created "model villages," where the state provided food, clothing, security, and infrastructure to indigenous populations. But there is no mention of this as a military tactic, nor is there any mention that Ríos Montt is currently on trial for genocide, a word that appears in the textbook but has not been spoken in the classroom.

Profe asks Guillermo to place a star next to the presidents who came to power through military coups. Students attentively copy Guillermo's list into their notebooks. As Guillermo continues writing, Profe offers the class yet another carefully balanced account. "There are two different points of view. . . . He created the PAC, the Patrullas de Autodefensa Civil, and obligated certain populations to participate. This is an authoritarian act, and I am not in agreement with these kinds of acts." he says, resting an open hand on his chest. "On the other hand, I'm not entirely sure whether he ordered the massacres to disappear thousands of indigenous from their villages, because I don't have evidence." Several students nod. "Why am I not sure? Because I would have to be *inside the head* of Ríos Montt to know for sure whether he organized those massacres or not. Right?"

One girl stands abruptly and grabs the bathroom pass, a clunky yellow block shaped like an arrow. Laura stares blankly at the hallway. Isabella leans over her desk to braid the hair of the girl sitting in front of her. Profe turns to the list of presidents on the board. "We are going to look at two presidents. . . . Between the years of 1978 and 1983, many people, thousands and thousands of indigenous were tortured, sequestered, and killed during these two presidencies." He circles Ríos Montt and Lucas García on the board.

A student confirms with the teacher, "Ríos Montt was pro-army, right?"

Alejandro can hardly contain himself. "Obviously, he was a general. And he killed more than one hundred thousand people in seventeen months." Guillermo finishes the list and returns to his seat.

Just as Profe finishes his sentence, Nicolás says flatly, "But they [his tactics] were effective."

Several students nod. Profe replaces the chalk on the ledge and visibly struggles to respond. Guillermo takes it upon himself to start teaching two girls sitting near him. "In the book I read, it said that the army ripped fetuses out of women's wombs and killed babies." He gets out of his seat and jumps on the floor, landing hard. "Pow, pow. They did this on women's bellies, and this is how they took out the babies." The girls make shocked faces and bury their hands in their sweatshirt pockets, but the class is hardly silent with interest. Several students shout titles of books and films they have read that confirm or conflict with Guillermo's examples. From across the room, Guillermo asks Alejandro if he has the book at home. Profe waves his hands to quiet the class and then offers his own example of the grotesque, illustrating how the army "threw babies like they were rocks," swinging his arm toward the class.

A student offers, "Like they were Frisbees."

In a soft voice, Mariella asks why. The desks creak as the boys shift in their seats, impersonating the army throwing babies out the window into the basketball hoop. Several girls have turned in their seats to confirm with one another that this is sickening. Profe manages to hear Mariella over the clamor and responds in a slow voice, "It's difficult to see the state's perspective . . . but if the state suspects there is a threat, the state has to respond, right? I'm not saying it's correct, but this is the manner of thinking like a state." Profe's call to *think like a state*, a rhetorical invitation he asserts regularly throughout the unit, suggests that students should take seriously the perspective and position of state actors, justifying human rights violations on the grounds of national security. Meanwhile, the guerrilla movement seems to emerge out of thin air as a violent insurgency that made no attempt to establish a peaceful dialogue with state actors, thereby justifying the state's violent response to an essentially terrorist threat (Bellino, 2014b; Oglesby, 2007a; Oglesby & Ross, 2009; Weld, 2012). The historical context and agency of actors and institutions implicated in this conflict are deleted in favor of telling a "myth of an orderly war [which] is more bearable" (Nordstrom, 2004, p. 33).

Profe's lesson reveals extreme caution and reluctance to simplify the moral lessons of the war that he urges students to take with them into their future roles. Although he tolerates and then participates in the construction of what Elizabeth Oglesby (2007a) labels grim "tales of death" (p. 79), he does so while discursively revealing disciplinary skepticism, a habit of mind central to historical inquiry (Boix-Mansilla, 2000). His restraint in constructing a cohesive narrative of war, then, might be taken for an elaborate demonstration of critical thinking in line with disciplinary goals such as perspective taking rather than as avoidance of a controversial topic. In his consideration of whether postmodernism fits in a history classroom, history educator Peter Seixas (2000) argues, "the lack of consensus is precisely what thrusts us beyond school history as consensual tradition, into the realm of history as a disciplinary practice" (p. 34). But Profe's lesson moves from postmodernist truth claims to nihilism, cloaked in an explanation that it is the discipline of history that makes truth unknowable. Like many teachers grappling with controversial topics, Profe later explains to me that his goal in this class was to denote historical objectivity and work to desensitize potentially personal and emotive connections students have to the violent past. Rather than engaging students in the reasons why conflicting historical accounts continue to exist, Profe renders the past unknowable by nature of these conflicting accounts.

Guillermo protests again, "But Profe, we can't deny that this is what the army did." Boys on the other side of the room seem to be rolling their eyes. Outside this class both Alejandro and Guillermo are affectionately referred to as "communists."

Profe responds, "Look, there are many sides. . . . There are versions of the indigenous—victims—who say the army protected them from the guerrillas, who love Ríos Montt. And there are other communities who say the army committed most of the violence." I recall my own bafflement when I met indigenous families in Comalapa, like Ixkat's sister, who defended Ríos Montt, long before the possibility of a genocide trial had repolarized his actions.

Profe now turns to the CEH and REMHI truth commission reports, the first evocation of historical evidence in this unit, though my conversations with students have revealed that most do not know about the existence of either commission. He notes that the findings attribute more than 90 percent of the conflict's deaths to the army. Given Profe's mention of these unbalanced numbers, I wait for the discussion to turn a corner, anticipating that it will end on clear moral grounds with the historical "lessons" Profe underscores in his classes. Instead, he turns back to the notion of relative truth. He says, "Now I can't say it's true, but I also can't say it's a lie. Why? Because the state army says the opposite in their documents." The girls in the front row giggle at his indecision, but he assures them that this is the work of historical analysis.

Profe Castillo then shares vivid stories about his college friends who lost eyes and limbs during the war. Each of the vignettes ends with a lesson about how these injuries left bitterness and rancor that the survivors had to overcome, realizing in the end that "both sides were guilty." "If you want to have a true historical memory, you have to . . . ?" Profe pauses for students to answer, but today only Guillermo completes the teacher's sentence. Softly he says, "Be objective."

Profe affirms, closing the class with a crystallized lesson: "To be objective, you must hear the two sides. . . . It wouldn't be ethical to say it was *all* the state's fault. Nor would it be ethical to say it was *all* the guerrillas' fault. Both sides have responsibility for this. And obviously the only thing we can do is interpret objectively, because *are we* living during the time of the conflict? . . . No. Therefore, we can never analyze the conflict in the way that people who really lived it can."

In moments like these, we are able to see the potential of schools to deepen the work of transitional justice, by expounding on the role of truth commissions; by exploring the complex linkages between historical narratives, truth, and power; and by asking deep questions about accountability and human capacity for committing mass violence. We also see how conversations in schools can undo or subvert the work of transitional justice, by denouncing the pursuit of truth as an absurd task that contradicts the work of objective historical analysis; by whittling asymmetrical violence down to the presumption of two devils; and by underscoring the impossibility of ever knowing what happened or why, not even by firsthand witnesses. Profe's lesson adheres to the national curriculum, yet it is also antithetical to the goals of civic education as they are laid out in the educational reform agenda. As I listen to him guiding students from biased accounts to an unknowable middle ground, I am conflicted about my role as an ethnographer. It feels morally wrong to sit there and say nothing, and I weigh my options for intervention in the conversation. Do I educate everyone at the cost of embarrassing the teacher, alienating the majority of students, and coming off as superior in my knowledge of their country's history? Certainly this approach would not lead to the deep relationships I am hoping to foster with students. This is one of the moments my own role as researcher seems to converge with Profe's call for historical neutrality, but it is more complicated than that, because in my notes lie deep judgments about what is said and what is not said that day in the classroom.

I am the last one out of the room, moving slowly as I casually explore whether Profe's personal convictions are more biased than he has let on. When he explains that the textbooks are insufficient pedagogical resources on the civil war, I offer to help select excerpts from the CEH report with him, an offer he declines. Although Profe does not give a clear indication that he was being intentionally cautious with his students, I wonder, could it be that I am not alone in my conflicted emotions about the allegedly unknowable past? Is rendering the past unknowable a tactic for moving the needle and better than risking the alternative—a narrative of state victory over an unequivocal terrorist threat?

Inspecting Our Wounds with Open Eyes

On the bus ride home Alejandro talks about Profe's social studies class as a "start," but, like many things at the academy, too "diplomatic." Leaning into the aisle, he says, "What is more important: to learn about history or to not offend anyone?" Alejandro argues that his classmates "should be offended" and "feel personally guilty for the terrible things their grandparents did," reasoning that without guilt, "you won't feel connected, and you won't care." For him, the issue goes beyond the elite's "personal" accountability to restore their family's "honor," extending to the entire population: "Guatemala needs to talk about its past, because the present problems all come from the Conflicto Armado. The government says all the time, let's not dwell on the past scars—but it's not a scar, it's an open wound and it's still bleeding. It's even getting infected, because people think they should forget about it. But you can't forget about it until you heal the wound. *Then* you can say, let's not dwell." Alejandro's words subvert attempts to characterize the memory act as putting a "finger in the wound," the metaphor Diane Nelson (1999) delineated as symbolic of the wounded body politic in Guatemala's divided postwar nation. They also evoke the troubling discourse of power that renders memories of violence essential obstacles to the construction of a postwar future, a logic powerfully reproduced in Profe's classroom.

We return home to an empty house. Rodolfo and Anastela are attending a meeting, planning the network's next steps in Barillas. They have taken the water jug with them, so we rummage through the shop for filtered water. "They do this all the time, take our things and bring them to meetings or the *campo* [rural area]. I hate when they do this." Though Alejandro admires his parents' persistence, he has grown more outspoken about his disapproval of their high-risk and high-cost choices. On many occasions his mother did not return from meetings and protests in time to pick him up at school or meet him at the bus stop. The driver was forced to bring him back to school, where a single teacher waited in the parking lot until someone came for him. He was not allowed to be home alone "because they thought it was a risk" and not allowed to spend time with friends "because they didn't trust them." Though Alejandro eventually managed to "convince" them to trust his friends, there are still classmates Alejandro is prohibited from socializing with outside of school, a notable few with family members implicated in wartime atrocities. Alejandro explains that in Guatemala, "you need to get good with names." Even when he would rather not know, he routinely asks himself, "Who am I talking to, is he good or bad? ... Because here, everyone has a dark past or a dark present ... even the good guys." Grimly, he adds, "Of course if they [my parents] were realists, they would accept that they can't do anything anyway, that if someone wants to kill me they can."

This fatalistic logic, which Alejandro terms "realism," lies in sharp contrast to his parents' ongoing commitment to the lucha—the struggle for justice. Anastela and Rodolfo's optimism about the protest in Barillas "made me laugh," he explains, because "it still doesn't matter." He estimates that they could gather half the pueblo in the streets and the government "still wouldn't care" because they are "more afraid of their debts to the companies than the suffering of the people." Again he repeats, "If my parents were realists, they would just accept that." On other occasions his implicit pressure to see his parents submit to the current order generates willful and painful arguments. When Pérez Molina was elected president, the family worried aloud about the possibility of a military draft. Anastela swore that she would "be the first mother in the street protesting this law." Alejandro insisted that she "wouldn't be able to do anything if it becomes a law" and forbade his mother from protesting if their fears were realized. In his passionate debate voice, he said, "You cannot speak out if they kill you on the street. No one can hear you then." This comment, punctuated by the thump of his fist on the table, ended the conversation.

Alejandro's grim "realism" applies to his classmates as well, as he consistently questions their need for bodyguards in a country where everyone is in a perpetual state of risk. Once his classmates outlined the topography of the capital city, designating safe and unsafe zones. At times these classifications appear straightforward: shopping centers and schools are "safe," while public transportation is "unsafe." Other times, these borders are more complicated and contingent on one's identity, "involvement," and accompaniment. For example, Nicolás reasoned, "You just don't go into the dangerous zones, and you don't interfere with narcos, and you're fine." He noted that "there is nothing to fear when you have armored cars and . . . men who are not afraid to die for you." By his own admission, Alejandro snapped at this in class. In front of everyone, he said, "Do you think they will really protect you if someone else offers them more money? You are fooling yourself, friend, because these are people who work for money. If someone wants to kill you, they can kill you." The teacher asked Alejandro to stay after class and explained that his comment was "unnecessary." Listening to Alejandro retell the story in an unsuccessful attempt to amuse his parents, I noticed a look of comfort come over him. Postwar violence knows no boundaries. Elites can purchase security in Guatemala, but money cannot guarantee their safety in a state globally recognized as a "good place to commit murder" (Alston, 2007, p. 20). Conceding the limits on human agency within a corrupt world ironically constitutes an exertion of agency in one's capacity to let go.

Alejandro and I heat up cheese sandwiches and stare out the store window at the steady rain. Anastela and Rodolfo have not yet returned, so Alejandro works the shop, with the doors locked and a small barred window open for exchanges. We part ways and prepare for bed, letting the house get dark, when the doorbell rings. It is a frightful sound at this hour, and the flood of stories I have heard about threatening late night visits comes to me. It is too late for a visitor, and Alejandro's parents would not ring the bell, not even if they lost their key. I listen to Alejandro ask in a deep voice, "Who is it?" while racing through scenarios: Could it be someone from the state, returning to warn Anastela and Rodolfo to stop their work? Has someone seen the network site and decided to silence its coordinators? Have they sensed the family's leadership in the Barillas protest? Could it be the father of Alejandro's ex-girlfriend, who reportedly put a gun to Alejandro's head and threatened to kill him? Or is it what Anastela's friend feared, that one of the hydroelectric owners would reprimand Alejandro for encouraging his children to ask questions? Without turning any lights on, I tiptoe toward the front door. Alejandro and I nearly bump into each other in the dark. He is already on the phone, calling his mother in a panic he makes no attempt to mask, asking if she knows a Señor Modlino. When she says not to worry and explains that Mr. Modlino sells them fresh cheese for the store, we embrace in a moment of relief, then laugh at our heightened fears. Alejandro assures me that he brought a crossbow to the door and that he is a "good shot."

The next day at dinner Anastela and Rodolfo make more plans for Barillas. More and more pueblos are coming together to protest the state of siege and all the repression and silence it represents. This struggle is also their struggle. Alejandro keeps his eyes narrow and tightens his jaw as they get more concrete about the time and travel commitment this next phase of work will entail. Finally he says, "Nothing is getting better. . . . Your protesting is not changing anything. The mining companies are still here; the hydroelectric companies are still here; we have a military government, a police state." Catching his breath, he says, "What is there to stay for? What is there to fight for?" Although Anastela is a Greek citizen by birth, Alejandro is not, and Rodolfo does not even possess a Guatemalan passport. Unlike his classmates, Alejandro does not have the unconstrained freedom to leave Guatemala, like the girls at school who announced that their parents are waiting for graduation before moving, worried that war is "coming." He longs for his family to find a new home in a safer country but doubts whether his parents would leave all they have built here, even if it granted them a safe exit.

Who Is Guatemala?

On the board Profe Castillo outlines the three components of the "civic identity" essay assignment: personal identity, social identity, and national identity. Alongside, Profe lists Guatemala's four ethnicities, forewarning students that they may not use the terms *indio* or *ladino* in their essays. He writes these terms on the board, then draws an *X* through them, instructing students to call Mayas *indigenous* and to self-identify as *mestizo*. In this classroom he can easily include all students in the same ethnic category, since there are no indigenous, Xinca, or Garifuna students in the entire school. Alejandro's parents are the only close exception, and even Alejandro is not indigenous by blood. The "four pueblos" is a cornerstone of the new civic narrative, a depiction of the Guatemalan nation aimed at fostering inclusion and pride in the state's pluricultural, multilingual, and multiethnic national identity (Ministry of Education, 2010). Departing from the monocultural depictions of nation that dominated past curricula, a strong sentiment conveyed in today's textbooks is that Guatemala's unity binds across diversity.

Profe Castillo offers a provocative statement to begin the conversation, "It's going to be grotesque what I'm about to say. . . . The indigenous are a dead weight on our country." For once, he seems to have captured the attention of everyone in the room, though students do not know yet what to make of this comment, which they have likely heard before in out-of-school contexts. "The indigenous are a nuisance, a dead weight. It's the fault of the indigenous that this country isn't developed. This would be a developed country of professionals if they were not part of it." He pauses, "Right?" Though it is now apparent that Profe is challenging the popular sentiment that "backward" indigenous culture has thwarted the country's progress, students appear to be waiting for their opening. Several hands slowly go up. Profe continues, "Let me ask you this—where would your family be without the indigenous?" He poses the question to no one in particular, and the students collectively make a deep *ohhhhhhh*, as if witnessing a friend receive a public scolding. "If it weren't for the agricultural work of the indigenous, your family wouldn't have what they have."

Though Profe typically responds to individual remarks, he now lets student comments fill the room. Luis offers, "But Profe, the workers protest, they organize the campesinos to revolt against the fincas. They don't just work the land for ladinos." After a pause, he corrects himself, "mestizos." One student repeats the deficit logic of another popular sentiment, "The indigenous . . . don't speak Spanish; they don't speak Spanish because they don't go to school; they don't go to school, because they want to have more children." Another adds, "When they [the indigenous] look for rights, they don't look for the same rights we have. They look for extra benefits. . . ." Another finishes his thought, "They don't want equality. They want privileges." The students are clamoring to participate and have stopped raising their hands.

Hale's (2002) concept of "neoliberal multiculturalism" is again clearly illustrated in this classroom, showcasing elite anxiety over the reversals of power that might ensue if indigenous movements were granted too much legitimacy. These anxieties are moving from one generation to the next, undisturbed in this school space.

Profe nods, looking unsurprised at these comments. He has heard them before, in this same room from a different class of students, the year before and the year before that. This is the nature of teaching at an elite institution, and Profe knows the job and its limitations. But he also sees opportunities to change the way his students see themselves in relation to Guatemala. His main pedagogical goal is to foster "dialogue about ethnicity" and help students "realize their Guatemalan identity," grounding these concerns in the lack of national pride he sees among young people, especially elites. Satirizing public ignorance, he says, "The indigenous are stupid, dirty, and have a lot of kids; Xincas are almost gone; and Garifunas, well they're black. . . . There's a lot of discrimination here."

Laura says matter-of-factly, "The problem with Guatemala is there are so many groups," positing that the groups share "almost nothing" in common. One student asks whether Kaqchikel is a "real language" with "an alphabet . . . and commas and all of that?" Without belittling the question, Profe affirms that each indigenous language has its own grammatical structure. The student responds, "But they sound like animal languages." Several boys burst into laughter. These conversations are both unexpected and unsurprising. Around the room colorful posters of student projects showcase a range of "national issues" that disproportionately affect indigenous populations, such as "Poverty and Illiteracy" and "Discrimination and Racism." Another poster is devoted to "El Movimiento Maya," with newspaper clippings of indigenous gatherings.

Student comments come to an abrupt pause when two indigenous custodians in International Academy button-downs appear at the classroom door and request permission to borrow a table for another classroom. The room falls quiet as the men briskly carry the table through the door. Next to me Laura finishes braiding Isabella's hair and knots an elastic band around it. Profe passes out textbooks and directs students to a passage titled "Construction of the Citizen." They take turns reading aloud, and when they complete the section, Profe dictates a summary for students to copy into their notebooks. Crinkly paper noises fill the room as students turn to a fresh page.

"Since the signing of the Peace Accords, Guatemala has been recognized as a multilingual, pluricultural, and multiethnic country. There are four ethnicities: Garifuna, Xinca—" The class breaks into laughter at the mere mention of Xinca. Several repeat in drawn-out voices, "Shhhhhinkkkaaaaa." Profe glares at the students, who straighten their faces when they see that he is not amused. "The Garifuna, the Xinca, the indigenous, and the mestizo. Unfortunately, Guatemala as a country lacks ethnic unity and a sense of national identity."

A student asks, "What about the ladino? Isn't that an ethnic group?" Students shift in their seats. "And don't forget the *shumo*!" another adds.[4] Profe responds with visible frustration, "Ladino is a *sinvergüenza* (scoundrel), someone who is not worth the trouble. . . . I don't want to hear anyone calling [himself/herself] *ladino* in this classroom. In this classroom *ladino* does not exist." Though students remain unconvinced of their "real" identities, as many continue to self-identify as ladino or European outside the classroom, for the moment they succumb to Profe's rule that this term "does not exist" in his classroom.

Profe returns to his steady tone. "We are talking today about what it means to be a citizen. Who was not born in Guatemala?" Three boys raise their hands. He points to each and asks where they were born. Two are from Korea. A boy with wavy hair says he was born in Spain, to which Profe replies with a flip of his hand, "You're more Guatemalan than a tortilla." Students laugh, and the boy grins. Profe continues, emphasizing that citizenship is "not just about where you were born, but where you grow up. It's where you have affection and respect for what is happening in your country."

Several students nod, but Nicolás disagrees, "But Profe, my parents are from Italy, so I am not mestizo, therefore I am Italian, or ladino. I don't have Indian in me, so it is not accurate for me to call myself mestizo." Other students chime in about their affiliations to other countries. Many have dual citizenship in European countries and travel with their foreign passport, not their Guatemalan one. One student notes that some of the Korean students speak Spanish no better than tourists, are they really mestizo just because they live here? Profe makes several efforts to get his students' attention, at last with a loud, revised proclamation that citizenship is less contingent on where they were born or where they grew up, but more "about saying, I feel part of my country. I may not have the opportunity now, but in the future I will do something for my country."

The bulletin board at the back of Profe's room is decorated with Post-it notes scattered under a question in large, wavy text, "What do you promise to do to make Guatemala a better country?" Students posted promises to abide by laws, to stop littering, to convince their families to vote "for the president who will make Guatemala succeed," and—a recurring pledge—to create jobs. Profe points to the number of students who want to contribute to Guatemala's economy as an indication of their connection to the country. Meanwhile, Alejandro worries that these statements display the hierarchical logic that "development depends on exploitation." He explains that the only society his friends want is "one where they are on top, forever."

Profe's routine reminders that his students are "Guatemalans for life" are not convincing for everyone. He worries that the school's internationalism tacitly exempts students from their civic duties and connections to the state. Privately, he explains, "We are a school for Guatemalans, but these students are also citizens of other countries. . . . The students need to sing our anthem; they need to know their flag. How else will they learn to feel proud of being Guatemalan?" Cultivating civic pride, loyalty, and investment in the future are explicit dimensions of Guatemala's civic education curriculum.

At lunch I find Alejandro standing against the tree with folded arms and a wide, knowing smile. He received a text from Rodolfo that the government lifted the state of siege in Barillas. Laura joins us as Alejandro explains that the news has not yet made national headlines, another triumph for the network. After several minutes Laura announces, "I don't know anything about what you are talking about."

Alejandro glares at her. "That's because you don't know what's happening in your own country."

I try to soften his words, although she does not look particularly offended. "Remember when we were talking with Isabella about her trip to Barillas?"

Laura recalls the place with a "ton of soldiers" but struggles so see what we are celebrating. She says, "I think it's not a good idea, lifting the state of siege. It's only going to bring more problems, and they're just going to put it back." She explains that the indigenous people in Barillas "cannot take care of themselves" and "know how to solve problems only with violence." When I ask why she thinks this is so, she connects violence to a lack of education: "The indigenous people . . . don't have education. So they know only violence." On Profe's wall Laura's Post-it promises to make Guatemala a better place by teaching "peace education." It caught my attention that several notes on the board promised the teaching of peace as a civic virtue, but if Laura's views were any indication, this approach to teaching peace was disconcertingly similar to colonial discourses of pacifying indigenous peoples.[5] She flicks an ant off her shoulder. Spotting Isabella across the lawn, she yells, "Isa!" and waves for her to join us.

Later I expect Alejandro to be disheartened by Laura's reaction, but he excuses it as ignorance and willful denial. "They [my classmates] don't mean to be racist; they just think it's true that all indigenous are stupid and do not know how to take care of themselves. It doesn't seem to matter that Mayas *started* this country." He explains, "It's *their* country. . . . We just live here."

By the end of the day Anastela and Rodolfo toast to their accomplishments in Barillas. Rodolfo elbows Alejandro, asking whether he believes in protests now, but Alejandro's earlier elation has faded. He assures them that it was not their protest that made the difference but the state succumbing to international pressure or else making some kind of strategic decision. He says, "You know what it is? Two words: *quitar esperanza*. They give you a little [hope], only so they can take it away." His words bring to mind the calculated maneuvers by those in power and their masterful delivery of a fundamental delusion: that people think they have control over their lives.

The Civic Virtue of Moving On

Alejandro straddles two distinct worlds, and the separation between what his parents' activism aims to accomplish and the reality that he confronts among his elite peers in school has led to a growing frustration with the limits of collective action to shift the status quo. In spite of his parents' ongoing commitment to solidarity and human rights movements, Alejandro encounters apathy and social distancing among his friends, who routinely dismiss indigenous movements as irrelevant to their lives and damaging to the nation. At home the Conflicto Armado has not ended but continues to marginalize indigenous groups in the form of megadevelopment projects that violate cultural rights codified in the Peace Accords. Meanwhile at school, these social movements are charged as misguided efforts to revive the past to make self-interested claims on the state, at the expense of national harmony and progress. Alejandro deftly navigates these worlds but refuses to settle in either.

Profe Castillo's social studies lessons are encoded with civic messages that he tailors for Guatemala's elite youth in an effort to harness their social and economic power toward national unity, peace, and development. Students are instructed to use particular words to categorize themselves in a "multilingual, pluricultural, and multiethnic" Guatemala but deterred from asking critical questions about how the country's ethnic diversity came to fundamentally divide them. In this sense, Profe makes great efforts to instill a "usable past" that will guard against the mounting shame and distance his students feel as members of a state with "no national identity."

Validating this usable past through the rhetoric of disciplinary analysis, Profe emphasizes the importance of perspective taking in reconciling conflicting evidence. Yet through measured accounts and a series of personal disclaimers about his own bias, Profe effectively subverts the work of his students' historical thinking in three distinct ways. First, Profe makes clear that historical memory has been manipulated as an "instrument of reproach" that promotes rancor and division and inhibits national progress. This framing creates a familiar divide between the partiality of memory and the objectivity of history, so that historical analysis becomes the critical tool to denounce these misappropriations. Second, he grounds his lecture in the two-devils narrative, explaining how "objective historical analysis" neutralizes accountability for past wrongs. Third, he makes repeated claims that the past itself is inaccessible: historical records are indisputably biased, and therefore truth lives exclusively inside the heads of its actors. If truth can be accessed only through lived experience, then the memory act belongs exclusively to those who survived to tell it. In the process, this exclusivity reinforces the notion that the war is not everyone's story to tell but rather belongs to selective groups.

Profe Castillo carefully constructs equal accountability as the entry point and end result of all historical inquiry, preserving the national myth that fighting took place exclusively between two armed groups who cannot be judged from outside their historical context and collective subjectivity. Nearly every claim he makes about historical analysis tips the scales toward a net of zero, ostensibly erasing accountability of all historical actors in committing a collective mistake. Imposing "parity" on the past becomes a collective pardon, so that "if everyone is either responsible or guilty, then no one is" (Barkan, 2009, p. 910). To be objective, a clear goal in Profe Castillo's classroom, is to consider the actions of "both sides" and ultimately recognize that oppositional accounts negate the possibility of a moral truth. What, then, constitutes the historical memory that Profe encourages his students to "conserve" to avoid repeating the "same mistakes of the past"? For Alejandro, the war's lessons are clear, and he likes to think that Profe "diplomatically" reminds students of the historical roots of contemporary racism. But for most, the lesson is more abstract: to avoid another war.

Profe's essentially "dogmatic transmission" of the past (Stearns, Seixas, & Wineburg, 2000, p. 12) comes with certain constraints: the past should be remembered but not reckoned with, objectively analyzed but not critiqued or judged. The past can explain origins and how things came to be but should not be used as provocation for the way things *ought* to be. Finally, Profe's juxtaposition of past and present violence further imbues historical analysis with civic duties in the context of Guatemala's alleged peace. Collectively, his message renders counterinterpretations as harmful to national unity, disruptive or naive in the context of post-postwar violence, and ignorant of the tenets of objective historical analysis. Throughout the unit there is no engagement with primary documents, so there is no practice in the "objective analysis" that Profe emphasizes as the key to understanding the past. Meanwhile, the uncontested authority of this predigested narrative positions students as passive receivers of this legacy; as members of the postwar generation, they inherit this history—it is not their story to interpret.

United hopes and desires for a better Guatemala are refracted through varied impressions of where social change begins, especially when so many before have failed. Memories of the high costs of popular uprising loom large when dissatisfaction turns to public dissent, as the risks attached to the public sphere multiply across actors and spaces. Eerily reminiscent of wartime repression, civic "involvement" remains a dangerous forum for exercising one's voice. Civic action and its historical links to "subversion" have become recriminalized within the discourse of postwar politics, portraying popular movements as self-serving, socially disruptive, and even constitutive of terrorist acts (Isaacs, 2010a, 2010b). Even when citizens willingly take on the risks of civic action, they confront fatalism, hopelessness, and the "quiet violence of dreams" (Swartz et al., 2012).[6]

Alejandro's "Open Letter," which brings to the surface the ongoing nature of historical injustice, becomes a site of contestation over the links between Guatemalan unity, security, and progress. While students dismiss these resistance movements as hindrances to national development and indigenous efforts to employ the past as grounds to be "separate" from the polity, the cultural deficiencies of indigenous groups become the scapegoat for both the nation's lack of progress and lack of peace. Alejandro's frustration that his peers have their "eyes closed" to the reality stems from his belief that the only way forward for Guatemala is to heal the "open wound" of the past. His paradoxical investment and skepticism toward social movements spiral toward a sense of civic inefficacy in the face of entrenched power inequalities. At times, his perceptions of the futility of civic action become an excuse not to act, not even to expect change. Hope is a risk, and Alejandro is a realist.

4

Paulo Freire Institute

The All-or-Nothing
Generation and the Spiral
of the Ongoing Past

Guate-psicosis and the Rules of Engagement

In the morning I wait for Paulina and her mother, María, at the bus stop near their home. Families walk together along the side streets, parents and older brothers accompanying girls to school. The main street is a blur of buses stopping, shuffling people in, and driving off in a column of black smoke. I am relieved when I spot Paulina's dark curly hair across the street. There are no shortage of buses this early in the day, but we wait for one of the blue ones that cost extra for their security cameras and police escorts. When none arrives, María suggests we take one of the regular buses so that we get to school on time. She loosens her watch and slides it into her pants pocket.

We climb onto a poorly maintained bus with a blessing written along the front window, sliced leather seats, and bent metal frames. The seats and the standing aisle are filled, so we squeeze in so close that I can smell soap on the skin of the person next to me. Despite the notorious risks of city buses, the majority of Guatemalans living in the capital are forced to rely on this system for everyday transport. The buses are far from safe, but they are affordable. Not many students' families at Paulo Freire Institute can afford to pay for the private school bus, a scattered route through the city and nearly half the price of school tuition. María makes her own schedule, selling clothing from catalogs door-to-door, arranging her route around Paulina's school day. She instructs Paulina to say a prayer each time they enter and exit the bus, one prayer to ask for protection and the other to express thanks, since one never knows what will happen on the ride.

Beti, Paulina's social studies teacher, calls this state of constant panic a "psychosis," affecting everyone in the capital. Everything in Guatemala has two sides. People carry guns to feel safe, but it is also a risk. "When people see a weapon, they shoot because they think you are a *marero* [gang member]." The city has undergone a massive public education campaign about a new gun law that prohibits the display of arms. Civilians can carry guns, but they must be hidden. Every man with a sweatshirt or a tucked-in shirt potentially hides a gun underneath. When a bus is robbed, there is no telling how many guns will come out.

The range of contemporary violence is often swept into the concept of *delincuencia* (delinquency), an overbroad scapegoat that largely attributes instances of petty crime and political assassinations to poor, young males, presumably gang members (Benson et al., 2011). The victims of *delincuencia* are allegedly either delinquents themselves—that is, drug addicts, prostitutes, and gang members—or their affiliates. By extension, the discourse of "involvement," once signifying guerrilla sympathizing or popular organizing, has been applied to a new kind of participation: that of criminal activities. Though youth gangs have grown dramatically in postwar years (Winton, 2005), young people are not the sole agents responsible for Guatemala's high homicide rates (Alston, 2007; Sanford, 2008). Nevertheless, the criminalization of youth has spread across the country, creating an alleged "youth problem" (Burrell, 2009, p. 97) in which young people are to blame for their apparent lack of opportunities, reinforcing the idea that criminal activity is the *cause* of youth struggles rather than a consequence.

I hold my balance pressed between bodies, fingers gripped over the handle of my bag. There are the people one would expect to see on public "death buses," as some students refer to them: men with baseball caps and oversized bellies, poor women in saggy tank tops, malnourished elderly women in traje with cheeks shrunken like dried apricots. But there are also well-dressed women with big earrings and men in dress slacks with ironed shirts. Several unattended kids in school uniforms, no more than fifteen years old, are squeezed four to a seat, hands folded on their laps. Bodies, mostly men, hang out the open doors. A pair of boys in school uniforms hops on the back ladder and climbs to the roof, where children crouch among sacks of corn. The driver and his assistant do not flinch when we pass the traffic police, who supposedly ticket overcrowded buses.

The man next to us exits, and María gestures for us to move into the empty seat. Paulina slides in and pulls the window up so we don't breathe in fumes. Her mother keeps her arm on the bar, her body shielding us from the throng of people in the aisle. Outside I count twelve soldiers walking in a line along the side of the road. "What is that?" I ask Paulina in a whisper, knowing better than to talk about anything remotely political in public. The students have instructed me not to talk at all, because "you never know what you might say that will provoke someone. . . . Or they might think you have money, or they will learn where you live or where you are going." Speaking makes you vulnerable. This is how you survive. The soldiers march beside a cement wall with graffiti that reads, "Otto Pérez = genocide. Otto Pérez = assassin. Don't vote for the military." Paulina glances at her mother and then back to me. She mouths the word *guerra*. War.

At the bus terminal, we take a stairway over the massive highway. Paulina teaches me that this is a very dangerous stairway and I need to be careful. Her mother explains, "People will rob you here, and no one will say anything. They won't call the police." Paulina adds, "If you call the police, they won't come anyway." As we head up the stairs, María's phone rings, and she slides a hand down her shirt to retrieve it. It is Paulina's father, and she tells him that we are still on our way to school and that she has to go because someone is probably about to rob us. We do not stop moving. This is one of the most important lessons—if we go out, we do not stand still. Standing still makes us vulnerable. We head quickly down the stairs to the other side of the road, past the woman with no legs who sells bruised strawberries in a basket, past the men selling newspapers, and the crowds of people searching for their bus while avoiding eye contact.

We switch buses and then walk the rest of the way to school. María walks behind us on the skinny sidewalks. When we turn the corner, two boys in school uniforms are in a heated discussion, blocking the path to the sidewalk. We step into the street to pass them. As we walk by, one of them unbuckles his belt. I feel María's hand on my shoulder, and I quicken my pace to match theirs as we pass the entrance to the public school just up the street from Paulo Freire. Paulina and her mother explain that the boys at the other school fight a lot, and some of them are in gangs. They take off their belts and wave them with the metal buckle facing out. Paulina laughs, saying, "When you hear a belt, that's when you move out of the way."

The Hazards of Memory and the Perils of Forgetting

Beti, a slim woman with dark features and a fitted suit, claps her hands until she has the attention of the thirty-six students in the room. The classroom's cement walls are painted bright yellow and blue, and a clean blackboard hangs in the center of the front wall, next to a handwritten class schedule. Cubbies line one side of the room, stuffed with students' textbooks, notebooks, and gym clothes. The other side of the room is enclosed by windows facing the hallway. Like in many schools, noise from gym class creeps through the windows, no matter how many doors are closed between us. The classroom belongs to the seniors, who will graduate in several months with a bachillerato diploma. Many of them will continue their higher education at Universidad de San Carlos (USAC), though a few students have their eyes on private universities, and one plans to take a year off from school to work and save money.

The students wear the required school uniform: dress slacks and a polo shirt embroidered with the school logo, black belts, white socks, and shiny black shoes. Everyone, even the newest student who arrived last month from the United States, wears the school jacket that signifies their status as seniors, a varsity jacket with white snap buttons and the name of the school stitched across the back. Students pile their social studies textbooks and notebooks onto the desks, some passing books from the cubbies to students seated on the far side of the room. Though the bell has not yet rung, their faces look up at Beti.

Beti begins, "Today we are going to talk about the causes and the consequences of the Conflicto Armado." The room is quiet, except for the steady bounce of a basketball on the gym floor below us. "Let's start with what you know. Tell me what you know."

Paulina has her hand up first, her ponytail dangling over the back of her chair. "There were armed conflicts all across Central America."

Javier adds, "The U.S. was a big part of the causes, because the land reforms affected the U.S."

Beti asks for clarification, "How did they affect the U.S.?"

Javier continues, "They felt threatened, because they couldn't keep developing the land for production."

Students describe Beti as one of their favorite teachers. During free periods they line up to talk to her about anything from school projects to family struggles. She knows when Mariana has a piano recital and when Paulina's church puts on a show. She also knows the secrets they carry. A number of them have confided in Beti about family and sexual abuse. "We talk about everything," Beti says.

Pedro, whose hair is shaped into a loose Mohawk, raises his hand. "There was a group of people practicing dictatorial and militaristic styles of government. . . . There were also many groups of intellectuals, and the indigenous who . . . had no other option but to become part of the revolution." Though Pedro is small for his age, he is the oldest member of the class, having repeated ninth grade.

Beti transitions into the contemporary political structure, referencing the present-day administration as a "military government" and noting that today's president "participated in the Conflicto Armado but also participated in the Peace Accords, and these are paradoxical. But the Guatemalan people are accustomed to paradoxes among our leaders." She does not elucidate what she means by this, but there is no shortage of examples: presidents who steal international aid money, judges who accept and offer bribes, antitrafficking units caught selling narcotics, and, today, a president who is a former military general, indifferent to the indictment of a génocidaire.

Ricardo, a boy with a round face and freckles, says that both sides were equally bad during the war. "They both had their motives for doing what they were doing."

Beti seems momentarily uncertain how to respond to Ricardo's comment, which rationalizes violence and circumscribes questions of accountability within the extreme context of war. Admittedly, she does not buy into the two-devils narrative, firmly believing that the state responded to the guerrillas with disproportionate force and committed grave rights violations, while the guerrillas organized people around a just cause. She actively works against zero-blame explanations in her classroom, believing that "it is their [the students'] *responsibility* as citizens to find out what happened," and "it is their *right* to know what the state did."

She says, "And we always say that the indigenous people are the ones who paid the price. We have testimony from many people, children as young as six years old, and the army massacred their whole family." She adds, "There are many stories of those who witnessed violence." Though they do not consult primary-source documents, Beti is confident that her students have been exposed to survivor testimonies firsthand and therefore do not need to read accounts of war. Though she makes a point to discuss the "difficult reality" with her students, she is also concerned that they already experience a low-intensity trauma in their everyday lives and does not want them "reading about rape and murdered babies." It is enough to evoke these horrors.

Gabriela, whose father manages a coffee plantation in the Highlands, says, "But the soldiers in the army were just following orders, whereas the guerrillas were making their own decisions about where to attack. They said, let's kill over here, over there." Pedro cups his hands into a microphone and radios General Tito, Otto Pérez Molina's wartime alias.

Beti describes incriminating videos of Pérez Molina speaking of the military attacks. Her hand covers her chin, painting the image of a younger Pérez Molina with a beard. "Imagine, he is now the president of Guatemala." The conversation moves backward and forward in time, from the president's covert identity during the war to his role in instituting a recent state of siege in Barillas, from Efraín Ríos Montt's tenure in Congress to his long overdue genocide trial.

Without raising his hand, Pedro offers, "My mother says that Guatemala is a country without a memory, which holds us back. We don't have cultural memory, so the people don't want to look back, they don't want to remember what happened in their country." He looks around, and several students shake their heads in agreement. Pedro continues, demonstrating the blurred lines between the authoritarian past and the militarized present: "We need to know everything that happened so that we can say, *'this is what happened*; let's improve ourselves; let's reform our culture and not return to what we had.' When we see massacres and militarized governments, we need to think about the present and tomorrow, and so we need to know our past well in order to know our tomorrow. . . . Otto Pérez Molina is a bad example, because he was in the Conflicto Armado, and Guatemala doesn't want to see. Guatemala doesn't want to say, '*this happened*.'"

Beti nods vigorously and explains that young people especially voted for Pérez Molina "out of ignorance" and contemporary fears. "The only thing they wanted was to find a soldier to take care of the violence." Reiterating her core belief about citizenship and an ethic embedded in the school's philosophy, Beti adds, "And this is because they don't have a civic education, so they don't know about the history. . . . Here [at this school] we talk about these issues so you have a historical memory." The reciprocal relationship that Beti builds between historical memory and good citizenship is evident in nearly every class discussion. Paulo Freire students have what many others lack: historical memory, political consciousness, and civic education.

The Paulo Freire Institute is a modest private school with a left-leaning curriculum. Most of the teachers have college degrees from Guatemalan universities, and several have master's degrees or are enrolled in part-time graduate programs. Nearly all the school's teachers have pursued post-secondary studies at USAC, some during the final years of the Conflicto Armado. A majority of teachers were involved in some form with the university student movement and their notoriously leftist agenda. Paulo Freire's monthly school dues are among the lowest of private-school fees in the capital, and the school directors take pride in providing a quality education for working-class families of "normal means" rather than the elite.

Beti continues, connecting historical memory to the REMHI investigation and juxtaposing contemporary instances of martial law with the writing of Señor Juan Gerardi. "He said that in Guatemala, *never again* would we return to violence, *never again* would we put power in the hands of military, *never again*." Students nod as Beti echoes the title of the REMHI report and a refrain that has deep roots in Latin America's histories of state repression. In a loud voice, she adds, "And what happened to him?"

Pedro motions a machete chop at his neck.

Javier says, "They killed him for thinking differently."

Paulina adds softly, "They assassinated him."

Beti confirms, "Yes, they assassinated him. Two days after releasing the report on historical memory." Her face tightens.

Ricardo protests, "But Miss, it's very controversial. . . . They say he was having a relationship with a man in the church—and that's why they killed him. It was a coincidence." Students break into laughter. Ricardo holds back his own laughter and insists, "It's true, he was a homosexual." Beti listens, patiently waiting for him to complete his thought. Outlandish theories about Gerardi's murder have circulated, mainly that his murder was a "crime of passion" but also that he was attacked by a wild dog who was later held under house arrest while authorities matched bite marks to the dog's jaw. Human rights groups have long argued that Gerardi's murder was a political assassination, a crime that set rigid parameters on what could and should be remembered and served as a vivid warning for all activists working on issues of historical memory (Goldman, 2007; Peacock & Beltrán, 2003).

Beti responds confidently, "This is called: how to confuse the population." She quickly moves on. "But the question is, *what* has this history left us?" She looks around the room, her eyes wide. "Do we have the consciousness not to return to this?" When class ends, a student helps Beti pack up her materials and another comes around with a bucket to collect trash.

The leaders of the Paulo Freire Institute, what began as a family-run effort to create affordable quality education, have come to view their students as future intellectual leaders. Guatemala lost many of its intellectual and political leaders during the Conflicto Armado, and teachers at the institute are actively shaping the next generation of leaders who, in the principal's words, will help Guatemala "recover." Several teachers and administrators remark that Guatemala would have ethical and just leaders today, if their generation's intellectuals had not been killed during the war. Beti actively supplements the curriculum with protest songs, critical documentaries and human rights films, and collaborative art projects, such as a portfolio of photos depicting the "two faces of poverty." She designs these projects to "raise consciousness" among her students, who know about the privatization of resources and that extreme poverty exists because of extreme wealth. One day after class Beti winks at me and says, loud enough that her students can hear, "We are really liberal here. We are forming leaders!"

Beti views her primary goal as an educator and her biggest challenge as one and the same: to "revalidate culture" among her students, many of whom suffer their own challenges at home, such as abuse and abandonment. This work is more difficult given the current context. "It is hard, because you have to be honest about the inequality and the violence that we live. . . . We talk about how the country is, and how we want it to be." Her eyes shift toward students gathering in the hallway. "They [the students] know what is going on in the country. Some of them are very angry. Some are angrier than I am."

Masks and Locked Doors, but Nowhere to Hide

The school day ends at lunchtime, so most students snack during school breaks and return home in time for lunch with their families. There is no formal teacher supervision during breaks. Students scatter, some texting at their desks, others chatting in the cafeteria, and still others wandering the hallways. There are no hall passes, and no authorities scrutinizing their movement, but students self-monitor their volume during breaks and return to class on time. Along the hallway outside the girls' and boys' bathrooms, there is a row of shared sinks and a long mirror, a design that the principal believes helps avoid chatter and disputes.

I follow Pedro and Luisa to the school roof to share a bag of dry cereal. The roof is off-limits except to retrieve loose soccer balls, so we tiptoe up the stairs. Pedro describes a tattoo sleeve that he wants from his wrist up to his bicep, his fingers tickling his bare arm. Luisa shakes her head, noting that people will discriminate against him, and he will not be able to find a job.

Pedro says, "That's just because people are stupid, and they think everything that's *different* is gang-related. When I'm on the street, people always think I'm a gang member or a delinquent, or I'm going to assault them." Luisa and I must look doubtful. Despite that his spiked hair is sculpted into a Mohawk, Pedro's scrawny arms, forehead scattered with pimples, and the perpetual grin revealing his silver braces make him look like an uncorrupted teenager. We laugh at the possibility. Pedro laments that "you cannot be yourself" in Guatemala. But when he tells us stories about wearing a ski mask on the street, Luisa's face changes from amusement to worry. "Why would you do that?"

I admit that even innocent Pedro with a ski mask would scare me. "I might think you were a gang member or a member of a vigilante group."

We laugh. Luisa gestures to Pedro, "You see, this is why I don't go out."

"It's just that I always try to see the good in people, and she sees only the bad," Pedro elbows her. Luisa is one of the students that Beti describes as "angry," and not without good reason. She gives me a serious look, and I can see in her dark eyes that she guards her secrets.

"She is just being careful," I say, hoping it is the right thing to say. Luisa seems won over by this and looks at Pedro as if to prove that she is right.

"Do you know what happened to Óscar's girlfriend?" she asks me.

Pedro's face goes white, and he tells her not to tell me that story.

"But she was . . . ," she begins. "It's not like she doesn't know. She doesn't walk around with her eyes closed." After a moment, she adds quietly, "She *should* know."

I am amazed at how often young people try to protect me, with their words, their heavy silences, their narrow shoulders; with their accents, their bus passes, their homes enclosed by cement walls, their eyes that they can will into threatening stares; by hiding, by withholding, by teaching me to blend in. I have more than ten years on them, but they know Guatemala.

"She went out, and these men grabbed her and . . . they assaulted her and . . . did ugly things."

"They raped her," Pedro finishes, looking away. There is never a moment in Guatemala where this dark reality escapes me, yet still I am never ready to hear these words. I search for something to say, knowing that if I make too big a deal of this, I become someone who does not understand Guatemala. I ask, "She is your age?"

They nod, and we all look at each other shaking our heads. No one needs to say anything.

Having made her point, Luisa says, "So no, I don't go out. I don't go out." She waves her finger no.

Pedro does not seem daunted by these stories. He says, "I just go out, and if someone takes my money, it's fine. Take it. I can't let it bother me forever." Pedro has endless stories about close calls, finding himself in the middle of a gang fight, witnessing domestic abuse among his neighbors, escaping an armed robbery in a neighborhood shop.

Luisa says, "But you're a man. I've been assaulted since I was thirteen years old. I've been assaulted four times in my own neighborhood. I can't even walk to the store down the street. I can't go anywhere." She goes on to say the obvious, that one cannot call the police when these things happen, because "if they come, they plant drugs on you and then arrest you. Because they just want money, they want you to pay them to not arrest you. . . . There is no one you can call, nothing you can do except hide." In Luisa's neighborhood, every house has barred windows, even on the second and third floors. Every door to every house has multiple locks.

"You just can't let it bother you," Pedro says.

"You say that because nothing's happened to you. Just wait, you'll see." Luisa pats him on the shoulder with knowing authority. "You'll be assaulted. Don't worry, it will definitely happen to you, and then you'll see." It is hardly an argument anyone wants her to win, but Luisa makes her point, and even Pedro backs down.

When the bell rings, Pedro heads back and Luisa grabs my wrist and waits for Pedro to turn the corner. "I also have friends who went to the mountains for a weekend, and a gang came and killed them all." She pulls back her hand, telling me their ages, all under seventeen. Looking at the floor, she adds, "They were my friends, and they killed them." I see now why Luisa keeps her eyes narrowed and her doors locked. Luisa knows how violence pulls things apart. She warns me, "Guatemala is a country where you *should* be scared."

Luisa and Pedro's contrasting, and distinctly gendered, experiences demonstrate their development of disparate coping mechanisms while inhabiting the same high-risk setting. Young people like Luisa limit their physical movement within and outside of their home communities, adjusting their "socio-spatial freedom" and in many cases withdrawing from public or shared community spaces (Winton, 2005, p. 173; see also Adams, 2011, p. 41). In contrast, Pedro's attitude is to recognize violence as routine, prompting him to develop internal coping mechanisms such as not letting it "bother you" and searching for "the good in people." But even Pedro recognizes the insecurity that derives from those who fear what is "different." In both cases, these markers of existential insecurity ostensibly work against civic connectedness, instead constructing a "relationship between fear, spatial exclusion, and a lack of social capital and social exclusion" (Winton, 2005, p. 180).

We walk down the stairs, past the Maya calendar printed on the wall, and sit at the wooden tables in the cafeteria. The school encloses an open-air courtyard with several trees growing through and past the roof, mounds of pink flowers scattered across the grass, a small fountain, and a ceramic statue of the Virgin Mary. This architectural layout is common in Guatemalan homes, enclosing living spaces within private walls, though it is not a traditional school design. The principal notes that it is one of the ways the school helps students feel like they are outside, but with the safety of the indoors, noting that, "These young people do not have much freedom."

We're Still There

Cristal moves her glasses into her hair and pushes them back like a headband, revealing thick smears of blue eye shadow. She wakes up an hour early to do her makeup, even when they have gym class. Though Xila (pronounced Sheila) does not have the facial features or darker skin of an indigenous person, I ask if she is Maya because of her name. She and Cristal burst into laughter. Xila's parents chose her name because they liked the Maya *X*. Offering me a cookie, Cristal admits it took her a long time to spell Xila's name correctly.

Beti taps her nails on the chalkboard, and the room quiets down. "Today we are going to construct the historical memory of Guatemala. . . . How do we begin? What is our origin?"

Pedro and Paulina say together, "The Mayas."

Beti draws her voice out, "Ahhh, and what comes after the Mayas?"

"The conquest. And then the colonization."

"And *mestizaje*."

Beti repeats what the students said with interest, "Colonization, *mestizaje* . . . and then what happens? . . . I am talking about the historical process. History is never linear. It is always in the process of unfolding, growing and growing." She makes loops with her hands. "So what happened next?"

"The independence."

"And then what?"

"The October Revolution."

"Very good, the October Revolution. And then?"

One student says, "The counterrevolution." Less certain, another says, "The Conflicto Armado."

"And then?" Beti continues, almost out of breath.

Cristal says, "We're still there." Students laugh, and Beti smiles until we can see all her teeth.

"We are still there." Beti tells the students to give themselves a round of applause at how well they know the history. We clap, and there is something tangibly emotional in the room.

Though it is difficult to imagine anyone at this liberal school countering the stability of this "counternarrative" with the story of a communist threat and two devils, each with their own excesses, teachers are aware that some of their students are from military families. On "very few" occasions, students have shared their disagreement with the historical narrative on the basis that their father or grandfather "is a soldier, and he is not like that." In response, the school has welcomed classroom visits from family members, regardless of their affiliation during the conflict, though it has been several years since anyone has expressed interest in a school visit. Cristal proudly confides in me that her father was a guerrillero but admits he does not like to talk about the war.

Beti dumps a pile of laminated black-and-white illustrations on the floor for a classroom exercise designed by the Oficina de Derechos Humanos del Arzobispado de Guatemala (2003; Office of Human Rights of the Archbishop of Guatemala). The premise of the ODHAG text centers on the need for future generations to understand the past and the "relationship between the everyday and historical memory" (p. 18). She instructs students to clear the floor. Students push the desks noisily to the borders of the room. The task is to make a visual timeline of Guatemala's history. We each select a page and unfold it to find a snapshot from Guatemala's history.

Students kneel on the floor, sliding images around. "This one is first." "I have the last!" They easily identify the familiar colonial images that begin the timeline, but at least three different students insist that they have the final picture. One holding the REMHI report with Gerardi's face says he is certain that he has the last. Another shows a group of people at a table signing a document—one side labeled the "URNG" and the other "the government." Cristal holds up a photo of an indigenous woman with a bandana covering her mouth, saying that her photo comes after the Peace Accords and REMHI. Reconsidering, she mumbles, "Actually, this could go anywhere."

"Where do we put this one?" Ricardo holds up an image of indigenous and mestizo students sitting alongside one another in a classroom and asks his classmates whether his looks like it should be the final image. Javier teases that Ricardo's photo is a fiction that never happened. I hold onto a page that depicts men and women, indigenous and mestizo, playing together and sharing garden tools, living as good neighbors in peaceful coexistence, believing it should be the last, except that I know it is not so. Javier points at my image and announces that I have another fiction.

Two boys argue over a picture of men fighting with sticks and machetes. One says, "That's not the past, that's today."

"No, it's soldiers fighting. This is what the guerrillas looked like."

"That's delinquency in contemporary Guatemala, not the army and the guerrillas."

Eduardo, whose classmates call him Huesos (Bones) for his skinny frame, says, "Cause and effect, my friend. Cause and effect."

The class finally agrees that the last photo should be an indigenous man with a blurb that says, "Fifteen years have passed, and I still know nothing of my family members who were disappeared." When the time is up, we squeeze into our desks, and Beti inspects the meandering shape on the floor.

Beti scans the first images and points to one depicting the "Eternal Spring." She asks the class, "What is the name of the man who generated land for all? Land for all, education for all, life for all, health for all?"

Most students answer confidently, "Árbenz."

Beti nods, "And after this, what happened? Who didn't like Árbenz's democratic polices?"

One student says, "Ríos Montt."

"The capitalists."

"OK, the capitalists. . . . So we are going to see, our story began with process of the conquest and then foreign domination over natural resources." She points to one of the pictures set off to the side. "So where should this go?" It is an illustration of a United States Fruit Company representative wearing a coat labeled USA, gripping Guatemala with his hands. Gabriela jumps out of her seat and slides the page into the timeline after the image of Árbenz. "Good. And here we have the beginning of the inequality we see today, and the militarism that is returning. . . . Today, is there land for all?"

Together, students say, "No." Some of them shout.

Beti guides them toward the language of political critique, "What is this called, when there is a lot for very few?"

"Inequality," Cristal says.

"And what is the small sector that has more?" Beti asks.

Javier says, "Oligarchy."

Beti smiles and crouches on the floor. "And so the big division emerges with the extremely rich. We have the rich who have their private land, and the workers who produce the food on this land but who are their slaves." The students nod. "Then we have the revolution . . . and the militarism that we have had since our colonial subjugation." Students' implicit beliefs that the state cannot be trusted and that the state works against people like them are reproduced through the telling of past events and the historical dimension projected onto contemporary justice struggles.

At first glance, the timeline elaborates the sequence the students outlined in earlier discussions, beginning with the "Spanish Conquest" and followed by colonization and forced labor laws. But the chronology also shows the ups and downs of the peace process, so that all the "peaceful coexistence" pictures that Javier denounces as "fictions" precede a "rekindling" of conflict (Booth, 2009, p. 364). The first wave of conflict is colonialism, the second wave the counterrevolution leading into the Conflicto Armado; another wave follows Gerardi's release of the REMHI report, and a final wave depicts contemporary delinquency. Though there is arguably no single correct order to these illustrations, the exercise is intended to end with the images of indigenous and mestizos living and learning side by side, committed to the difficult and ongoing work of peace and reconciliation, as the culture of peace is the guiding force in the ODHAG text. The students' ordering of time demonstrates their resistance to the postwar narrative of peace and harmony. It also suggests that they struggle to bracket the conflict in a "parenthesis," instead constructing an "ellipses" of ongoing and recurrent eruptions of ethnic, class, and political conflict (Booth, 1999, p. 250). Moreover, it evokes the "blurring of categories and distinctions between wartime and peacetime violence" (Scheper-Hughes & Bourgois, 2004, p. 19).

Beti uses this timeline exercise with all of her classes and notes that it provokes interesting discussions about the rough edges of Guatemala's transition. She is less concerned with their recall of the chronology than the way they make meaning of the violence and attempt to "harmonize the country." Her intention reflects strong alignment with the ODHAG goals for teaching the past, despite that she allows her students to express their frustration and skepticism. "What I want them to see is that they can change the culture of violence with a culture of peace." She does not view these disjunctures or broken promises as cause for disillusionment. After a moment she adds, "I think frustration can help provoke the desire to change." Beti's philosophy contradicts claims that young people crave a positive past that is "usable" toward nation building; instead, she teaches with the presumption that it is the *unjust* past that is "usable" toward empowering her students as critically conscious civic actors. Although they do not spend much class time complicating the historical narrative students co-construct, at Paulo Freire students are able to make historical linkages that are not easily permitted elsewhere.

When the bell rings, several students climb out of their seats and collect the illustrations, piling them neatly onto the teacher's desk. The rest move the desks back into rows.

Reclaiming Public Spaces

From the school building, where Saturday morning detention is in session, I follow marimba up a hill to a small, nameless park, where a band plays traditional music. Several volunteers lean against the wire fence, chatting and texting on their phones, while Javier, Xila, and Paulina dig their knees into the ground, scratching off graffiti from cement benches with paint spatulas and screwdrivers. They walk me around, anxious for me to take pictures to document a before-and-after comparison of the work they will do, confident that they will transform this space. There is a square patch of grass with several trees, two stone tables with curved benches, and a small basketball court with pebbly cement bleachers and bare hoops. Javier leans over the steps to the court and tells me to look down. The stairs below are covered in layers of graffiti, mostly tags that he identifies as signs of gang intimidation and territorial control. They have made progress on scratching the paint off the benches, but the basketball court will be the big challenge, with paint on the bleachers, the walls enclosing the court, and the backboards.

The graffiti is not just a blemish but a visible marker that the neighborhood is under gang control. Javier explains that there are two sides to the risk of occupying the park in its current state: either the gangs will come or others will presume that those in the park are gang members merely by being there. "People would think you painted the graffiti and that you were a gang member. You could get arrested or . . . worse." He pulls a bandana from his pocket and describes the blowout fight he had with his mother this morning about whether wearing a bandana signifies *marero*. It does not matter who you are but who others think you are. It is important to be careful.

Paulina adds, "Anyway, we can't [come here]. It has been privatized because of the gangs." The town cleaned and repainted the park three times in an effort to eliminate gang graffiti, before deciding to privatize it. A year ago they enclosed the space with a locked fence, accessible only to residents. Although few Paulo Freire students live in the school neighborhood, Javier explains that the city arranged the cleanup and granted volunteers access for their service. The plan is to scratch off the graffiti, repaint the walls, and patch up the holes in the fence. The key to the park will be accessible to the school so that everyone at Paulo Freire can use it.

Javier laments that he used to have dates with his girlfriend at the park, and it was a safe place to sit and talk, but now the park is off-limits unless "you are a resident with access. You need a key." He notes that there is no easy solution, since privatizing the park has only kept "good people" from using it; meanwhile, gangs continue to find ways in. We walk onto the basketball court and Javier points to the holes in the wire fence where delinquents have cut their way through.

Xila wrinkles her face. "This area used to be one of the best zones in Guatemala City, clean and safe. And every time there is a clean and safe place, the delinquents come to take advantage." Xila lightly kicks the bleachers. "This always happens. They keep cleaning places, and they keep getting ruined."

Paulina adds, "They clean up only the colonias, not the municipality. And in the city they fix the roads where they feel like it. The mayor decides to fix the roads near his house and the roads he uses." Javier agrees that city resources maintain private spaces, while "people in the middle" need to do their own work to maintain public areas. Paulina points out, "There are better roads in the safe zones where the rich people live. Why should that be?" Despite their professed goals for participating in the project, naming the reasons why this work has fallen to them—those "in the middle"—while other parts of the city get cleaned up through state resources becomes a marker of "disjunctive democracy" (Holston, 2008; Holston & Caldeira, 1998). It is a reminder that "democracy's distribution and depth among a population of citizens in a given political space are uneven" (Caldeira & Holston, 1996, p. 717).

Just outside their school walls there is a cement wall with graffiti that reads, "We want justice for genocide" and "We are fighting for pride in the Maya pueblo." Old campaign flyers glued to the walls urge citizens not to vote for militares. But for Paulo Freire students, there is a clear difference between gang graffiti or tags that vandalize public walls and the political graffiti forced into marginalized spaces. They explain that one is "criminal" and designed to intimidate, while the other is an "act of social justice" meant to spark public dialogue and do the work of democracy. They would not be here cleaning if the park were covered with political graffiti.

We head to the bleachers and begin the grating work of scraping paint off uneven cement. The work is slow with little to show for long stretches. We stop periodically to shake out our hands as they go numb. Not long into the afternoon, it begins to rain. The volunteers line up under a small roof affixed to a neighbor's house. A woman wearing a municipal vest hands out lunches to the marimba players and the volunteers. As we bite into the sandwiches, the school principal and his wife pull up in their car. They roll down their windows and ask us how the project is going. Paulina gestures to the rain, saying she is not sure what they will accomplish if it keeps up. The principal says he is proud that so many students are here to help improve the community. When they ride off, the students ask one another how the principal knew they would be there. "Beti," they guess.

The woman who gave us lunch soon returns and announces that the project is over for the day, because they need dry walls to scratch off paint. She says they will try again on another weekend but does not know when. At the time no one seems disappointed to have their Saturday afternoon free again, but at school the following week Javier expresses his frustration to Beti that the project began late, ended early, and the neighbors "were just watching, not helping." Beti gives this a positive spin, noting that it helped him see "the attitudes toward civic participation in our society." He does not see civic value in the project, noting that city officials hired a band and documented the event with a number of posed photos, but no one posing in the photos picked up a tool. In class the students agree that the project was a "farce."

Anger and Forgiveness

We meet Cristal up the street from Xila's house, near the bus stop. She wears wide sunglasses that cover most of her face, but when she gets close we can see that she is upset. Too tough to cry, Cristal yanks off her glasses and reveals lines of frustration around her eyes. She tells us about the man on the bus who sat next to her and put his hand on her leg and said she could be his girlfriend if she wants. "No, thank you," she kept saying, and she tried to move but he followed her to another seat and got off the bus when she did, calling after her, "Come here, my girlfriend." He left her alone when she turned down a residential street and was off the main road. And yes, she adds, this happened on the municipal bus that charges extra for police protection.

Inside, the girls borrow Xila's lip gloss and put makeup on in front of the mirror, flipping their hair and kissing their lips together. We pile into Xila's mother's car so she can drop us at a pedestrian street with shops and "good security." Xila's mother kisses each of us good-bye and says to be extra careful since it is market day. Off to the side, rows of police trucks are parked on the cement tiles. A line of soldiers in fatigues marches across the street, hands wrapped around oversized guns. Men with carts weave through the crowds selling ice cream, while women flip tortillas and boil ears of corn. Boys with machetes chop fruit and fill bags with pineapple, watermelon, cucumbers, and mangoes. Women and girls stand in front of baskets of hot food covered by towels and boiling pots of *atole* (corn-flour drink). We meet the boys near the Evangelical Mass in the courtyard, a crowd of people with arms up and heads bowed.

As we head for the main strip, Cristal tells me she is my bodyguard for the day. She puts one of my bag's straps on her shoulders so we carry it together and walks the same pace so she can keep an eye on me. She touches me on the shoulder to guide me away from the tight crowds, like the one forming near the stage with girls in bikinis dancing around a man playing guitar. She leads me around the people, to the side of the street, where the crowd is thin and we can see one another. Along the street there are performance artists painted in silver, Transformers who stand up and then crouch down and fold into cars, waiting for passersby to drop change in their basket. Cartoonists draw pictures of famous singers with oversized heads and tiny legs. Cristal stares longingly into the window of a tattoo parlor that boasts expertise in Maya art. She draws small curvy designs on her hip in pen, knowing that she cannot have the real thing. Like Pedro, she wants a tattoo but fears the dangers of self-expression.

From the other end of the street, a swarm of mostly young women heads toward us, led by a marching band and baton twirlers. They carry a banner the width of the street that reads, "The people want quality education, not quantity." Another sign says, "3 years yes, 5 years strike." Together they shout, "Quality not quantity!" Cristal whispers, "It's the *normalistas* [teachers-in-training]," pulling me toward a storefront. Although the proposed Ministry of Education's reform promises to professionalize and improve education, the additional years of teacher training have spawned national protests among the poor and working class, many of whom have been funneled into teaching careers with minimal prerequisites. Now prospective educators will have to finish a bachillerato, apply to college, and complete an accelerated university-level program before becoming eligible to work in public schools. Like the bus protests that periodically keep Paulo Freire students from arriving to school on time, students have mixed feelings about these expressions of popular resistance. Even as their collective undertaking stands to benefit them in the long run—notably as members of the working class—students vacillate between frustration and solidarity, resenting the inconvenience of protests but recognizing that state negligence demands action.

Every few steps we check to make sure we are all together, the six of us. They scold one another when they veer off from the group. "Javier, you need to tell us if you want to stop to call your girlfriend." "Where are Xila and Paulina?" We move as a group from store to store, so when we lose Diana and Javier, it seems like they must be right around the corner. When it starts raining, things get confusing. The crowd watching the performance scatters, and columns of people gather under small ledges. The thumping drums of the normalistas fade into traffic sounds. Cristal taps us on the shoulder, and we follow her into a clothing store to brainstorm. Everyone pulls out a phone to text Javier, but no one seems to have Diana's number. Javier does not answer. We call again and again. Cristal assures us, "Don't worry, Diana is with Javier. They must be just up ahead."

We move toward the door, standing on our tippy toes and looking into the crowds for Diana's flannel jacket and Javier's black T-shirt. The rain is picking up, and people join us on the steps until we are shoulder to shoulder under the small store awning. Cristal's bangs fall from their sculpted arch into her eyes. Several minutes go by. Then Diana and Javier reappear, separately. Exasperated, they tell their stories. Diana starts crying as soon as she catches her breath. She clenches her purse, saying that they were pulling it off her shoulder and grabbing her by the waist the other direction to pull her into the crowd. With Javier's help she was able to hold on to her purse strap and extricate herself, but that's when they got separated and Javier got pulled in. Javier holds back tears and does not look us in the eyes when he tells what happened. He was not holding a bag, so he gripped the pocket with his wallet and braced himself. Then he felt his watch loosen and fingers along his wrist. He grabbed the watch and kicked his way out of the crowd. Students have experience with flash crowds that entrap them, hands running along their body grabbing at anything they can remove, snapping chains off their neck, yanking on earrings until they fall from their lobes, sliding into their pockets and pulling out everything, sometimes taking off their sweater or their coat. Javier has his watch off his wrist and drops it in his pocket.

We take turns comforting them, normalizing Guatemala's exceptional violence. I tell Javier that I am sorry this happened to him.

He shakes his head. "You shouldn't be sorry. It's just the way it is here."

Cristal says, "Let's walk," and Javier and Diana agree that any direction is fine as long as it is away from Tenth Street. We head to the bakery with the smell of warm bread and the cashier that Paulina has a crush on.

On the walk back, Cristal explains,

> People steal because they need to survive. They don't have anything, so they steal, to sell your watch, your earrings. If the state would just take care of the poor people, we could decrease the amount of violence we suffer today. But the state will never do that, never. They never have. . . . This [type of assault] happens to me all the time. It makes me really angry, but this happens all the time. Like once a week. And every time it happens, I get really angry. I start cursing and hitting the person. My dad worries about me, because he says I'll get killed that way. . . . I'm supposed to just say nothing, do nothing. That's security in this country, you have to let yourself be a victim and accept that you can't do anything about it.

In the face of petty crime, these young people experience anger and impotence but also display instant forgiveness, recognizing that delinquents are so poor that they are forced to steal to survive. They do not see delinquents as persons committing violence for individual reasons. Instead, committing crimes against fellow citizens to feed one's family reflects the structural inequality and lack of state services for the poor. Petty violence is an expression of the powerlessness of those forced to become delinquents. While violence is a controlling mechanism of the powerful, it is also a coping mechanism of the powerless, who assert their agency through crime (e.g., Levenson, 2013a). These instances serve as a reminder to these youth that the country has to resolve problems of violence and delinquency on a national level, necessitating stronger punishments for violent criminals and a reallocation of resources. Students believe this is the "only way" to remove the incentive to steal from fellow citizens.

Becoming San Carlistas

Between classes the principal visits the senior class to talk about college. He recommends that students register to take the entrance exam at USAC, even if the public university is not their first choice. When he asks who is planning to take the exam, everyone raises a hand except Gabriela and Ricardo. He reminds them that USAC is a good backup, even if they already have plans to enroll in a private university. After sharing a few anecdotes about students whose parents unexpectedly came on hard times and had to transfer to the national university, he gives them a wink and passes out a sign-up sheet. Paulo Freire has arranged an early dismissal so that students can travel to the university campus to register for the exam. Some years students can spend the whole afternoon waiting in line. Later that morning, when Beti introduces the United Nations' Human Development Index, Pedro asks if it is true that Guatemala has a "really bad" education system. She notes that the problem is that "here, the government thinks that education is learning to read and write at the primary level. . . . They think this is all the people want." As in many cases, Beti employs sarcasm as an indirect invitation for her students to challenge dominant beliefs and practices. It is as if she is saying: *prove them wrong.*

We leave school early and hurry over to Xila's house so the girls can change out of their school uniforms to look pretty for college guys. They put on stretch pants and T-shirts with collars that slide off one shoulder. They pucker their lips in the mirror and pass around makeup kits. Cristal has convinced her older brother to pick us up in his truck as long as we chip in for gas, so that we do not have to endure the long and unpredictable bus ride. He waits for us with the windows down, music thumping. He chain smokes the whole ride there; meanwhile, he and Cristal debate how much money each friend should contribute. Once on campus their argument shifts toward whether he should drop us off or park and risk his car getting stolen.

The line to register for the entrance exam is wrapped around several buildings, but we have arrived earlier than other students who took buses. Students from across the country will arrive today to sign up for the exam, and the wait is expected to be several hours. Students light cigarettes and fan themselves with their identification cards, then shuffle into the administration building when it is their turn. They exit the building after a few minutes with a confirmation card and the date of the entrance exam, another school day for which Paulo Freire will excuse their absence.

Historically independent from the state and long associated with liberal intellectualism, the national university is the only option for most Guatemalans desiring a college education. In recent decades a number of costly private universities have been founded in the capital and a few urban centers around the country. But unlike private universities, tuition at USAC is affordable, and the academic quality remains well regarded. Several years ago, in part because of its inability to meet the demands of increasing student enrollment, USAC instituted an entrance exam, a merit-based assessment that private universities in Guatemala do not require. Beti and other teachers at Paulo Freire frame USAC's exam as an alternative to the elitist prerequisite of private universities, that is, family income. But even students from decent private schools like Paulo Freire worry that the exam is a proxy for socioeconomic status, measured by the quality of one's secondary education.

After registering, we walk around campus and study the famous murals painted by those in the student movement over the years. Paulo Freire students have been raised on stories of the radical idealism at USAC. Xila complains that these are the stories left out of their social studies textbook, the "urban reality" of past and present. During the Conflicto Armado USAC students and professors mobilized support for labor and indigenous rights and endured violent police attacks for their positions. After the war the ones left alive painted murals, and the corridors between university buildings continue to feature vendors selling Che Guevara and Jacobo Árbenz T-shirts alongside woven bags and indigenous textiles. Campus walls are marked with political graffiti about contemporary issues and recurrent calls to remember the October Revolution.

The student movement continues to be a mainstay of the public university experience, although the prestige of this movement never fully recovered the blows it suffered during the Conflicto Armado (Taylor, 2013). Students with older brothers and sisters attending USAC admit that their college education has granted them "critical consciousness." To be a San Carlista is synonymous with developing "critical consciousness," "political consciousness," and "historical consciousness" of the country's experience with injustice and inequality. This is more than a symbolic stance. When USAC's independent status was threatened, students protested and classes were canceled for weeks. And now, in support of the normalista strikes, the student movement is serving as an advisory and collaborator.

Yet the expectation that all USAC students identify with the radical movement is a source of anxiety for Xila and Paulina, who simply want to study and become skilled professionals. Paulina is committed to carrying out "good works" through her church, and Xila resents that being born in Guatemala dictates that she shape her life around a pursuit for peace. Cristal is anxious to participate in the student movement but worries that she may not pass the entrance exam. Meanwhile, Ricardo's reason for not pursuing higher education at USAC is his parents' belief that "one loses a lot of time" due to frequent protests. This perception of "losing time" is not unique to USAC, reemerging in response to strikes across various sectors of society, such as the normalista movement deterring progress on students' school projects, and the bus strike impeding their already strained ability to navigate the capital and arrive at school on time. As usual, it is the people "in the middle" who pay the price for the deficiencies of the government, just as it falls to them to do the work demanded of democracy.

Late afternoon we head off in different directions. Cristal leaves with her brother, and I wait with Paulina at the bus stop for her brother to accompany us on the ride home. He stands in the aisle next to our seat, his arm extended in front of us, and outside he walks on the traffic side of the sidewalk.

In the kitchen María is cooking up sausages and a large pot of rice and peas. I help peel cucumbers, and Paulina squeezes limes. María dumps a half bag of sugar into a pitcher of cantaloupe juice and asks me to make sure it is sweet enough. Paulina piles clean dishes to set the table and answers her cell phone. Her soft voice lowers as she steps into the hallway, finishes her conversation, and slips the phone back in her pocket. "What is it, *mija* [my daughter]?" María asks. Paulina says that Mariana is missing. Paulina's mother twists the faucet closed and asks for details, her face expressionless. Paulina explains that they rode the bus together to USAC, but Mariana forgot her identification card. She got off the bus alone and ran home, assuring them that she would be fine and they would meet on line at the university. "But she never showed up," Paulina says. Her voice gets softer as she mentions that Mariana has not been answering her phone, and now it is going straight to voicemail. That was her father calling, worried that she never came home. This last part is like a punch in the gut, because we know what it means when a young girl is not home by early evening. This is how many stories begin in Guatemala.

Without sounding angry, María says, "You shouldn't have let her get off."

Paulina pleads, "I know. We told her not to. We said, 'Are you sure?' and she said, 'It's not a problem.' . . . But now we don't know where she is."

"She's not old enough to take the bus alone."

"I know." Paulina bows her head.

María covers the pot of food and explains that the situation in the country is very difficult right now. "One cannot ride the bus alone, because there are delinquents that will assault you, rob your things, or . . ."

"Or much worse," Paulina finishes.

María instructs her daughter to call every classmate who may have seen Mariana this afternoon. If we had a car, we would canvas the streets, but, if we must, we will take buses all the way back to the university. Paulina nods, and it is so quiet in the kitchen that I hear the cockroaches scurry across the bare floor. Paulina scrolls through her phone, making calls to all the girls in the class. They either have not seen Mariana or last saw her on the bus to USAC. When Paulina places her phone on the table, we know she has called all her friends, and the panic returns. It will be dark soon, and the rain is coming down, flooding the streets. María unties her apron, and we put on our coats. No one says a word.

Through a cloud of black smoke, we climb onto a red bus, pay the fare, and head downtown to connect buses, weaving our way back to USAC. The bus fare doubles in the evenings to compensate for the increased risk, and the doors close between stops. We sit behind a teenage boy with loose jeans and a neck tattoo that says *thug* in tight script. We get off in a part of town that I am told never to go to alone. A man is stretched across the sidewalk, motionless. As we approach him, I am not sure if he is alive or dead, remembering what Pedro and Francisco have told me about walking over dead bodies near their homes, like they are rocks: "You pretend to not see what you see, just keep walking." I am relieved when he lets out a snort and realize he is passed-out drunk. I watch Paulina and María to see what to do, stepping over and to the side of the man. Like Francisco says, "It's normal here. You just get used to it." In Guatemala, the normal and the exceptional are braided together.

Once we reach the second bus, Paulina gets a call from Mariana. She squeezes my hand and reaches over me to wrap her other hand around her mother's long fingers. All I hear is, "Mariana, you had us worried," in a breathless voice. We begin the journey back to their house. We heat the food on the stove and do not speak about people going missing for the rest of the evening.

The Spiral of Time

Beti draws a large spiral on the blackboard. "Today we're going to talk about the spiral of history." She identifies the inner rings as the past, with time coiling outward. Tapping the chalk on the widest rings, she asks, "And what's our challenge today, as a country?"

Student suggestions begin, and before long the board is filled with negative words: corruption, violence, extortion, threats, robberies, assaults, violations, rapes, exploitation, and discrimination. Before Beti writes each contribution on the board, she asks students to clarify: "What kind of violence? What kind of violation?" They share critical reflections on the differences between extortions, threats, and robberies, insisting that each warrants its own category. They talk about the different ways people discriminate, by ethnicity, gender, and age, noting that old and young people's perspectives are often ignored. Many teachers see the need for this kind of open discussion with their students but worry they will leave students feeling disempowered. When students comment that the list is "all negative," Beti reminds them that they have the power to transform the culture of violence. She says, "We need to break these habits, these stereotypes, that do not have to be ours."

The spiral is an epistemic symbol of Maya cosmology, reflecting the belief in a nonlinear path along which spiritual and material pasts, presents, and futures coexist and travel concurrently. Though the notion of time repeating itself is erroneously linked to this circular ontology, the spiral does not convey social life as trapped in an inevitable loop. Rather it illustrates how similar challenges reemerge throughout time and that "no given time, whether past, present, or future, can ever be totally isolated from the segments of time that precede or follow it" (Tedlock, 1982, p. 202). Corresponding to the spiral shape, one of the principal elements attributed to the Maya conception of time is the idea of accumulation, so that reforms and transitions are never wholly new beginnings but always building on what has happened before.

Some of the students have prepared spirals in their notebooks for homework. Paulina's contains dense, curving text, beginning with the Spanish Conquest and ending at the Peace Accords. Her story of Guatemala is grounded in collective suffering. In one long sentence, from the inside of the spiral and coiling outward, she writes, "Guatemala is a country that has suffered much since the Spanish conquered us, after they began to enslave and degrade us, after this the army recruited people against their will and then began the invasion of land and homes, destroying homes and killing innocent people, after this began a new government with Jacobo Árbenz, in which the US intervened, after the citizens began to demand their rights and the return of their relatives who were forced into the war, and after this tragic situation was the signing of the peace treaty." Her story demonstrates Guatemala's accumulation of loss through a "continuum of violence" (Manz, 2008), with unresolved wounds at the core.

Javier is not convinced that changing the "culture of violence" is all up to them. He asks, "But Miss, how can we make political change, how can we touch the political consciousness of others if we have a president who says, 'I'm not going to take care of my people'?"

Several agree that the poor are neglected by the state, the indigenous rural poor above all others. Pedro asks whether it is possible that Guatemala can be "harmonious with all the different cultures we have."

Beti asks how fourteen million people of twenty-three ethnicities can all "share the fatherland," to which Xila responds that Guatemala binds them by birth. Paulina says they all "have the same origin," in that they are all descendants of the Maya. Although no one in the room self-identifies as indigenous and only three Paulo Freire students' parents wear traje, students decide that pluricultural Guatemala is like a Maya textile, with multicolor threads woven together. Despite this sugarcoated ideal, there is consensus in the room that just because everyone from Guatemala is Guatemalan does not imply that all Guatemalans are equal. Beti does not argue with their conception of Guatemala's democracy as "disjunctive" (Caldeira & Holston, 1996; Holston, 2008) but easily transitions from critical moments of disjuncture to the abstract guarantees of democratic citizenship.

Beti reserves the end of class for an essay assignment. Several students read aloud as she writes on the board: "What do I hope for from the social covenants in the search for peace? And what/how can I contribute?"

When students ask about social covenants, Beti reminds them of the Peace Accords, educational reforms such as bilingual education, and the idea that "we are all equal in our rights and duties to the state, and the state is obligated to protect our life, liberty, and property." Students make sarcastic displays at this ideal expression of the civil contract, but when Beti closes the door, they diligently lean over their notebooks and begin copying the questions.

Pedro, who struggles with a quiet room, says aloud, "I can help make peace by fighting. Don't you think I have to fight if we want peace?"

Beti answers to the class, "No, I don't want to see you *fight* for peace; I want to see you help struggle and *maintain* peace."

Xila raises her hand and says, "Why do I have to do something for peace? What about other things that can improve the country . . . like writing novels?"

Beti agrees that writing novels is a nice idea, but gestures to the spiral and notes the list of challenges that constrain one's choices in Guatemala. She encourages Xila to do both.

Despite these initial interruptions, the students write continuously for the remainder of the class. Even the students who claim to hate social studies stretch long lines of text across the page, filling the blank space. Some students fill two pages of loose leaf, and only one hands in a single paragraph floating in white space. One by one they pass in their papers. The essays reveal deep frustrations and the struggle to remain hopeful that Guatemala can change. Most express uncertainty about how they as individuals can work within and against the existing structures of power.

Several students refer to the social covenants as "propaganda," "lies," or a "mask that hides the reality." There are numerous references to the government and state authorities as "thieves" who "care only about money," "cheat the people," and favor "a sector" of citizens who compose the "elite oligarchy," often privileging "their [own] well-being over the country" while neglecting the "common good." A majority of students direct their frustration toward the state or extensions of the state, such as Javier, who reflects, "I think that in Guatemala it is difficult to find someone who is honest and cares about Guatemala," and Cristal, who writes, "We are very bad with violence because the police are also thieves." Marlon's paragraph is filled with superlatives. He writes, "It is the worst to have to live with fear, and it is the most ridiculous that instead of intervening in the matter, the government of Guatemala tells the people that they have to be careful in the streets. . . . This is the most illogical, a mediocre government that is intimidated by delinquency instead of delinquents who are afraid of the government."

Nearly every student grounds his or her essay on the idea that Guatemalan citizens should have, but currently lack, "the right to walk freely in the streets" without fear. This is the way that Guatemala's contemporary violence most affects their lives, causing fear and suspicion of others and distrust of police and state authorities, limiting their social movement, and in some cases directly impacting their lives through rape, kidnapping, and murder. One student writes, "I hope that one day we can have the peace that we signed for in Guatemala, and we do not have to suffer violence daily."

Several students write about their ability to contribute to peace by "avoiding violence." Pedro, preoccupied with how Guatemala could accomplish peace without fighting, writes, "I can support peace by offering peaceful solutions and demonstrating that it is possible to be happy without being above or below someone, with everyone equal." Cristal's suggestion focuses on structural reform, such as purging corrupt officials from public office and vetting police forces while offering social services for the poor. Rodrigo identifies a tangible action step, recognizing the slow and committed work that peace demands: "I hope that we can change each one of us, little by little. . . . I could help the organizations that are looking for peace, to be a promoter of peace, and not living simply to live but rather living to make a change in our country. . . . Although it would require a big effort among all of us to change even a little bit . . . it would be worth [it]."

Similarly, Paulina anticipates a long-term process with young people as principal actors: "We students can help create peaceful environments in our homes, then with our neighbors and our classmates." Following this statement, she identifies two chief obstacles: government corruption and repression against freedom of expression. Closing the circle, she connects these authoritarian conditions to the resurgence of civilian violence.

Several students make explicit references to the Conflicto Armado when they write about the contemporary political situation. Mariana writes, "I would like to contribute by helping people understand the history of Guatemala that we *cannot* repeat . . . giving them historical consciousness so that they have a foundation and consciousness about what is happening. And in this way they will not repeat the past, so that there will be no violence, robberies, discrimination. So that there will be no inequality!"

The student essays display the same unevenness as their timeline, at times expressing a clear and confident vision for eradicating violence, only to talk themselves into circles and realize that they are wedged between the possibility of change and those in power who directly benefit from the status quo. Francisco, whom I have never heard speak in class, writes, "We can never hope for what we desire, because we will never have peace for the simple reason that in Guatemala we are constantly fighting." Luisa reflects on what she can do for "my Guatemala," concluding that "they [unclear subject] can teach us to be better people, but it doesn't matter if at the corner down the street there are injustices, corruption, and *violentaciones*." Combining *violence* and *violations*, Luisa creates a compound word for a "violent violation," making the point that speaking the language of peace cannot work against the ubiquity of violence. She presses her pink pen into the paper on that word, so hard that the page almost tears.

When class ends Luisa turns in her seat to tell me, "The problem here is corruption. Everyone wants money. This is why nothing changes."

Xila glares at Luisa and leans over my desk. "It's not *all* bad. We have nice things in Guatemala too."

Luisa does not seem put off. "It's true, there are nice things in this country."

For the first time, I sense genuine conflict in the room. Luisa and Xila debate whether things are getting better or worse with a bitterness alien to both of their soft voices. From across the room, Huesos agrees that they should "let go" of hope, while Xila argues that believing "how bad we are" is "part of the problem." She worries for Guatemala and does not understand why people line up to leave the country when it is their duty to stay and improve it. Xila places blame on the failings of the state but also on the people themselves, who "spend their lives complaining about the situation but don't do anything to change it." Luisa faults Xila's optimism as denial, a lie that Guatemala has been telling repeatedly rather than facing real problems. The people are victims, trapped within a criminal state. "There are only *corruptos* in the government. . . . They all want something."

Despite Xila's plea that they "not talk as if the future is hopeless," Luisa's glare is unyielding. Huesos puts his hands on Luisa's shoulders and notes that she cannot walk down the street without fear of being killed. "People kill you over anything. What kind of hope is there? . . . No, let go of it. You can't have hope here."

Evasion and Inversion

Though chaos is the only life Paulo Freire students know, they are mindful that Guatemala is an upside-down place, where criminals roam free while victims hide, where citizens take care of the state while the state takes care of itself, where the rules of survival require masks and silence. Because they are young, and because they are in "the middle," every risk has at least two sides: the risk of falling victim or the risk of being taken for a criminal. Who they are does not matter as much as who others decide they are. If they are in the park with gang graffiti, they are a *delincuente*. If they wear a bandana, they are a *marero*. If they have a tattoo, they must be a prostitute or a criminal. These social categories are often imposed on them, stemming from broader discourses and imagery of criminal youth. Young people are forced to contend with the labels assigned to them, even as they work to resist and distance themselves from their meanings. They recognize the need to be invisible, yet invisibility carries its own risk, in that they can be easily eliminated. Their daily lives oscillate between the dual risks of invisibility and hypervisibility.

Recognizing this no-exit situation, Beti embraces the pedagogical risks of engaging her students with their lived experience of democratic disjunctures, acknowledging fault lines so deep that their recognition brings on a collective state of psychosis. The path to collective empowerment, she believes, is through collective anger. Some students follow Beti's intended path from anger to action, yet there is also fatalism operating within Guatepsicosis. As Luisa demonstrates, normalizing violence casts hopelessness and relinquishment of agency as adaptive strategies. This chapter describes key moments where power and inequity, as well as hope and fear, are felt, sometimes in ways that contradict themselves.

One of the casualties of the war was the "urban *barrio* culture of class solidarity" (Levenson, 2013b, p. 196), a loss that Paulo Freire tries to compensate for by educating a generation of new leaders. Students' experience with violence becomes the organizing frame for their collective identity, a reminder that they suffer and struggle together. This like-minded community at Paulo Freire is strengthened through a shared interpretation of historical injustice and of the lack of historical consciousness apparent in other communities who are not enlightened to the "difficult reality" that the state never escaped the counterrevolution. Class discussions, the timeline exercise, and the spiral of historical memory reiterate that the violent past is an integral part of Guatemala's ongoing story, a story with no discernable ending. Although reliant on some crude conflations between the war and "postwar," what is powerfully captured in these gestures is historical and interpersonal connectedness, that these students and their teacher inhabit the same Guatemala, one where violence and repression formulate an "ellipsis."

Young people's perceptions of Guatemala's deficiencies at times hinge on their impressions of the unresolved past and the way a history of violence resonates in democracy's failures. Beti illustrates the outlook of many survivor-generation parents and teachers when she frames historical memory as the critical foundation of Guatemala's civic education and its deficiency among postwar youth as the reason why a former military general would be democratically elected. The students at Paulo Freire are not the young people who voted for Pérez Molina—though they may share the fears and fall victim to the same "psychosis." Students uphold this partnership between the *nunca más* and the future, believing that good citizens know the violent past and participate in the ongoing struggle for justice. Good citizens do not celebrate the growing number of soldiers in the street as "security" but are reminded of Gerardi's warnings about militarizing society. Voting for *militares* is a violation of this reciprocal duty to the country's unjust past and its hoped-for future.

Paulo Freire only outlines the path to renewed working-class solidarity. A changed Guatemala depends on these students' decisions about their own futures, in part their adherence to the USAC student movement. But college life at USAC comes with two central anxieties: gaining access and the risk of "losing time." Teachers and school leaders openly discuss the educational reality with students, noting that families with wealth easily pay for access to higher education, while the poor and working class need to earn it. Students fear that their education at Paulo Freire, though private, still has not adequately prepared them for the university entrance exam, yet another block toward equal advancement.[1] A more acute concern for these students, however, is the reality that education at USAC is notoriously uneven, interrupted by protests organized or supported by the student movement. In this sense, studying at USAC comes with the erratic cost of losing time. Despite that many students are eager to join the movement and the working-class struggles poised to improve their own trajectories, they are not equally prepared to bear the burden for their democracy's failings. Like much else in their lives, transitioning to college requires enduring sacrifices in the present for the uncertain promise of a better future.

Unlike most public spaces in their lives, Paulo Freire is a place where students can express themselves physically, emotionally, and intellectually, without fearing repercussions for being themselves. These young people can make lists of *what Guatemala lacks* in their sleep, and they seem to do so almost ritually as a demonstration of their awareness of the global perception of their country as increasingly violent. They are also aware of what flows in abundance, assuring me that weapons, drugs, and assassins are as easy to access as water. Yet, despite what they say about the civil contract unraveling, they make great efforts to protect one another. They walk shoulder to shoulder in the capital; they cry in each other's arms over the unwanted caress of a stranger's hand on their knees, the violations done to their bodies, and the stripping away of their belongings; and they keep one another's secrets hidden. Together they shield me from the violence, teaching me what they know about survival. They make efforts to differentiate themselves from youth criminals, to prove that they are not like Guatemala's reputation, that there are exceptions, that living under extreme conditions makes one grateful for the smallest gifts. They do all this, even as their selective disputes dig a hole so deep that looking inside requires abandoning hope. Amid everyday struggles to stay safe, there is the added work of guarding hope, not only from outsiders—who see what they will see—but also from one another, who believe they know better than to put their faith in fictions.

5

Sun and Moon

The No-Future Generation and
the Struggle to Escape

Options and Opportunities

It is a myth that roosters make noise only at daybreak. The roosters in the backyard have been crowing for hours, and I am the last one in the kitchen, still rubbing my eyes. Leonardo and María Carmen are seated at the table, drinking hot milk with sweet coffee. Their youngest son, Josué, waves hello, his eyes glued to the blurry television screen. With his other hand he offers warm mango slices to his pet parrot. Pati emerges from the yard, carrying a pile of tortillas. María Carmen studies the tortillas and yells to Pati that they are too thick. To us, she says, "The girl is still learning to make tortillas. When she first came here, she didn't know how to make them. Look how much I have taught her." She holds up a steamy tortilla. "But they are still too thick," Leonardo agrees, chewing quietly.

Like many of the young women in Río Verde, Pati comes from an *aldea* (hamlet) where there are no opportunities to study past elementary school. Río Verde has several public and private schools, one of the main reasons why this village has become a rural migrant community. Several months ago Pati turned fourteen and her parents sent her to help María Carmen, a distant relative, with cooking and cleaning in exchange for room and board. Leonardo and María Carmen's nephew Werner also lives with them and four of their five sons, so that he can finish middle school.

Ricardo, in his early twenties and one of Leonardo and María Carmen's eldest sons, is dressed in dark pants and a button-down shirt, formal attire reserved for church affairs. The heat is heavy even in the morning, and Ricardo already has sweat beading along his forehead. He swallows a bite of eggs and announces that he will return before going on duty as a taxi driver. María Carmen looks at her cell phone and announces the time to Josué and Martín, indicating that they should get ready for school. The youngest brothers walk together to Josué's elementary school, and Martín continues on the main path to get to his middle school, a private institution that he boasts is "the best in the entire department."

María Carmen scrubs dirty clothing on the sink's washing stone. When the coals cool, Pati begins scaling fish for lunch and rolling corn for the next batch of tortillas. Together they clean the breakfast dishes, mop the floors, feed the chickens and change their newspaper, and head to market for vegetables, oil, and soap; when they return they begin preparing lunch. Today is especially busy, because Leonardo is traveling north to volunteer as a mediator in an escalating conflict between townspeople and the mining company that is encroaching on village life. It is not the first time that indigenous people have been dispossessed of their land at the hands of a wealthy foreign corporation. The legacy of colonial destruction lurks in the foreground in this recent decade of renewed foreign development, which for many has brought about new forms of exploitation. To no one's surprise, they much resemble the old forms.

María Carmen does not hide her concern that the journey is dangerous because of the poorly maintained roads, not to mention the number of delinquents and narcos who stand between here and there. Leonardo's mediator position is not without its risks, and yet he continues to volunteer, while his family struggles to make ends meet. He earns little money selling vitamins and occasionally a chicken door-to-door. The family scrounges all resources when it is time to pay school fees and the electric bill. While it is clear that Leonardo cares deeply about helping others, he is also bound by hierarchy to his former guerrilla commander, who initiated the volunteer organization. Leonardo clips his sunglasses to his shirt collar and heads out into the heat. He walks with a slight limp, suffering injuries from five separate bullet wounds during the war. His sons say they can still feel one of the bullets circling his kneecap.

Fighters and Martyrs

Pati walks me along the dirt path to get to school. We cross a dry riverbank, which has become an unofficial garbage dump, avoiding several oversized pigs feeding on trash. At the top of the hill, we part ways, Pati heading to her public school with uneven grass and swampy patches, rotted wooden bleachers, overflowing toilets with unhinged doors, and stifling classrooms with no windows or fans. The cement walls that surround the school, like many village storefronts, are covered in hand-painted advertisements for cell phone carriers.

Next door is Sun and Moon, the only high school in the village, a newly opened, indigenous-run private school where students can earn bachillerato diplomas. A hand-piled stone wall encloses the buildings, free of advertisements and graffiti, an architectural style that the principal explains is meant to evoke the ancient Maya. Classrooms are housed in a long, slim building with open-cut windows and doorless entryways for ventilation. Several stand-alone huts are scattered across the grass: the cafeteria, the computer room, the front office, and a parking area for bicycles and motorcycles. The walkways between structures are decorated with recycled bottles tied together with odd strings and shoelaces. Students arrive before the teachers and administrators, who pull up on motorcycles just minutes before classes begin.

Social studies class begins with a student volunteer to lead the morning prayer. Students scramble out of their chairs to stand with their heads down and their hands folded, many with their eyes closed. This is not a religious school, but administrators and teachers at Sun and Moon actively encourage the students to "find God" so that they know they are loved. Many of the teachers express concern that the students come from families without love, some enduring habitual abuse, and they want to prevent the children from taking the all-too-available path toward delinquency. The walls and floors of the classrooms are cement, painted yellow and stained with dead bugs, despite their newness. A whiteboard hangs at the front of the room, but otherwise the walls are bare. Teachers have made various attempts to hang materials, but the heat is so dense that nothing sticks.

Though the rooms fit nearly fifty wooden desks and a bare table and chair for the teacher, the school does not yet have the enrollment to fill the classrooms. There are twelve students in the senior class, all of whom identify as Maya, though only one of the girls wears traje rather than the school uniform.

The teacher, César, born and raised in Río Verde, rests an open textbook in his palms. It is an outdated social studies text with a hard cover whose graphics have worn away. The students have bound photocopies of text excerpts, most of which are jam-packed with facts about Guatemala's natural resources, population statistics, descriptions of the country's departments and their topographical features, and an appendix with global health indices. When I ask how he addresses the Conflicto Armado in class, César notes that the subject does not get much attention in schools anywhere in the country. It is "not in my book," and, besides that, it is "irrelevant" given the distinct challenges facing rural Guatemalan youth today. César is initially hesitant to invite me into his classroom, emphasizing that it will not be useful, because his students are less connected to their history than they are to their declining culture. I am better off consulting historical texts—though he cannot recall the title, he directs me to the truth commission report, where I will find "all the answers." With some time, I convey that I am more interested in the thoughts of his students than their historical knowledge.

Most of César's classes begin with dictation exercises, though today he holds up the front page of the newspaper and gestures to the cover photo, a violent standoff between the national police and the normalistas. Since the Ministry of Education proposed extended training for future teachers, normalistas have organized protest movements across the country to demonstrate their discontent and to persuade ministry officials to establish a dialogue. Tensions have been rising between both parties, with student protests increasingly becoming conflictive, and riot police violently stifling their actions at the orders of the state.

César glares at the cover page and mumbles something about how the lucha never ends. A few students take this as a rare opening to share their opinions. Rosa says, "I identify with them, because we indigenous have to fight for every little thing."

Gregorio says, "How are they going to better themselves? Who is going to help them or give them opportunities? This is why they look for illegal ways to be heard." From the news it is difficult to tell whether the students came to the protests armed with sticks and rocks or whether the police overreacted from the get-go.

David says, "Yes, but on the news they say the police threw tear gas at them . . . and that the government is not going to change the law, no matter what. So why do they keep protesting?"

César nods. "Well they might not change the law, but it's important to listen to what the students are proposing. To see how the dialogue is taking place—"

Álvaro interrupts, constructing an affinity between the rural poor and the normalistas, who largely represent the urban working class. "It's not about dialogue; it's about the rich. The police, the army, they always manage the country, and they always take care of the rich. We don't have a chance to get out from under [salir]."[1] Most of the students in the senior class are between seventeen and nineteen, but Álvaro is in his midtwenties.

César responds, "That's why it's important to get ahead [salir]. . . . And let's remember that the laws exist for this reason, to allow for dialogue." Almost in the same breath, he adds his own counterpoint, "But it's important to remember that the government right now is military, and they are repressive. They have already demonstrated this." There is a small back-and-forth over whether it is useful to protest at all when opportunities for change are so slim. Though the Sun and Moon students do not sound particularly optimistic that the normalistas will succeed in fostering a dialogue, they exhibit empathy for the application of more "extreme" tactics, linking the students' turn to illegal means and the necessity of being heard in a country where the state would otherwise not listen. They further defend their position by acknowledging power inequalities, explaining that bending the law is acceptable for those who are "underneath."

César continues, "I'm not sure how many of you read the newspapers. But I can't do it anymore. Our newspapers are an embarrassment—not their quality, but what the pages are filled with. Everything is violence, massacres. . . . How shameful." He drops the paper onto the table with visible disgust.

Julia disagrees. "But this is what we are living."

Álvaro confirms, "Guatemala is a meat factory . . . and we are the meat."

The students consider this. Rosa says, "But no one wants to read newspapers because they are filled with violence. When someone feels like reading, better to read a good book." Students share concerns that the news inadvertently leads readers to praise criminals for outsmarting authorities, so that children see that delinquents have money and power. "They say, 'This is what I want to do: I want a gun. I can be a delinquent. Then I can have anything I want.'" More than once a day I hear students lament that criminal violence has become the language for social interactions, while discounting their participation in this production. Currently, there is an e-mail circulating among the students with photos of a busted narco mansion, rooms of money stacked like books, a mound of jewels sparkling like wet limes. These linked symbols of criminality and material wealth are the markers of a high-risk setting where violence shapes identity, status, and self-presentation (Edberg & Bourgois, 2013).

Víctor shares a story about an instance of *justicia propia* (vigilante justice) that took place the previous night. A drunk driver hit a family crossing the street, and quickly a crowd began to gather, throwing rocks at the car. "The people were angry. Of course they were angry, but we have violence over everything. And we're never going to progress because of it. And the worst was . . . the women carrying babies, with their little children, throwing rocks, teaching their kids to be violent. . . . They learn violence this way." Classmates confirm details about where the incident took place and who was involved. The police arrived, but only after "the people responded," because they "wanted their own justice." This story brings on a flutter of student comments about how authorities are "corrupt delinquents," who cannot and will not do their jobs. Though the police managed to prevent a lynching, the driver is free today because he paid off the authorities. There is consensus and almost ritual repetition of the statement, "They *sell* justice."

Víctor ends the story with a rhetorical justification of vigilante justice: "What option do we have? . . . What option do people *like us* have?" The way he emphasizes *like us* knots my stomach. These young people are aware that they experience insecurity and lack of justice, "because they are certain kinds of citizens" (Holston, 2008, p. 7).

Without hesitation, Álvaro opens his mouth. "Revolution . . . it's the only way." Students look at one another, with slight laughter at Álvaro's conviction. "The people here are sleeping. I don't know when they will wake up." Álvaro conjures a familiar image of Guatemalans who live with their eyes closed to the suffering around them. The image, in his view, applies to both elites, willfully oblivious to their privilege, and to the disenfranchised, who passively tolerate injustice.

Rosa theorizes that the key to change is "improving education at home." By this, she means steeping children in strong moral values such as belief in God and the absence of family abuse.

Álvaro takes education to mean support for pursuing one's studies, noting the challenges they all face as the first generation to pursue high school—not just financial struggles but a lack of trust that education can lead to better opportunities. "Many [of our parents] have this idea that education is not important. They say, 'Why are you going to school? You don't need it.' This is ridiculous. This is how we have generation after generation that stays the same, that cannot get ahead [salir]. I want to see us learn, organize, and start this revolution. . . . This is the only thing we can do."

Students talk over one another, teasing about whose parents are least supportive of their studies. As it gets loud, César leaves the room and talks with another teacher in the hallway. Though his exit initially surprises me, I soon realize that this is not an uncommon practice at Sun and Moon. César often leaves the room during formative moments when controversial and painful issues surface among his students, not out of uninterest but conceivably out of uncertainty as to how to respond. Other teachers at Sun and Moon also take part in this practice—arriving late or exiting in the middle of a class session—believing that students come to respect teachers more when they are made to wait.

In César's absence the students carry on, shushing one another when they see that timid Amílcar is trying to tell a story. He begins, "My neighbors where I used to live, the parents were abusive. On many occasions we saw them hitting or pulling their children by the hair . . . and I felt really bad. My father called the human rights office [to report them]. . . . The mother found out, and she screamed at us, 'Why are you meddling? These are my children! Don't talk to them; don't look at them.' And what happened is the human rights office tried to register a complaint, but the husband was a friend of a judge, and so they couldn't." Students nod emphatically, recognizing what it means to pursue justice to the abrupt end of its line.

Álvaro comforts Amílcar, who looks troubled. "What could you do? The law was on your side, and it didn't matter. . . . What else *can* we do if our authorities don't do anything to take care of us? What else can we do, other than start a revolution?" Amílcar's story sets off a series of similar stories about civic action interrupted and justice denied by corrupt individuals and institutions.

David connects the impossibility of achieving justice back to Víctor's story about the drunk driver: "This is why people here . . . make their own justice."

Some rural communities in Guatemala have identified strategies for working together in order to "fill the gap" left by a weak state, giving rise to illicit expressions of civic engagement and community organizing. Rather than report criminals to a corrupt police force and funnel them into a dysfunctional justice system, citizens make their "own justice." In some cases, communities forge vigilante units in the spirit of neighborhood watch groups, using posters to display with pride and caution that they are "organized" (Bellino, 2015a). In other cases, communities spontaneously come together to capture and punish alleged criminals, displacing the state's role and reconstituting justice as a "common good" to be collectively upheld, even when it requires violence or self-injury to the community. These public displays, ranging from meticulous to mob-like formations, serve the immediate purpose of delivering justice while vocalizing dissatisfaction with the current system. In the process, citizens demonstrate the incompetence of state security structures to respond to crime (Alston, 2007). For this reason, lynchings undoubtedly "comprise a story of failure" (Santamaría, 2012, p. 45). On international measures, Guatemalan youth tend to support popular appropriations of justice, tying with their peers in the Dominican Republic for the highest levels of support in the region, "if the authorities fail to act."[2] Moreover, Guatemalan students expressed "very significant" skepticism compared to their Latin American peers that peace could be achieved through dialogue and negotiation (Schultz et al., 2011, pp. 65–66).[3] Both of these civic stances are on display in this classroom, where students' attitudes toward violence and justice are shaped through everyday experiences with local and national impunity.

Students recount recent instances of mob violence in Río Verde, including lynching of criminals and arson of the local police station and law enforcement vehicles. There is a combination of shame and defense in their comments, as students are well aware of the dangers of reacting too quickly. Víctor says, "Sometimes the people just do it to do it. . . . There is no dialogue."

Another says, "They don't open the space to talk. They just come with gasoline and start pouring it on the road. They don't listen to what people have to say."

But considering the dangers of taking justice into one's own hands leads the students back to their instinctive beliefs, that *some* justice is better than none. Rosa says, "On one hand, I'm in favor of taking justice in your own hands, because what does justice do here? Right now, here, justice doesn't do anything."

David agrees, "It's true. Even if you capture a criminal, they let them go. . . . And when they are set free, they say, 'Tomorrow we steal.' This is how the cycle continues. This is why people have to take justice into their own hands."

Álvaro reasons that justicia propia is a form of resistance against "ladino laws" and the corruption and impunity that hollow these promises. He explains that every pueblo has "its own form of fighting back. This pueblo burns." Though extreme, these expressions of extrajudicial justice mediate the people's anger at being gravely neglected on a national level (Snodgrass Godoy, 2002). Despite that students know by heart sections of the national Constitution, the Peace Accords, and international human rights laws, they also know that these guarantees have limited applicability for people *like them*. Rural areas of Guatemala have historically functioned in isolation from the state's capital and central policy making. In particular, indigenous populations have been excluded from the benefits of state membership. At best, marginalized Guatemalans have experienced "low intensity citizenship" (O'Donnell, 1993, p. 14; see also Sieder, 1999, p. 110), in that their civic identity has been more strongly rooted in local communities than in the strained relationship they have experienced with the state. For much of Guatemala's past, this has served as a "functional distancing between the governing elites and the people they govern" (H. Mack, 2011, p. 453) but has since become a challenge to state efforts to construct a pluricultural national identity. Many Guatemalans living in rural areas continue to view the state as ineffective, irrelevant to local realities, and indifferent to the structural inequalities that shape their lives.

When I ask whether there is an opportunity to stop popular justice before it escalates, the students look at me with regretful amusement. Gregorio explains, "If you say anything—if you say, for example, 'let's call the police instead of all this'—they will say you are working with him too."

Amílcar adds, "Or else they will say, you're just a youth."

Rosa says, "What you want to do—the only thing you can do—is *apartarse* [remove yourself]."

Like many conversations at Sun and Moon, this one gives way to the relative powerlessness students have to change the course of their lives and communities. Rosa attempts to explain, "One can try to change things, but ..."

David finishes her thought, "You try to improve your life, you try to escape [these conditions (salir)] . . . and they keep pushing you down, so why try to change anything?" He holds out his hands flatly and then moves them toward each other, shrinking the space in between. "You want to stay in the middle." This theme of "staying in the middle" by achieving invisibility or neutrality runs through many of the conversations during formal class sessions and unstructured time at the school.

Rosa nods. "We can only change ourselves; that is the only way. We cannot make others change."

Álvaro says, irritably, "But someone needs to do it. Someone needs to do it."

"But when they do it, they kill them. He will not be a *luchador* [fighter], but a martyr." After a moment, Gregorio adds, "And we don't need any more martyrs."

César returns to the class, his smile out of place in this stoic moment, to announce an extra-credit assignment centering on the Conflicto Armado.[4] He does not overtly connect today's conversation to the assignment, and it is unclear whether he intended or managed to follow the discussion from the hallway. Students negotiate how many points the assignment will be worth, some more interested in participating than others. César holds out his arm and divides the class in half, so that two groups will present the results of their research independently. "You have just a few questions to answer, because this theme is big: How did the Conflicto Armado originate? Why did it happen? And who were the populations most affected?" As an afterthought, he asks, "Do you all know what the Conflicto Armado is?" A few students nod, but several have blank faces. Álvaro, who rarely raises his hand before speaking, catches César's look to keep quiet. Several years older than his classmates, Álvaro's contributions can come off as reproachful of his classmates' naïveté. The teacher calls on Claudia, undoubtedly the shyest student in the class and the only one who wears traje. She vigorously shakes her head no. With some prodding, she stands up, smooths her skirt, opens her mouth, and then sits back down without saying anything. The teacher looks around the room and explains that Río

Verde, like many pueblos, was "affected" by the conflict. Students nod. "It was the time when . . . basically the Maya community disappeared."

César says, "How do you not know anything, living here? You didn't learn about the conflict in elementary school?" Students shake their heads. "Not from your parents?"

Julia, the only one who seems unafraid of her own voice on the subject, explains, "The little bit I know is what my parents told me. They didn't want to leave the population in peace. Rather they wanted to fool them and get them involved, and the people were mistreated."

César asks, "By whom?"

Julia says, "By the guerrilleros. But the soldiers were the ones who were more powerful . . . or no?"

Some of the students begin to regret their decision to participate, remarking that there is a lot of information to investigate for the project. One student says emphatically he doesn't know *anything* about the conflict. Julia announces that she has a video about Guatemalan children being kidnapped by guerrilla soldiers. César promises that they will make time to watch the full video, even if it means borrowing class time from another teacher, a statement that garners some vocal support.

Despite his initial insistence that his students are "not the generation that cares about the conflict," César seems frustrated at his students' lack of historical knowledge. He promises them that the assignment will make clear "why we study history, so that we don't repeat the same mistakes we committed before, to not fall again."

Stories That Hurt

Over dinner María Carmen tells stories about how she and Leonardo met during the war, "in the mountains." When she mentions the Conflicto Armado, she gestures with her lips to the hills at the outskirts of the village. She and Leonardo were both guerrilleros. Casually, she reminds me that not many women joined, and fewer returned from the war. "Two of our [five] sons were born in the mountains. I had only a kindergarten education, and I could barely speak Spanish. . . . We were very lucky to return from the mountains together." She places a stack of plates on the table. "We were very lucky. . . . But we suffered through hunger, cold, rain. When you are a guerrillero you withstand a lot of suffering."

Josué, Martín, Isaac, and Werner pour themselves tall glasses of soda. When I ask whether her children know her story, she laughs. "Of course they know, they all know. My two eldest were born in the mountains. They are *guerrilliños* [children of guerrillas, born in the mountains]. These three are *hijos del pueblo* [children born in the village]." She looks at me, gesturing to her three sons at the table. Leonardo's brother, Werner's father, also joined the guerrillas, but Werner is too young to be considered a guerrilliño because he was born after the war. He too is a child of the pueblo, not the mountains.

I give Josué, the youngest, a playful look, wondering what this twelve-year-old might know of his parents' suffering. "Is it true, Josué, you know all about your parents' story?" He giggles and tucks his mouth into the glass, letting soda bubbles tickle his face.

María Carmen assures me, "He says yes, he knows."

I keep my eyes fixed on Josué until he looks up. "I know some."

María Carmen portions out a plate of fried egg, noting that this is what she cooked for her commander when she was in the mountains. "In the mountains, I have to cook for all the soldiers. I stay in the camp and take care of all of our things. I stay there alone, only me." María Carmen often slips into the present tense when speaking about the Conflicto Armado. One explanation for this is that Spanish is not her native language and speaking in present tense is easier than tracking past tenses, but it may also be that the present tense captures for her the immediacy of the past and the ongoingness of its legacy.[5]

"Alone?" I remark, and look again at her sons, their heads bowed over their plates.

"Yes, only me. Like this, in case the enemy comes." She holds her hands over her body, wrapped around an imaginary rifle.

The boys look up to see her gesture, and I realize now they are listening, looking up because her verbal cue requires visual attention. I catch eyes with Martín, who is fifteen. "Have you heard these stories before? Do you know all about this?"

Martín turns his eggs with a slice of tortilla. "Very little." Isaac adds with some embarrassment that he likely knows the least of his brothers.

María Carmen shakes her head and assures me, "We tell them all about our story. They don't know, because they don't care." Gesturing to Martín, she imitates their ambivalence about the past, "He says, 'Why should I care about that if it already happened and it's over?' My two sons who were born in the mountains, they know a lot, but not these ones."

Though I risk disrespecting María Carmen, I playfully pursue this opening with Martín. "Is that true, that it doesn't matter to you?"

Looking up, Martín says, "No, it's not that I don't think it is important. It hurts to hear these stories."

María Carmen cuts him off before he finishes. "It hurts. Because sometimes we have food; sometimes we don't have food. Sometimes we have clothes; sometimes all of our clothes are wet. Sometimes we have water; sometimes we don't have water. And always under the rain."

Martín seems to lose interest and concentrates intently on the TV. Josué also twists toward the TV, occasionally turning his attention back to his mother. María Carmen continues, describing how she came to join the guerrillas, partly out of desperation for the massacres in her village but also because of the cruelty of her first husband, who insisted that she accompany him even though she was too young to know how to make tortillas. She was around twelve. The boys turn back to their mother when there is another verbal cue, "We walked through a river this high to arrive." Without reacting, the boys note that María Carmen's hand is up to her chest, and they look again when she curves her hand to demonstrate how the guerrilleros moved stealthily through the mountain, their mother at the back.

Folding a tortilla, she continues, "Life is very difficult, very, very difficult. Sometimes the enemy comes, and you have to leave everything. What am I going to do, all alone? And I think to myself, *why did I come here?* I cry. I miss my mother. I miss my family." Slipping back into past tense, she finishes, "Life was very hard. A lot has changed since the war."

When I ask what has changed, she says, "Everything about our lives has changed. There is no more violence. No more thieves. Life was much more difficult. Thank God the war is over."

A smirk comes over Martín's face, but he does not let his mother see. "There is violence in the capital," he says, looking at the television.

"Yes, but that's the capital."

Martín lists off the names of several villages with prominent violence, and his mother explains that those are very poor places, and that's why there is violence there. But at the mention of a third pueblo, she changes her tune. "There is always violence. That's why we don't go out much. That's why our doors are all closed, even though it makes the house hot." She gestures to a door on the side of the house, near the bedrooms. "That door, we never open, because thieves can enter." She describes one late night when thieves broke into the front gate and stole two bicycles and a radio off the porch.

She explains that people in the village know that she and Leonardo were guerrilleros but prefer not to be reminded. Several times she says, "it is not safe," because some people don't respect the guerrillas. Her sons know not to mention it outside the house, because it might "stir up problems." Ricardo, one of the guerrilliños, has tested these waters and found that members of the community tease him, calling him a monkey and in some cases dismissing his contributions with claims that he thinks "differently" because he was born in the mountains. Still, he remains proud of his parents' courageous actions and his unlikely survival. Isaac, on the other hand, locates his lack of knowledge about the Conflicto Armado in both his frequent absence from home and his vocational education: he is not exposed to the violent past in either informal or formal learning environments—and "besides," he adds, "I am an hijo del pueblo [not from the mountains]," an identity he falls back on when he wants to distance himself from political discussion.

Boomtown Revolution

After the morning prayer César begins lecturing about the municipal political structure and the relationship the pueblos have with the state, emphasizing both their de jure autonomy and their de facto invisibility. "What are the resources that we have in this municipality?" Who could know what César means for them to answer—perhaps the lake system and the fishing traditions, the large number of schools for a pueblo, the small medical center staffed by qualified nurses and a traveling doctor, or the network of community leaders that maintain the traditional system of local governance. But the students immediately recognize that he means *natural* resources, not human resources or community assets. Several confidently say, "The mines."

At César's request, students whose families are in the midst of land conflicts with the mining company raise their hands. About a third of the class raises their hands, though a bit shyly, looking around to see which classmates are affected or at least who has decided to own up to it. He points to Renée and asks how long his family has been struggling for their land.

Renée stands and obediently recounts his story.

My mother was living on our land for twenty years. And six years ago they kicked her out and told her she had to start paying them for the land. So my mother started paying monthly installments, and, with this, it began. But when she began to pay, she did not ask for the papers. . . . And this is why if you do not attend a meeting or do not ask for your papers, you can go under. And this is why you have to be vigilant and pay attention to what is happening with your land, and you have to ask for papers.

Many of the aldeas surrounding Río Verde have been taken over by the mining company to build their grounds or swept into their system of fincas, though hundreds of families continue to negotiate land rights, with little help from state agencies.[6]

Some of the land now owned by the company was formerly controlled by the state, intended for conservation. Even among the most informed adults, there is little knowledge of the historical ins and outs of the land exchanging hands. The chronology gets murky during periods of conflict and transition but usually moves through the following stages: in the precolonial era the indigenous inhabited the land without a formal title system; land was incorporated into European fincas during colonization and independence, and indigenous were forced off the land or into positions of indentured servitude; many businesses fled the country during the Conflicto Armado, fearing the guerrillas; peace negotiations then distributed selective lands to displaced indigenous populations and designated other territories as under the protection of the state; and in Guatemala's recent neoliberal turn the state has granted land to international companies to encourage their return and investment, "knowing full well," in Leonardo's words, that indigenous were inhabiting the land without documentation.

The nature of these conflicts is not confined to property rights and range the gamut from manufacturing runoff contaminating the drinking water supply, industrial practices that damage ground soil necessary for crops, deliberate erecting of infrastructure such as electricity only to limit its accessibility to the company grounds, and employing a private security force whose role is to quell popular opposition to any of these practices, or in some cases even their vocalization as valid rights issues.

In addition to displacement, the people of Río Verde worry that they will lose their right to fish the local waters or that the waters will become contaminated once the company begins mining. Historically, the local economy of Río Verde has centered on fishing. Gregorio explains, "We are afraid that the army will arrive and take away the tools of the fishermen and tell them that they cannot fish anymore. . . . This has happened in other areas, so we are afraid it might happen here too." His tone is didactic, as if he is teaching the students why adults are anxious about the presence of the mines, though it appears that the students already understand the layers of fear operating in their town. At one of the entrances to Río Verde, there is a billboard snapshot of military officers marching in neat rows. The sign states, "We are all working together for peace." On the back of sign, *NO MINERIA* [no mining] is spray-painted in black letters, with a skull and crossbones filling in the *O*. When I first arrived, I did not understand this connection, but I see now why all the way in the capital there is graffiti that swears that *mines = genocide*.

Looking at me, Amílcar says, "All of us live with this conflict."

César explains that the mine has not yet begun extracting, but once it does the state will receive a small percentage of its profits. With some bitterness, he adds, "We need foreigners to come here to exploit the wealth that we have in Guatemala."

Álvaro shares in his frustration that every country seems to have a hand in Guatemala's economy "except Guatemalans."

David agrees that the companies should pay more for natural resources, theorizing that the company will find more metals than what they are looking for. When they exhaust one element, they will move on to the next and the next, until they have taken everything and the people have nothing.

Concerns shift to the river system and the local water supply. One student comments that mines routinely contaminate water to do their work. Again, students note that they have seen it happen in other villages that have suffered the presence of mines and factory plants—water systems become polluted and crops cannot be maintained, children develop rashes from washing in the lake. Mysterious illnesses appear, and the company leaves with profits. Álvaro puts it this way: Río Verde is at the "beginning of a boom." "When it becomes a 'boomtown' suddenly there is money, and they build bars and prostitutes come and thieves and delinquents . . . and then they [the company] leave and all that is left are the prostitutes and the delinquents." Cindi Katz (2004) conceives of development as the "structured transformation of [a] local environment" (p. x), through which the "relationship between [material] production and social reproduction is thrown open and reconfigured" (p. 21). Development implies more than the remaking of rural spaces. For many indigenous groups, the loss of land is "not just an economic issue . . . but a historical and ontological one," akin to war (Bacigalupo, 2016, p. 162). In Guatemala today's displacement and dispossession is the war after the war, or the war that never ended—depending on how one conceives of the historical connections between past and present injustice.

Julia agrees, "They bring a lot of delinquency. When there is money, delinquency follows. And this is what is happening here."

David mentions a nearby town where the community organized in an effort to close the mining operation, only to find that the company responded with violence. Several students fill in the details: they burned people's houses and shot at them, they burned hospitals, *hospitals* of all places. "It was a good attempt at resistance, but the companies are powerful." They do not need to say the implicit, that the companies are powerful, in part, because they have the direct support of the state in the form of the military or indirect support for taking "necessary" measures when populations pose a threat. This is why there have been states of siege, to "subdue the people," as David explains.

Álvaro reaffirms his earlier claim that the only escape is revolution. "Only if the whole population rose up to do something. Then maybe." He closes his eyes as though imagining the possibility.

Rosa says, "We want to change things. It's not that we don't want to. But we cannot change our lives, not alone."

Gregorio echoes, "We don't have support."

All over Río Verde, young people express an interest in pursuing change, in the *salida* (exit) from poverty and exploitation, but they know all too well the obstacles that stand in their way like thick cement walls. At times they seem to adapt their desires for change to their perception of its limited possibility, cultivating a position of self-imposed submission as if it were an active choice. For example, despite their anxiety about the monopoly of the mine over their local economy, and even the company's appropriation of public spaces—all trash bins in Río Verde are painted with the initials of the mine—young people express their desire to join, rather than protest, the company.

César echoes a sentiment shared by many of Río Verde's inhabitants: "They [the corporations] should come to the community and work with the community. The community should benefit. We are not asking for much, we are not asking for their profits. We simply want jobs." He adds, "Me, I would like to work at the mine." Perhaps noticing my surprise, after listening to accounts of the years of struggle over land rights and the repressive presence of corporations, César reasons, "This is why the people become angry with the company, because we don't have job opportunities here." I look around to see whether students are betrayed at their teacher's admission that he would leave them for a chance at a more stable job, no matter the corporate practices that go along with it. Instead, students nod in agreement, hoping aloud that when they graduate they will find jobs at the mine, because otherwise "you study, but you don't know for what." As César has confided, in spite of completing their secondary education, most of the students who graduate from Sun and Moon will likely remain in the village and not pursue professional careers or even work in the formal sector. If the mine began hiring, it could change everything. Young people's imagined possibilities could be "thrown . . . open and reconfigured" (Katz, 2004, p. 21).

After school Amílcar takes Rosa aside and instructs her to tell me not to discuss the mines with just anyone. He reminds her of the two students in a nearby pueblo who started organizing, only to turn up dead. She nods, verifying details about this recent tragedy. The nausea comes over me in moments, and I interrupt them, fearing the worst—that my questions have put them in danger. I quickly replay the class conversation in my head, confirming that the students were actively sharing their experiences and frustrations, and all with the teacher's encouragement, so that if there were signs of discomfort I had not picked up on them. They assure me that no one is in danger, but they want *me* to be careful. It is safe to discuss these topics in school, because "we know one another here," but I should be mindful about asking people I "don't know" about the international companies. Instructing me to be careful, they explain that you never know who you are speaking with and that "people talk." They might say that gringa is "stirring up trouble"; she is "agitating people." Gregorio concludes with a succinct contrast, "Here you are fine. You are with us. . . . But outside the people are vigilant. They are watching." This warning represents a new constellation of threats: the repressive forces of the company and the negligence of the state, coupled with the town's xenophobia and increasing tendencies toward vigilante justice. Many of these risks converge on the status of a *cualquiera*, someone of unknown social and political allegiance, akin to the orejas of the past. Fears manifest along the relational boundaries of social trust and vigilance: they cannot talk if there is no trust, and they cannot trust unless they know who is listening.

Two Devils or One?

Two days in a row students carry their notecards and laptop to school, comb their hair back, and press their shirts for their class presentations. Without notice César misses school or arrives late. Students do not seem particularly disappointed or surprised, explaining that sometimes their teachers "forget" to come to class. They sit in the shade under a tree and wait. When César returns, he is unapologetic about his lateness, explaining that he had work at the university. Like most Guatemalan teachers, César's highest level of education is his high school degree with a specialization in teaching, though he is currently supplementing his basic training with university classes. Also like many teachers in rural communities, César teaches several classes at different schools, cobbling together sufficient income to support his family. It is not surprising that he cannot remember all of his students' names.

When it is time for the presentation, the first group of students stands at the front of the computer room, their slides projected onto a large white screen with one of their laptops. They have selected a variety of images to depict the subject of war: women sobbing with their hands covering their faces, children with distant looks holding wide banners of missing faces, a cadre of guerrilleros posing in three tight rows like a soccer team, a young guerrillero snaking his way through dirt, grisly shots of organs that have escaped bodies with the blast of a shot at close range, and campesinos peering into the gaping hole of a mass grave as the forensic team below sorts bones into bodies.

Claudia begins, in a voice so small that I would hardly know she was speaking if I didn't see her mouth moving. What little voice projection she has is lost in the noise of the fans and air conditioner. César motions with his hand for the students to speak up. They take turns presenting a small portion of summary material on the Conflicto Armado before passing the slide remote to their classmate. There is quite a bit of repetition in the largely generic statements. "The Conflicto Armado in Guatemala began in November 1960, and in this era there were many massacres of indigenous populations and many assassinations. And this was because of the intervention of a U.S. company. . . . This is how the conflict began."

David continues, "The Conflicto Armado in Guatemala began in 1960. What determined the beginning of the conflict? It began because of the leftist movement. They tried to fool the people, and this is how many people were killed."

Their narrations read like excerpts from many of the textbooks used in schools across Guatemala, with bland generalizations about war and a striking prevalence of passive voice. Yet these students have never had access to these textbooks. Either the narratives students have been exposed to in other spaces have erased historical agents, or the students themselves engage in this act of erasure through their retelling.

Gesturing to a photo of a young boy, maybe fifteen, holding his rifle to the camera, David says, "As you see in these photos, youth were obligated to participate. They did not want to, but if they did not participate, they would be assassinated."

Desperate for a historical agent so that I can gain my footing in their reading of events, I raise my hand. "Excuse me, who made the boys participate?"

David says, "The guerrillas."

Gregorio says, "The army." It is unclear whether he is contradicting his classmate or conveying joint responsibility.

Turning in his seat to face me, César says, "Both. It happened on both sides. Both groups wanted the men and boys to participate." Pausing, he adds, "The army came for me three times," and holds up his fingers for what seems like minutes. I look around the room, noticing that most of the students look uninterested. Some have their heads tipped back toward the cool air, a few with their eyes closed. The school computer room is their only exposure to air conditioning. The direction of the conversation does not surprise me. César's correction is representative of broader discourses circulating Guatemala and zero-accountability frames resonant with other postconflict settings. These young people are being asked to narrate war in ways that conform to the preconfigured structure of the "two devils." Elizabeth Jelin (2003) views the myth of two devils as a discursive effort to strip victims of their agency as political actors. Reflecting on Argentina's commemoration of a similar period of state repression against liberal ideals, Jelin writes,

> The transition government constructed an interpretation based on a scenario in which two violent forces were confronting each other (the "two demons"), while the population at large, the "good citizens" who favored peace and democracy, were caught in the middle, unarmed and defenseless. The "silent majority" was allegedly external to and absent from these struggles, suffering the consequences of the conflict rather than being an active participant in the confrontation. This middle ground enabled this alleged majority to

identify itself with the notion that "*por algo será*" (there must be a reason for repression)—a position that implicitly justified the repressive acts of the military regime. (p. 54)

Similarly, Susana Kaiser (2005) finds that younger generations actively draw on the two-devils trope when discussing Argentina's period of state repression, contrasting the political actions of the disappeared with the seeming nonactions of "innocent victims" (p. 41). Their "postmemories of terror" became problematic when, as Jelin anticipates, youth blamed victims for their political agency. Kaiser writes, "The belief had been transmitted that the danger of disappearing was based on "being involved in something" and the possibility of survival on "not being involved in anything," implying that the victims were to be blamed for their suffering" (p. 41).

In this way, the two-devils narrative gives way to the justification of repressive violence to quell an unruly citizenry who became "involved" and thus deserved their fate as victims. In line with Jelin's and Kaiser's accounts, the students do not grant political agency to those trapped in the middle—the position they understand their parents to have endured. But as their discussion continues, it turns out that acknowledging the presence of two devils largely serves to reaffirm the *real* criminal actors, the guerrillas. Their story, which begins as one of innocent people caught between two devils, thus becomes recast as a story of radical manipulation by rebels to join in an unjust cause.

César waves his hand for the students to continue. "In the Conflicto Armado there were many people who died because they did not participate in what the guerrillas were asking them to do." Flipping to the next image, "And here, we see people who are looking for their dead family members. After a long time, they are still looking for them. Here they find the remains, and they are remembering their family members who died."

Renée begins, again, at the very beginning: "In the year 1960, on November 13, the Conflicto Armado began in Guatemala. . . . There were families who suffered a lot because their husbands were ordered to fight, or their children, and because they didn't have food to feed them." Flipping to an image of the Peace Accords text, he continues, "They signed the Peace Accords in 1996, and this is how the Conflicto Armado that affected all Guatemalans came to an end. There was a lot of harm and violations of human rights of the citizens."

Another student adds,

When the military arrived, the soldiers, they fought the guerrillas, and the people hid in the mountains to save themselves. The Conflicto Armado caused people to go to the mountains. They did protests, but—but they couldn't. We see here in the image that many people in Panzós were injured. There was a lot of suffering in Panzós. The other image is in Cobán. . . . There are mothers who were left without husbands and without sons. Only recently they have found the remains of their family members and can let them rest in peace. . . . Today, they still protest so that the wars will end, because they still continue here in Guatemala.

At this last statement César shakes his head and clarifies that the war ended in 1996. "You should not be confused about the violence we live with today in Guatemala. We are not at peace, this is certain, but the violence today is different." César distinguishes between past and present violence in a way that facilitates a nonconvertible rupture between the war and the postwar. "In the capital there are gangs. Here, no. . . . In the capital the gangs demand money from businesses; they extort. Here, that doesn't happen. That's why I left Guatemala City to come back here. This is not what the war was about." Without clarifying what the past violence was, he identifies contemporary violence as derived from gang activity and extortion. Simultaneously, he upholds the divide between high-risk urban areas and peaceful rural communities, despite obvious evidence to the contrary. The student who made the statement about ongoing wars nods in agreement with his teacher's distinction and later tells me that he was confused when he elided them.

David confirms this rupture, "Today it's all about gangs. It is different." The corporate repression and vigilantism they have discussed does not seem to factor into their depictions of postwar violence, as if these are something else altogether.

César waves for the students to continue, but they announce that they have finished. We clap loudly. While César was absent, Álvaro dropped out of Sun and Moon. It is his fourth time not paying his school fees on time, and the principal says he had to put his foot down. As if just putting this together, César asks where Álvaro is. Students are tight-lipped, but they all know that he is home, packing for his move back to the capital to work a job in security. Though Álvaro has been outspoken about both the need for revolution and the importance of an educated Maya population, he will be the first student to drop out of the twelfth grade since the school's opening.

César's cell phone rings, and he excuses himself to answer. We wait in silence, staring into the hallway.

When he returns, he asks if there are any questions. The students shake their heads no. When I ask about the historical sources they drew on for their reports, students explain that there are no books about the conflict, so researching the past requires consulting the Internet and listening to the stories told by elders. Their claims that books do not exist about the conflict are largely true for their experience. Much of the research about the Conflicto Armado is published abroad and either censored in Guatemala or confined to a few liberal bookstores in the capital. Additionally, there is no town library, and there are no bookstores in Río Verde. Even in schools, books are so rare and coveted that only teachers have them, while students carry excerpts.

When I ask students about the consistency of accounts, assuming their families' former political divisions presented them with conflicting evidence—not to mention the range of views they might encounter online—students state with some perplexity that their parents and grandparents confirmed the written narrative with their lived experience. They all heard the same stories about women who hid in trees to avoid rape, men who fled to the mountains to avoid being dragged away, babies in their parents' arms suffocating as their mothers stifled their cries, children hiding under logs in the woods, guerrilleros who lurked in the mountains and could see in the dark, and the rare survival stories of those who were captured and managed to escape. Their stories delve into the wounds of war, eluding its causes and escalation but most poignantly its agents. "*They* threw hot chili in *their* eyes." "*They* hit *the people* with stones." Ambiguity has characterized the stories to which students have been exposed, their parents shielding them from the identities of those who committed violence—likely neighbors—in the name of security or protection. In some families parents shape their children's historical consciousness with great care to the historical circumstances, outlining which group was at fault, which group organized around more principled ideals, who was selective, and who was indiscriminate with their violence. But what is emphasized above all in survivor accounts is the phenomenological experience of war. Suffering is the essence of a family's right to promote *historical memory*, distinct from the "objective" historical analysis that institutions like schools are expected to disseminate (Bellino, 2014b, pp. 141–145).

César explains, "Everyone has their own experience. And from there they know their history, from their own story."

"Who killed more people, the guerrillas or the army?" This question comes from Julia, who initially shared with the class her understanding that the guerrillas "fooled" the people, despite that the soldiers were "more powerful."

Almost at the same time, one student says it was the guerilla, another says it was the military, and a third says it was both parties. Rosa sums up what seems to be the collective opinion: "It was both. But the guerrilleros didn't let the people have peace. They could have let the people be in peace, but they didn't. They wanted the people to be involved, so they fooled them into joining or killed people when they just wanted peace. And from here, this is where the conflict began."

The teacher elaborates, "The reality is that it was a power struggle, so both groups were responsible. . . . The guerrilleros wanted land, and the army did not want this. So you see, both were responsible." César makes explicit rhetorical moves to guide his students toward the two-devils compromise narrative and the construction of the "apolitical" Maya victim, but he does not directly counter their claims that the leftist movement deceived people into becoming involved. Álvaro's unexpected absence from this group's presentation may have impacted the arrangement of material and the unfolding of discussion. Students claim he left them with few notes. Given his radical stance, Álvaro might have shifted the balance from confused coexistence of disconfirming evidence to uneasy juxtaposition and the evocation of a critical counternarrative.

The second group shuffles to the front of the room for their presentation. Their slides are black with white text and only one image appearing on each slide: a man burying several dozen caskets in a massive hole, a crowd of indigenous people standing over him. Julia begins, "The subject we are here to talk about is the Conflicto Armado and the guerrillas. It began in 1960, and this civil war lasted thirty-six years. It ended when President Arzú signed the Peace Accords in 1996."

Another student takes over, "Why did the Conflicto Armado take place? When there is a war, there comes pain and suffering for all the people, all the people who were assassinated at this time. The guerrilleros—no, the soldiers—obligated the . . . combatants not to attack the population, so that the army could kill the guerrillas. . . . This is how the army protected the people."

Another adds, "In Guatemala this tragedy . . . left two hundred thousand people dead and forty-five thousand injured, who were injured forcibly by the guerrilleros."

Amílcar flips to the next slide. "The poverty of the Conflicto Armado. When the guerrillas began, many people were left without money, without jobs or livelihoods. They could not afford to feed or clothe their children until the government helped them. During this time, they were moved to different places, where the military was finding new *tierras* [lands]. And the people didn't have food, jobs, or places to live."

The students continue, much in the same way that the first group presented, with starts and stops through the chronology, agreeing with the other group on accounts of the geographic regions and populations affected, pinning down some of the key dates, and similarly applying passive voice to the actions of vague, collective historical agents. When they finish César again invites questions, noting that the other half of the class researched the conflict themselves and might have specific comments. The room is silent, and students' expectant faces look to me.

I pose the same question about how this group approached the investigation and whether they encountered conflicting accounts. In contrast to the first group's reliance on oral history, this second group largely consulted the Internet and was not able to access testimonial narratives of survivors. Amílcar explains that most of the students in this group have deceased grandparents, and their parents don't know about the conflict to tell them stories; they lived it but were too young to understand it. The students' distinction between lived experience and textual accounts reemerges on the subject of consistency. Julia says flatly, "There is only one story. . . . The second story is what our grandparents lived, and that is the reality, but that story is gone. The only story we have [now] is what is on the Internet."

Hopeful of encouraging a class-wide discussion, I ask how these stories are different. Víctor explains, "No, they are the same [story]. What we are saying is that sometimes there are specific things that happened in the aldeas that are not written."

Another confirms, "There is only one truth."

Impatiently, as if I am not grasping something utterly obvious to them, Julia repeats, "The only truth there is, is on the Internet. There are no books on this. And most of the grandparents who lived the conflict are dead, so we cannot know their experiences." With some hesitation, I press a bit further, asking which sites on the Internet tell the true story. As if embarrassed for my adult inexperience, Julia assures me, "All you have to do is type 'Guatemala Conflicto Armado,' and you will find pages and pages. Any website will have the same information, because it is history. It is *history*, so it is the same wherever you find it." Several students find this amusing, asking whether I have Internet access at home, as if my questions indicate confusion rather than interest. This assertion that all narratives circulating the Internet are *the same* contradicts not only my own experience carrying out Web searches in Guatemala but also the experience of young people in other communities who have explained to me that the Internet "confuses" them because written narratives about the armed conflict do not match their understandings.

In accounting for legacies of the violent past, Jelin (2003) posits that, "It is often new generations, those who did not live through the period that left these marks, who render them [legacies] visible and ask questions about them" (p. 101). Karen Murphy (2013) similarly argues that young people "[inherit] not just societies that have experienced war and mass violence but the transitions themselves, their legacies and the legacies of the remedies" (para. 5). This critical questioning is indeed taking place in some communities. But at Sun and Moon, a class of Maya students living near one of the most prominent wartime massacre sites, in a village forged by displacement, in visible sight of a mountain where townspeople whisper that weapons buried after the ceasefire remain accessible, students are expressly uninterested in the historical evolution of injustice. In their understanding, what they live today is not only "worse than war" (Moodie, 2010) but also disconnected from it.

Admittedly, students' overreliance on passive voice, the tendency to speak in generalities about the suffering that comes with war, and the slight incompatibility of the conflict's provocations (e.g., external corporate interference, the rise of the insurgency, a power struggle between the Right and Left) may be due more to students' unfamiliarity with the practice of collaborative presenting than their discomfort over corroborating divergent historical evidence. Further, there is a general lack of exposure to constructivist pedagogy and the classroom practice of discussion and deliberation. Despite the student autonomy and constructivist leanings implied in César's assignment, interactions like these ultimately affirm and uphold the nature of power in his classroom: questions are asked for clarification and identification of correct answers, not for exploration of ambiguity and certainly not for the experience of debate. My persistence that students reflect on their process of constructing a historical narrative and consider whether all sources were in agreement is a foreign practice, uncomfortable for both the students and the teacher, who are anxious to provide "right" answers that will settle inconsistencies. This is apparent in César's encouragement that I consult books rather than attend his class and his routine interruptions to student comments, concerned that their interpretive inaccuracies might lead us all astray, as well as in students' deference to his explanations. I believe the stilted and recursive nature of this conversation is further entangled with students' collective expectations about what I am researching and why—why would I have come from so far away only to hear their assumptions and erroneous stories when I could have done a search for the apparent single historical truth online from my home?

Responsibility Begins with Involvement

César leaves to teach his evening classes, and the rest of us opt to stay and watch the film that Julia brought to class. Julia introduces the film as a documentary about the Conflicto Armado in Guatemala, emphasizing that the documentary nature of the film is what makes it a representation of the truth. The girls fiddle with the projector, but the glare from the afternoon sun blanches the center of the screen. Several minutes into the film, after we have missed the opening text frames (which describe the film as a reenactment based on true events of the civil war in El Salvador), we resolve to crowd around the laptop. We sit close together, our knees touching.

The film, *Voces inocentes* [Innocent Voices] (Mandoki, 2004), is based on the life of Chava, a Salvadoran boy who grew up during the height of the country's civil war. The story encapsulates the experience of people caught between two armies, though it is somewhat tilted in favor of the guerrillas: the state soldiers occupy the town center and routinely intimidate civilians, round up young boys in schools and pile them in the backs of trucks to become soldiers, mercilessly beat the priest who tries to protect the children, and assassinate the protagonist's friends. Meanwhile, the protagonist's uncle is a bearded guerrillero hiding in the mountains, and when the boy and his friends run away from home, they seek out the guerrilla camp. To be to sure, there are gritty scenes with innocent civilians caught in the crossfire of a war whose causes and stakes they do not fully understand, but during the film's climax sequence, guerrilleros rescue the protagonist from near assassination. At the heart of the story are Chava and his family suffering in poverty, everyday close calls and efforts to find safe spaces to live, and their meticulous attempts to fake Chava's age so that the army will not take him away. There are many light moments, opportunities to distance oneself from the dark reality unfolding in the background of Chava's unlikely friendships and innocent first love. Ambiguity is central to the storyline, perhaps intentionally so, conveying a people forced into war without a choice.

Throughout, there is a great deal of confusion in the room surrounding the political identity of the characters, and students casually deliberate over which soldiers are members of the guerrillas and which are members of the army. They believe that Chava's uncle is a member of the state military, until we see him hidden in the mountains, and it becomes clear that he is a guerrillero. In the frightening scenes that take place at the school, the students first assure one another that it is the guerrillas kidnapping the boys with their lists of names, but in later scenes they concede that it was indeed the army.

Given the students' clear evocation of the "criminal guerrillas" in their presentations, I expect some of the students, especially Julia, who was most vocal, to change their tune about the guerrillas after the film: to recognize how blurry and complex it was to choose sides, how brutal the army was, and that in fact it was the army that famously recruited young boys from schools and forced them into combat. Not that the guerrillas were wholly innocent—this remains fraught, but the insurgents are depicted in desperate attempts to match the scale of the professionally trained and well-armed state military. The film arguably endorses and undercuts the parity implied in the two-devils trope.

Throughout the film the students are confronted with historical evidence (albeit in the genre of a memoir) that disconfirms, or at the very least challenges, their earlier claims. Yet students do not interpret the film as a conflicting account, nor do they dismiss the film as a whole as inauthentic or insufficient historical evidence; rather, they adjust the film's narrative details to fit into their preexisting framework, even if it means fabricating off-screen events. For example, now that they have seen on-screen confirmation that the army officers forcibly recruited boys to join their ranks, they reason that the army was mimicking the strategies that the guerrillas had first adopted and explain that the army must have had to go to schools to fight the guerrillas. Further, most of the students construct the film as explicit support for their conclusions that it was the guerrillas that caused the Conflicto Armado, a claim that leaves me baffled, given the storyline.

In studies of young people's historical understanding of conflict, scholars have found that in some settings of public denial, students are able to distinguish and tolerate divergent accounts between official and unofficial histories (Wertsch, 2000, 2002; see also Barton & McCully, 2010). Although some students "know" but do not "believe" the histories they are taught in school spaces, in Sun and Moon we see what James Wertsch (2000) has identified as a pattern of "believing but not knowing" (p. 39). In a similar vein, Jonathan Jansen (2009) finds that second-generation youth in postapartheid South Africa have developed "knowledge in the blood," which is "emphatic," "defensive" and highly resistant to change (p. 171). Although we watch the same film together, the students and I hear different narratives about the conflict and notably the position and experience of allegedly apolitical victims. Whereas Chava's story lends support to my understanding that the guerrillas were undermatched for the state army; that soldiers took part in unnecessarily brutal intimidation; that the state censored music, repressed civil liberties such as freedom of expression, prohibited gathering in public spaces, and forced underage minors from the safety of their classrooms onto a battlefield, they see confirmation that the army fought, repressed, and occupied the village *because of* the guerrillas. In their eyes, Chava and his family would have been safe if the guerrillas had not been hiding in their mountains, if the guerillas had not "fooled" the people into joining their struggle.

Realizing that we both find ways to validate our preexisting frameworks, I finally see what is for these students a critical distinction: even if the guerrillas did not commit the majority of the loss and suffering during the conflict, their presence and the threat that they posed to the state order caused the suffering all the same. For them, there seems little value in exploring whose hands actually pulled the triggers and dropped explosives or even whose minds authored the campaigns to massacre entire villages. What matters is that there was peace before the war and the guerrilla organizing disturbed what, at least in retrospect, seemed to be a tolerable way of life. At one point, David blurts out, "All of the deaths were caused by the guerrillas. *All of them . . . they* are responsible."

There is no mention that the film is actually about El Salvador, not Guatemala. This point seems irrelevant or is not entirely clear, despite confusion about which village and civilian population Chava and his family are meant to represent, since the characters are clearly not Maya.

The Privilege of Ideals

At home Leonardo tells stories about his trip up north, how the bus broke down and he trudged through the mud, how they flagged another bus and had to pay their fare again, how the men he traveled with wanted to eat a second dinner in the middle of the night. He jokes, "During the war, yes, you could wake me up to eat at midnight, but not now." He finishes with a grin, and we all laugh. But he says little about the reason he was traveling, to attend a meeting with other municipal leaders to discuss ongoing conflicts between indigenous villages and foreign-owned mines. Like César and the students at Sun and Moon, Leonardo was once boldly opposed to the mine but revised his position when he realized that the company's presence was both powerful and permanent. Leonardo's estimations at the local level are that only 1–5 percent of the townspeople have documents that prove they own their land, and inevitably some will be displaced. "They have lived here for years and years. Their grandparents died on this land. Their parents were born on this land. They have given birth to their children on this land. But they do not have the papers to say that they *own* this land."

Leonardo insists that the community leaders of Río Verde are not asking for anything radical like removal of the mine or profit sharing. In fact, they desire development and ask only that the mine act as a "good neighbor," providing jobs and public services. His comments construct a hopeful role for the company as a "parastate" agent, more likely to respond to local concerns than the state itself, if for no other reason than because they occupy the same physical space: that is, poor roads in Río Verde no longer simply affect the townspeople; they mean poor roads for the company's delivery of supplies, transportation of workers, and shipping of exports.[7] Despite his optimism about collaborating with the mine, I am stunned to hear that Leonardo has also "dropped off his [hiring] papers" to be considered for work. Aside from the obvious limitations of his leg injury, he is well aware of the dark side of their corporate practices—not to mention he is likely banned from employment due to his involvement with land conflicts. It is as Gregorio reasons: when employment at the mine is the best chance for survival, "one cannot [afford to] live by his ideals." All decisions, all morals, are relative. And besides, "having strong principles can get you killed."

The boys whine during dinner, asking when they can watch the soccer game. Patting his chest, Leonardo admits he is as big a soccer fan as the next guy, but he needs to know what is happening in his country first. On the news they show flashes of gridlock traffic in the capital. The normalistas have organized roadblocks, obstructing the highway with their bodies and piles of school desks. Leonardo shakes his head, noting that the normalistas are a negative example for their conflation of peaceful protest movements with delinquent acts and a lack of respect for the rule of law. Ricardo agrees that they should hold signs along the side of the road rather than organize these "illegal acts." Leonardo adds that "irresponsible" teachers have planted these ideas in the students' heads, to break the law "as if it were their right" when they should recognize their civic responsibility to obey the law.

The next segment centers on the state army gaining the trust of the population by monitoring the streets and setting up military checkpoints. Military vigilance, the newscaster announces, is achieving its goal of increasing everyday security. Martín looks at the screen and says, "*Que* cool," at the soldiers marching. He turns back to his plate and says, "So many police."

"Those are not police, my son, those are soldiers," Leonardo says in a soft voice.

The boys jump out of their seats to change the channel when Leonardo answers his phone. It is their eldest son calling from Guatemala City, where he lives with his wife and their new baby. Leonardo and María Carmen want to plan a visit to the capital but have not found a way to leave the house in safe hands. María Carmen explains that the children are too young to be left alone to mind the house. "We cannot leave . . . because thieves may enter and steal my things." When I ask whether she could ask a neighbor to check in on the house, she reasons, "I am a good person. If my neighbors asked me to look after their house, I would look after their house. But if I ask them, they might steal my things. You cannot trust your neighbor." They have the same dilemma with church; they want to attend services as a family but cannot risk leaving the house empty, not even for a few hours. Leonardo comforts his wife and promises they will meet their grandchild soon.

After dinner the boys take turns using the ironing board as a desk. Werner races through the front gate with a handful of limes, running to the kitchen so fast that I wonder if he stole them. Villagers have lynched over infractions as small as this. But it is not Werner who is in danger. Struggling to catch his breath, he announces that two women in the street are fighting, hitting each other and pulling each other's hair. He doesn't know what they are arguing about, but "people are gathering." Leonardo motions for the boys to join us in the kitchen and says in a firm voice, "Stay inside." What ensues is not what we are afraid might happen, that without pause and without consulting authorities, there might be another instance of justicia propia. But we lock the gate and stay inside until it gets quiet, until all we can hear are the roosters.

Becoming Invisible

Ricardo's taxi is broken, and he is losing potential earnings every day he waits for the part he needs to fix it. With enough free time on his hands, his thoughts return to the mines and whether he should drop off his papers again. This will be the third time, and his knowledge of the company's lies that they are employing the majority of the Río Verde population adds to his frustration. He stays up late to retype his hiring papers. In the afternoon we borrow bicycles and head up the hill to the company headquarters. We ride through town, past the muffled sounds of church choirs, past the beachfront narco mansions, through the next town and the next, past the military checkpoint where the young men's vigilant eyes squint in the sun, past schoolyards where teachers' voices travel through broken classroom windows, past frail houses with long strings of laundry, through dirt roads and thorn bushes. We ride fast, Ricardo with hopes of securing a job, and me so that I can look down at the hollow of the mine, to see how far its arms reach. People say you must see it to believe it.

But before we make it, the afternoon rain comes down and Ricardo's chain falls off his bike. We huddle in the bushes and wait for the rain to pass, knowing that his papers are wet inside his bag and that we will have to turn back. We look out at the billboard for the mining company that promises, "Development is the new peace." Two peace doves, wayward symbols of the war's end, flutter at the edges of the sign. I think about what Ricardo says, that "the best way to stay safe is to be invisible, to not become involved." The rain comes down, harder now, until our clothes stick to our skin, and we stare at the sign until its edges become one with the sky.

The Legacy of Neutrality

Río Verde is filled with guerrilliños and *hijos del pueblo*, as well as children of state soldiers and of the local paramilitary groups that organized against the rebels, and the many families who were forced to endure the tentative and perilous space in between. At Sun and Moon, the story of the Conflicto Armado, partially constructed by the students themselves, draws from the official narrative of two devils. Their reliance on passive voice and ambiguity of actors, coupled with the evocation of culturally available archetypes, contributes to its narrative reproduction. Meanwhile, this narrative outlines apolitical neutrality as a safe space that young people resign to occupy in the postwar period. What other space is there when there is no one to trust, no one to hold accountable, and when luchadores too easily become martyrs?

In their account of the Conflicto Armado, nearly every sentence students utter lacks a clear historical agent ("Many people were affected"); even when they use active voice, they rely heavily on pronouns ("If you didn't do this, they killed you"). This "systematic vagueness" (Edwards & Potter, 1992, p. 162) is an artifact of war, so that ambiguity serves as a protective rhetorical device, avoiding potential threats and promoting solidarity through the testimony of shared suffering. What is important is the personal experiences of fear and loss rather than the political conditions that gave rise to them. Telling the story this way honors mass suffering without constructing accountable agents, as youth have been distinctly taught not to let history lead to rancor. To an extent, María Carmen's stories perpetuate this ambiguity of agency for her own sons. Who the guerrilleros were, and what they were fighting for, is partially obscured by her personal circumstances and motivation for joining—not only the inexplicable and horrific massacres in her native village but also her abusive husband's insistence that she accompany him into the mountains. When she describes in vivid detail who the guerrilleros were holding those guns toward in the dark, in the cold rain, she resorts to general language of "the enemy."

Whether students' narrative ambiguity permits the coexistence of multiple perspectives is questionable, though they are highly tolerant of interpretations that counter their existing understandings of the conflict. Though the film we watched complicates their readings of the past, students find ways to insert new information into their preexisting schemas, which have been partially constructed in private spaces and confirmed

through family oral histories. What initially seems like silence or refusal
to engage with the past as anything but a particular manifestation of a general pattern of war recedes when students are guided by their teacher to
tell a clearer story, one in which two devils are responsible. Emphasizing
indigenous populations as innocent civilians trapped between two armies,
students evoke familiar archetypes that have been well cast in Guatemala's
official history: the protective state army, the criminal guerrillas, and the
neutral Maya.

They tell the story from the perspective of apolitical victims, condemn-
ing guerrilla involvement as reckless, dangerous politicking, and deceptive
in the guerrillas' entrapment of people who wanted nothing to do with
their lucha. Like many victimized populations, Mayas have embraced apolitical status to be recognized as legitimate victims—to claim material reparations from state agencies, to garner support for international humanitar-
ian aid, and at times to coexist at the community level. In this sense, the
construction of apolitical Maya victims has offered proximate "usability"
for the survivor generation, not to mention its convenient fit within the
international human rights discourse.[8] Much of the global world seems to
find usability in apolitical Maya innocence.

But the innocent-victim construction has been preserved at the expense
of recognizing Maya political agency more generally, and specifically in the
context of collective struggles for equal rights and full citizenship. Even
when these roles do not hold—when the state is menacing, when ordinary
people become "involved" of their own volition, students assign approval
and responsibility only where there will be no consequences for doing so.
The two-devils trope denotes a space between well-defined perpetrators,
occupied by people anxious to remain safe: the only agency they can fea-
sibly exercise is self-protection through abstention. Youth in Río Verde are
bound to this in-between space today, desiring change but fearing the risks
of taking action. Their village is physically bounded by symbols of powerful forces that comprise the new "devils": the military, the mines, and justicia propia.

Rather than empathize with a (failed) movement that mobilized on
their behalf, these students distance themselves from the guerrillas on the
basis that they took up arms and broke the law. The causes of the conflict
are central to these claims; as Rosa makes transparent, "they [the guerrille-
ros] could have let the people be in peace, but they didn't." Meanwhile, the
dominant interpretation that the guerrillas caused the Conflicto Armado

leads to a critical rejection of resistance as a suitable expression of civic engagement, because it is consequentially dangerous, morally corrosive, and not pragmatically useful. Like the guerrillas, the normalistas stretch the law to be "heard," despite the state's insistence that they will not adjust their position. But when the students listen, all they hear is the sound of young people unsuccessfully battling the state. The normalistas have been misled, not only for their application of "delinquent" tactics, but for their mistaken beliefs in dialogue and the utility of public protest. Although Álvaro pushes for the ultimate form of resistance in a revolution, his classmates argue that the risks are too high. Perhaps more telling, Álvaro himself resigns to chart his own future within the status quo by leaving school and moving to the capital for a job that he fears and loathes.

The narrative of apolitical neutrality becomes newly fraught with perceptions of Guatemala's "continuum of violence" (Manz, 2008) and the constraint this apparent changelessness places on the capacity to dream a better world into being. Young people are cognizant of the allure of neutrality and the lack of support for action designed to seek change rather than assimilation in the current order. As Gregorio explains, "[People here] don't believe in anything. I told my friend I want to plant some peppers. He said, 'What for? The dogs will ruin them; the pigs will eat them; your neighbors will complain that you are attracting weeds and animals. They won't grow. You will waste your money; you will waste your time.' They won't even support me growing peppers; they think everything will fail."

Río Verdenses' youth calculations of safety, efficacy, and usefulness intersect with their beliefs that the guerrillas caused the war and ultimately failed anyway, as they make everyday decisions about how they will participate in their communities and how their communities figure in a perpetually unequal state.

6

Tzolok Ochoch

The Lucha Generation and the Struggle to Overcome

Rules Are Rules

It is already dark when the senior girls return to the dorm. They shuffle in, stripping to their underwear to cool off. The dorm, a wooden cabin with spiders wide as fists living in the rafters, is crisscrossed with clotheslines. Girls fold their sweaty clothing over the wooden supports of their bunk beds and race to the few wall outlets to charge their phones before the power shuts off for the night. Tonight there is no time to think about homework, nor will there be light long enough to study. The girls were asked to stay late at the boys' camp to make tortillas, because, to everyone's surprise, they had run out during lunch. A boarding school specializing in ecological career paths and community leadership, Tzolok Ochoch depends—somewhat erratically—on the shared labor of the students, whims of volunteers, and the financial support of international donors.[1] To keep fees down, students contribute to the everyday order of things. Boys and girls share all responsibilities, such as cleaning dishes in the kitchen, sweeping dorms and classrooms, carrying buckets of water to the toilets, washing their clothing in the river, and staffing the souvenir shop. The only gendered labor requires that women make tortillas, and men collect firewood. Several miles of river separate the male and female camps, a pair of motorboats transporting students between sites. The gender separation reflects a concern that high numbers of indigenous youth abandon school to have families. This is the school's most rigid policy: there are to be no romantic relationships here, and if girls become pregnant, they (and often but not always their male partners) are forced to leave. Yet the high cost is not a perfect deterrent, and every year at least several female students return to their families pregnant, their studies left incomplete.

Telma, the dorm "mother," begins evening role call. Angelica? Present. Gloria? Present. Rubi locks the door. Telma calls a meeting to announce the arrival of a new volunteer group from the United States. As the girls drag chairs to the front of the room, the lights go out. Girls in the neighboring cabin squeal. Always prepared, Telma lights a candle and continues. The girls shove fresh candles into old mounds of wax along the windowsills and pass around a book of matches. Telma explains that the gringo volunteers are planning to paint the dorm tomorrow, and we will have to sleep in the computer room for two nights while the paint dries. In fact, we will have to pack most of our things and move some of the furniture out as well.

The girls note that this is the first they are hearing about the plans. Several protest that there isn't enough time to gather their things. Running their fingers along the wall, a few girls remark that the paint looks fine to them. Diana, the class president, raises her hand. "Please, Señora Telma, can we talk to someone to change the date?"

Telma sympathizes but says it is out of her hands. "This is the schedule, and the date has been set." She goes on to explain that they will have to be on the boat earlier than usual tomorrow morning, because the volunteers are going to photograph the ride for their project. She adds, "I want you to show everyone that you are [seniors] and have good manners—you can arrive on time having bathed, done your washing, and put your things in order."

The plan implies that the girls will need to wake earlier than the usual four thirty in the morning to make preparations and do all of this in the dark because the power is not turned on until midday, when the solar panels have accumulated a charge. "But Señora," one girl says, fanning herself with her shirt collar, "This is a lie. They say they will leave at six, but they won't." Others agree that the boats never leave on time. The discussion continues, until one girl has fallen asleep leaning against the wall. Her quiet snores put a light end to the meeting.

Diana says with some authority, "This is a pointless argument. We should be spending this time getting ready." The girls scatter, some tossing clothing into suitcases and others crawling into bed.

As we prepare our mosquito nets, Rubi says to the floor, "What are we going to do? Rules are rules." Though within the dorm, the girls easily critique school decisions and offer viable alternatives, Telma's dismissal that nothing can be done serves as a reminder of the power of volunteers in a school that is dependent on international donations.

In predawn darkness, we pile our things onto the mattresses and slide them off the bed frames. Some of the senior girls are already on the boat and have been sitting dutifully since before six. The drivers scoop rainwater out of the remaining boats, and girls line up on the dock, their hair pulled tightly into wet ponytails. We hold each other's hands as we step from the dock onto the boat and share folds of toilet paper—a precious commodity—to clean the seats dirty from our shoes. Tightly, six to a row, we pile in. We wait and wait, until the sun dries our wet hair. We wait until the volunteers emerge from their cabin, waving, and pile into their boat, which leaves promptly. We wait more than an hour after the scheduled departure time. No one complains, but when I ask what we are waiting for, the girls say without expression, "They never tell you. 'Just wait,' they say."

Parents send their children to Tzolok Ochoch, because the low-cost tuition is subsidized to cover room, board, and school fees but also because its isolation makes it safe, or "safe" as the students characterize it, making the point that there is not a place in Guatemala that is truly secure. Most rural areas where the students live do not suffer the extreme level of street violence that pervades the capital city, but there is a growing presence of delinquency and local gangs (*pandillas* rather than *maras*), along with community responses to meet violence with vigilantism. Nearly every student I meet at Tzolok Ochoch has been exposed to domestic abuse, if not directly suffering it in his or her own household, then witnessing it among extended family or neighbors. And, increasingly, the northern region and the Guatemala-Mexico border have become a stronghold for drug cartels. A year ago in Petén, the nearest city to many students' home villages, there was a massacre attributed to the Zetas so horrific that Tzolok Ochoch's enrollment skyrocketed. They had to increase their school fees to accommodate the growing number of interested students, expand and construct new dormitories, and begin a wait list. Though the students remind me that the school campus is not immune to the occasional robbery, "at least it is safe to walk around," and this alone makes it "one of the safest places in Guatemala."

The boats start their engines and skim away from the dock. As we move farther from the shore, we can see the tall trees rooted among buildings and the slippery paths winding between them. The girls' campus contains one dorm for each class cohort, various quarters for volunteers, several empty spaces such as the "computer room," a damp kitchen with a fire pit, a boathouse where extra parts are stored, and a medical clinic staffed with a medic and a volunteer who serve the students and twenty-eight nearby aldeas. The boys' camp is home to the boys' dorms as well as the main school campus and administration offices. It also holds the school souvenir shop, designed to attract tourists to the important contributions of the school to its local communities. Several girls close their eyes and tip their heads back, enjoying the day's only breeze until the return trip in the afternoon. When the boats arrive, one of the new volunteers with a flashy camera asks us to remain seated so that he can film our exit. Diana, again taking her role as class president seriously, says, "*Chicas*, don't get off yet," and the girls listen, even me.

Struggling for a Voice

The classrooms at Tzolok Ochoch are humid, with dirt floors and open slots for windows, and the furniture is eclectic. Some rooms have blackboards, others whiteboards, and others no boards at all; some desks are small and others wide, with metal or wooden chairs attached. As students enter the classroom, they pull desks into a circle, boys on one side of the room and girls on the other. Students settle into their desks, and their teacher, Lisandro, begins, "Today we are going to talk about the Conflicto Armado and issues that are important to rural well-being." Lisandro, who teaches classes on human rights, ethics, and "rural well-being," has just turned twenty. Like many of Guatemala's rural teachers, he has completed his teaching degree, the equivalent of a high school diploma with a certification in education. He has slender limbs and wears thick, tinted aviator sunglasses. With some embarrassment, he explains that he wears them indoors because they are prescription and his only pair. Diligent about practicing English with the American volunteers, sometimes Lisandro substitutes as the school's English teacher. In total, he balances three teaching positions, working at this school during the day, another in a nearby village at night, and a third during weekends. Yet his full schedule does not seem to exhaust or overwhelm him.

"Who of you come from outside this area, where your parents were affected by the Conflicto Armado?" The students shrink into silence, but it is a familiar silence that I have observed in class after class, day after day. It is not the shocked response to a question with sharp edges, but a routine avoidance of being put on the spot.

The whiteboard is crammed with notes from the previous class, names of Guatemala's departments. Lisandro pulls a cloth from his pocket and wipes the board in frustrated circles, leaving a smear of red ink. In defeat, he opts to write at the bottom of the board: "Conflicto Armado" and underneath, "genocide." He looks out at the room: girls staring at their notebooks and boys gazing back at him.

Just outside the classroom a cluster of students hovers on the stone enclosure, unfolding banana leaves from their tamales and slurping homemade ice cream from a plastic bag. They may be skipping class, they may be on a break between chores, or they may have been selected by the volunteers to be part of their video project. When volunteers come, the schedule changes so unpredictably that even the administrators claim they don't know the order of the day. In the quiet we can hear their aimless chatter.

Finally Alfredo, a small boy with spiked hair and a brown MTV T-shirt stands at his desk. Alfredo's voice is low and scratchy. He talks for almost five minutes without a pause, giving testimony to the horrors his parents survived:

> For any type of problem that you had with a friend, you worried that they might go to the army and then the army would come and *BAM* they would take you away. It didn't matter if you were involved or not. Many peasants were killed for any reason. They were persecuted and killed. My parents tell me that for anything—anything—you could be taken. You never knew if you would be next. Sometimes you woke up and didn't know if you would be killed that day. You passed the soldiers in the village, and they would look at you, trying to decide if you were a guerrillero. Many in my pueblo were affected. One day in May, the day of our town celebration, the soldiers started shooting

everywhere, and there was a big massacre and many people died. And not just this day, but many days. There was no day when they didn't have to take bodies away or look for bodies. During thirty-six years my mother grew up with this conflict, and she said it was so difficult, because you didn't know if you were going to make it another day. And you didn't know if you were going to eat or not. It was very hard.

As Alfredo speaks, his classmates give him their full attention. He returns to his chair, and Lisandro thanks him for sharing his story, noting that it is important to know about what happened.

Though many students at Tzolok Ochoch grow up with tangible consequences of the Conflicto Armado, such as deceased family members or a loss of land documentation due to displacement, and despite their school's explicit project to educate the next generation of community leaders, nearly half of the students here have never heard of the conflict, confuse it with the Spanish Conquest, or only know that it was a war in Guatemala's past with a high death toll. Yet these "children of war" also know the violence in their bones in ways that escape rational explanation, such as their fear of soldiers and other instruments of war. Rubi tells me how she and her brother grew up with an acute fear of helicopters. "If we were in school and one flew over, we would leave school running." At the time, she did not understand her fear but later realized that it was connected to her parents' trauma. Perceptively, she notes the connections and distinctions between the lived experience of violence and its legacy, juxtaposing how her parents live with "trauma," whereas she lives uneasily with a "history" of collective suffering.

Many students share Rubi's fear of soldiers, both the extreme acts of violence members of the military have committed in the past and their capacity to return to the streets and the *campo*, reining in new youth. Rubi confesses that the sight of soldiers scares her and forces her to "remember" and "feel the terror. . . . It makes me really think that this [violence] could happen again."

One of the teachers has seen his students' bodies' tense up and even slip into a "state of panic" upon seeing a soldier in uniform, like the indigenous widows on the news who fainted during the state of siege in Barillas. He recalls wearing a camouflage print sweater on a rare cold day, and he swears the students were scared of him. "They were acting very strange, like there was a fog of fear. You could sense it. When I took off the sweater, it was like I lifted something from them. They were normal again with me. All because of a sweater, so just imagine what it is like for them when they see a soldier." He too connects the students' intense fear of soldiers to the history of violence and what its legacy implies. That same teacher reminds me, "The *dueños* [owners] of the government are soldiers. They can invent any reason to kill people. . . . We have seen this, soldiers arriving in pueblos and all over the country. . . . I'm not referring to *then* [during the conflict], but *now*." Implicit in his warning is the state's recurrent use of physical violence as an instrument of structural violence.

Students groan when Lisandro announces that it is time for the group presentations they prepared over the weekend. Each group was asked to research national statistics on education, poverty, and health, a challenging assignment given their inconsistent Internet connection and the outdated resources in the school library, details that the students mention several times as disclaimers for potential misinformation.

As each male student comes to the front of the room to present, Lisandro waves his hands until the boy realizes that his shirt is untucked or his collar is uneven. The students giggle at the boys' frantic attempts to make themselves presentable, pointing to where their collar is flipped or a patch of skin is showing between their shirt and pants. Tzolok Ochoch requires no uniform, but there is a clear message that self-presentation is important, and nonnegotiable when presenting to an audience, even informally among classmates. Audiences carry a reciprocal responsibility, to listen respectfully and applaud after closing remarks. The classroom walls are cluttered with Maya calendars, stencils of *nahuals*, and handwritten signs that outline the rules for each class that shares the room.[2] For English class, the first rule is to speak as much English as possible. On most other lists, the first rule is "No Q'eqchi'. Spanish only." Not all the students are Q'eqchi', though this Maya group constitutes the majority of the student body. There are a handful of Kaqchikel, K'iche', Mam, mestizo, and two Garifuna students. The language rules are "for the good of everyone," students explain, reminding me that they need to know Spanish if they are going to make any social impact.

When it is Silvia's turn to present on education, she drags her feet across the floor to the front of the room with obvious distress. Her blouse is securely tucked into her skirt and her hair pulled into a ponytail with no loose strands, but her face is tight with anxiety. She folds her notebook open and looks up at the room, then back down to the page. She opens her mouth several times as if about to begin, but no words come out. The teacher encourages her, inviting a nervous smile and another false start. Finally, she sucks in her cheeks, stares intently at her notebook, and begins reading. "Many indigenous are illiterate, especially women. There are many parents who will not let their daughters study, because they think it is useless for them to be educated. . . . The majority of times, it is our culture that is [in the way]." Silvia speaks clearly and slowly, taking exceptionally long pauses between sentences. Twice, Lisandro asks if she has finished, her pauses are so long. When she finally finishes, she closes her notebook and sits down to her classmates' applause.

Students agree that Silvia's claims have validity, that Guatemalans do not value education the way it is valued in other countries, and that women, poor, and indigenous disproportionately suffer the lack of opportunities "to improve themselves" and *superar* (to overcome). Many of the girls at Tzolok Ochoch have had to convince their parents that they want to pursue a career that requires a high school education. Some, like Daniella, were presented with the opportunity to study only when her brother decided not to continue his schooling. Others relate to Rubi, who waited several years between middle and high school, declining more convenient opportunities to study accounting or education closer to home. Many girls plead with their parents during semester breaks for the opportunity to return to school. Sending young women to school is not always about increasing the family's chances to overcome marginalization (superar); sometimes it is a strategy intended to maintain, rather than overcome, the status quo. For example, Reina confides that her father calls incessantly to ask whether she has found a husband at school. "I am one of nine girls, and he needs me to be on my own so that I won't depend on him. He cannot support all of us anymore."

As the conversation moves toward projections that most female politicians have been selected merely "for show," one student named Mario asks the teacher whether education is required to work a job in private security. When Lisandro gives him a baffled look, the boy explains, "I have heard there are a lot of jobs in security in the capital." The private security sector has grown dramatically in recent years, from bodyguards for individuals to security guards for gated communities, shopping centers, and even small shops. A few of the male students nod with interest, but Elvin, Ramiro, and Alfredo look offended at the suggestion. Later they use this exchange as an example of one of the "clashes" that takes place between students who are committed to bettering themselves (superarse) "for and with the people" and those who want to advance for their own gain and by any means necessary (salir).

Lisandro is unable to mask his irritation, as he explains, not at Mario's comment but at the pervasive belief that working in urban centers, even in the most dangerous positions, is superior to remaining in rural communities. He tells the class, "You know, a lot of people leave here, leave rural areas, for the capital, because they think there are better conditions there. But I can tell you that if you go to Zone 1 in the capital, you are going to see a lot of women, indigenous, selling their tortillas in the street or bringing their kids with them to clean houses. . . . Or you will see the men working at the gates of communities where they will never have the opportunity to live. Believe me, there is poverty and suffering in the cities too."

On the board Lisandro begins outlining the country's education system, critiquing the unequal opportunity structure and noting that social services have been transformed into private goods: "At four to five years old, you enter preprimary, *supposedly*; then you spend six years in primary school, three years in middle school, then the [high school] level, where there are two tracks: bachillerato (general high school diploma) or a technical accreditation. . . . And what happens at this [upper secondary] level? Most of the schools are private, so only those who have money can continue. . . . So education is no longer a right. This is why many parents do not let their children continue their education. . . . Many women want to work at home because it is cheaper, because there are fewer costs involved. . . . How many of you here live in good houses?" Not one student raises a hand, despite the vague description of "good." Whatever *good* might mean, it is certainly something they lack. Students look around, murmuring that they are all poor. Lisandro finishes, "This is why many youth do not continue their education, because their families cannot afford it."

Lisandro moves beyond the cultural and individual explanations for illiteracy, into the politics of structural inequality, where students easily make connections to their own available choices. Students are acutely aware of how they, as members of poor and indigenous populations, are routinely excluded and tokenized by the polity. Tzolok Ochoch students synthesize the relationship they have with the "supposedly democratic" state through the common refrain: "The pueblo has no voice."

The class is not wholly convinced, however, that individual attitudes and cultural norms are unrelated to the lack of educational advancement.

Nor does Lisandro's explanation sufficiently respond to Mario's implicit questioning of formal education's capacity to serve upward social mobility. One boy raises his hand. "Profe, many girls who graduate from school have children and stay at home and don't do anything with their education." A few boys verbally agree, mentioning examples of female cousins or neighbors. The girls shrink further into silence.

Lisandro's body turns to face only the male side of the room. His response is simple, "This happens because they give up looking for a job." He goes on to lament that many Guatemalan youth are uneducated, and think only about parties, sports, games, "everything *light*." But he also recognizes that it is a singular challenge to find a job. "When you leave here, you cannot stay at home waiting for a job to find you. No, you need to keep fighting, keep persevering. We have to keep fighting for opportunities." Securing a job is a lucha, a struggle, when one is born on the margins.

Lisandro ends class with a passionate call for rural involvement and a reminder that if the students do not commit to their communities, they will be reined in, manipulated, and "dominated" by the Guatemalan oligarchy. "The oligarchy needs to leave our economy to *us*. We, the developers of rural areas, are going to break this history [of domination]—we are going to improve our communities. . . . Remember, *we* are developing our rural areas, and no one is working with us." This image of working alone, meant to provoke collaboration and solidarity among the students who unanimously come from the margins, leaves a lonely and heavy feeling in my gut about the roads that lay ahead for everyone in the room.

Voces Inocentes and the Culture of Orating

Valeria makes her way to the center of the cafeteria and looks out at the nearly seventy boys who have gathered. She is the school's sole Guatemalan volunteer, and she has grown close to the students. Even when there is a crowd, she greets each student by name. Tonight she has partnered with Henry, a male counselor, to show *Voces inocentes* (Mandoki, 2004), touching on a subject that is important to her personally because of her father's disappearance during the Conflicto Armado. Addressing the group in the dark, she asks whether anyone knows what day yesterday was. There is a drawn-out *nooooo*. Many of the boys have arrived topless, in shorts and sandals, a few draping their shirts around their neck like towels. Valeria announces that it was the Day of the Victims of the Conflicto Armado and explains that they will watch a film about the armed conflict in El Salvador, "but it was the same as ours here." With this minimal introduction, she starts the film. The event was her idea. When the school directors explained there was not sufficient money for travel between the sites, Valeria decided to kayak on her own to the boys' site and do everything twice, once for the boys and once for the girls.

I lean over and whisper to Elvin, Alfredo, and Ramiro. "This film is about El Salvador?" Like Valeria, they nod and emphasize, "It was the same as here. The same." Throughout the film, I try to corroborate the film's representations with their understanding of Guatemala's Conflicto Armado. During the scene where the army arrives at school with names of boys who have become twelve years old and are now fit to serve in the military, I ask whether this happened here too.

Alfredo nods and says, "The same."

Ramiro adds, "This is what happened. This is what they tell us in the stories."

Pancho, nearby, affirms with sunken eyes that his father was taken from a school and enlisted in the army in exactly this way, his future laid out for him by a list.

Anticipating my next question, Alfredo whispers that "only the army" did "these kinds of things," while "more than anything the guerrillas tried to protect the people."

During the scene where the family hides under the mattress during crossfire, Chava's uncle kneels and plays a song on his guitar, singing to calm the children and symbolically rivaling the sound of bullets with his poetic call for the lucha. The song is "Las casas de cartón" (Cardboard houses), by Marco Antonio Solís. It was one of the prohibited songs during the Conflicto Armado, and its significance is not lost on these adolescents, despite that it is from their parents' generation. Unprompted, the boys begin singing along with the character in the film, lamenting that "their people" live in cardboard houses that lose their form in the rain. The song encapsulates not only the lived experience of poverty but the collective suffering bestowed on a people whose misery inhibits their ability to dream up a better future:

Hoy es el mismo que ayer	Today is the same as yesterday
Es un mundo sin mañana...	It is a world without tomorrow...
Que lejos, pasa una esperanza	How far away hope passes
En las casas de cartón.	From inside the cardboard houses.

The song is about them, their families and the sound of their fragile homes enduring rain, the unjust pasts that narrowed their presents, and the future they long to change, their unanimous desire to better themselves and transform the exploitative conditions in which they live (superarse). The film stretches on: the scenes where the family packs up their belongings and moves to another village hoping to escape the war, more tragic scenes in the elementary school collecting children for military service, and finally the assassination of Chava's friends and his own close call. The room never falls silent. Instead the boys almost incessantly comment on what is happening in the film, often filtering through the lens of what they know to be Guatemala's experience. In the dark there are whispers about how this or that "really happened" and "how terrible" it must have been.

When the film ends Valeria and Henry take the floor. Valeria begins, asking how many of the boys had the opportunity to learn about the Conflicto Armado in school. Only several students raise their hands. "How many of your parents or grandparents told you about it?" Boys begin to nod, but the room is mostly quiet. Valeria says with some irritation that there are not many opportunities to learn about the Conflicto Armado. She goes on, "As you know, the film is about El Salvador. This is very similar to the Conflicto Armado in Guatemala. There are many who had to leave because of the army and the guerrillas, the two groups that were fighting." Valeria explicitly self-identifies as a member of the postwar generation, linked to the students in the room, some her own age. "Maybe we don't remember, because we were just being born when this was ending, but our parents do remember. And it is part of us, part of our story."

Several years older, the male counselor positions himself as both a survivor of the conflict and a receiver of its legacy. His words anticipate the students' disbelief and the popular trope that today's youth conceive of the war as a "tragic fiction." "Maybe it seems like this is a film and it didn't happen, but it really happened. During my childhood I couldn't go outside to play. . . . You couldn't talk the way we are talking now. You couldn't have this conversation." His words evoke familiar recollections that meeting in a group and speaking openly, especially to discuss anything construed as political, was prohibited.

Usually the evening films end, the lights go on, and the boys shuffle back to their dorms. But tonight is different, and the boys patiently remain in their seats listening to the instructions for what Valeria and Henry have planned. They count off and split into five groups, a mix of ages and cohorts, each given a single question to consider.

I visit each of the groups as they meet in separate corners of the room. In Elvin's group, he unfolds the slip of paper and reads, "Are any of you from villages that were affected by the Conflicto Armado?" In silence the boys pass around the paper as if it were the kind of question you need to read a few times for it to sink in. With some impatience, Elvin asks who is from the north or from the department of El Quiché, because whoever came from this or that part had to be affected in some way. Patting his chest, he says, "I am from Alta Verapaz, and my area was affected." After a few boys insist that they were too young for this to be relevant, they begin to make tentative contributions. The denial that they know anything about the Conflicto Armado befalls its own ritual, a rhetorical permission to discuss the violent past.

One boy shares, "My father was a guerrillero. He lived in the mountains."

Another says in a soft voice, "I was one or two when the army's helicopters flew over my pueblo, shooting. My mother tells me that she held me in her arms and ran. They—we . . . lived in the mountains and then fled to Mexico."

In Alfredo's group the question is more oriented toward historical content than personal experience, asking students to identify the causes of the Conflicto Armado. In the absence of resources and Valeria's recognition that Guatemalans are rarely exposed to this history in formal schooling, this seems a particularly challenging question. Even if the film were about Guatemala the causes of the conflict are unclear, yet the question communicates that young people should have sufficient background knowledge to respond without consulting historical sources: it is expected to be basic civic knowledge. Looking at me, a boy with bony knees asks if it was about land. He twists his face, indicating that this is a wild guess. Alfredo, who has already demonstrated deep knowledge about the conflict, subtly encourages the younger and more timid students in his group to take the lead. Rather than situate his knowledge as a collective starting point, Alfredo asks the other members questions and waits for them to consider their answers. "What do you know about the international companies?" he asks, crossing his arms.

When Ramiro unfolds his group's question, his face becomes stiff. He reads aloud, "Do you think there could be another war in Guatemala?" It is a frightful question, though the boys do not hesitate in their small group to say yes. They seem satisfied with answering the question so succinctly but less interested in imagining this potential return to violence. One by one they begin looking away from one another, at the floor, at other groups. After some contemplation, I break the silence, asking who would be fighting if there were a war today. They agree that the collective actors would be the same as in the past: "the army remains" and the guerrilla groups might reform, they theorize, especially if the draft law is passed.

For weeks Pancho has been intensely worried about the threat of a military draft or a law demanding a period of compulsory military service. His uncle has warned him to be careful when he travels so that the army does not "steal" him. Though I can find no evidence of a potential law to instill a draft, Pancho insists that it has already been "approved by human rights" and that "no one cares how many of the Peace Accords it breaks." Ramiro and Pancho commiserate about how the state will likely start by placing homeless people and delinquents in the military against their will, but the police might collect kids like them off the street if they look like vagrants. This policy would put them all at risk. If they are forced to join the military, they would have no chance to transform their lives or the oppressive conditions that marginalize them (superarse).

Young people in other communities theorize that if there were a new war today, it would be between the military and the narcos, but I have heard little concern about drug cartels at Tzolok Ochoch, even when students recall the recent state of siege in Petén, brought on by a Zetas massacre. For them, the military is still the principal repressor, an entity that survived the postwar transition and is unlikely to suddenly protect people like them—even if people like them were drafted.

When it is time for the group presenters to take the floor, the room becomes quiet, and there is clear attention directed at the speakers. Without instruction, the boys form a large circle, almost to the borders of the room, and take turns moving into the center. The first volunteer, Max, walks into the middle. His jeans are rolled to his ankles so that we can see the broken buckle on his sandals as they glide across the floor. He begins with an almost ceremonial greeting, "Welcome everyone, and good evening. I am from Group 1, and our question was, 'Why did the Conflicto Armado begin in Guatemala?'" He unfolds and refolds the slip of paper before tucking it into his pocket. As soon as his hands are free, he begins to use them to conduct the room. His gestures are almost constant, but natural. "More than anything, it began because of the foreign companies and their desire for our land and resources. For this reason, it began in the areas where businesses had a lot of land. The workers there began to be afraid, because they began to kill people. And their fear grew and grew and grew. And they arrived at a problem, which was the Conflicto Armado, so the people organized to rescue the land."

Other boys look on, most of them intensely interested—if not in his words than plainly fascinated by his form of speaking, his confident Spanish, his assertive stance and gestures. Their attentiveness outweighs any that I have observed in their classrooms. Max speaks for several minutes, as if building a case for his position. The details he draws on are particularly vague, never naming the companies, the geographic regions, or the guerrilla groups. But his story succinctly captures the experience of suffering shared by many in the room, invoking "knowledge in the blood" (Jansen, 2009), legitimized through experiential claims rather than grounding in particular historical facts. He finishes by thanking everyone for listening and returns to the border of the circle to vigorous nods and loud applause.

The next boy, Tippi, keeps one hand in his pocket the entire time he speaks, though he experiments with gesture with his free hand. He, too, begins with a welcome,

> Good evening to all. I am in Group 2, and our question is, "What do we think of the Conflicto Armado?" More than anything, we could see in the film different examples of violence. A conflict is painful for everyone. . . . And it matters how the conflict began, because before they didn't live well. They repressed them, and also, before, they didn't treat the people well; the people were suffering. So it is like my classmate says, the landowners came after us, the poor. And the poor, they looked for strategies to get out of the conflict. So the strategy they decided on was to form groups. And there was fighting between the groups, and this was the Conflicto Armado.

As he speaks, a stray dog makes his way to the center and lies at his feet.

Elvin represents the third group. Though he barely moves out of the circle, his voice instantly commands the room. He takes pride in his

appearance, wearing fitted jeans and always tucking in his shirt, even outside of class when there are no teachers to correct students' physical presentation. His hair is carefully combed and tucked behind his ears. As he takes
the floor, he reformulates the question, representing it as his own subject of
interest.

> Good evening, fellow classmates. What I would like to talk about is who was
> affected by the Conflicto Armado, and what we learned is that it affected
> everyone in different areas, in different ways. It doesn't matter if you were in
> Alta Verapaz or Santa Rosa or at USAC in the capital. It affected everyone all
> the same. And so you may not think you were affected, but everyone in this
> room was affected in some way. This is what we discovered. . . . It was because
> of the government, and their form of governing, because they made the PAC
> into the police so that they would harm and kill the people. Imagine. Imagine,
> many times the army came to a village and killed someone, maybe a boy or
> a leader, for whatever reason. And then the guerrillas would come, and then
> the PAC. And what violence would come! A lot of people say, "oh, but there
> was the guerrillas." . . . But the military continued like this, just killing people.
> Imagine.

As he prepares to close, he quiets his gestures and looks around the room
slowly. "A lot of people say let's reform the guerrillas, let's fight like the
guerrillas. But what good is force, when all it does is kill people?" Softer,
he says, "They say, how could we have a revolution without killing people,
and I say, we do it with this." He points to his head, and lets his finger linger
there. After a pause, he thanks his classmates and steps back into the circle,
beaming to their loud applause.

Notably, each group veers slightly off topic to contextualize their
response. When Tippi discusses his thoughts about the Conflicto Armado,
he incorporates his impression of their causes. Elvin most explicitly deviates from the assigned task, moving from a realization that everyone in
Guatemala was impacted by the war to a spontaneous call for nonviolent
revolution. Though occasionally the student presenters make clear that
they are representing a collective view of their group, more often they speak
as individuals whose views have been shaped, challenged, or intensified
by discussion with their peers. This sense of ownership is an accomplishment for youth who lament being socialized into conformity. All speakers
use their voice to make broad claims, speaking in axioms such as Tippi's

statement that "conflict is painful," and they condense decades of struggle into sweeping accounts such as Max's facile claim that "they arrived at a problem, which was the Conflicto Armado." Finally, all speakers rely on pronouns as substitutions for historical agents. In most cases, the eventual plural first person (we, us) becomes the collective agent in the room: they attacked *us*, it was *our* land, *we* are Guatemala's poor, and *we* suffered.

Gesture and ritual are central to each of the presentations. The performance of oration as a device through which to call others to action is central to community leadership. In some way, each of these boys attests to their growing comfort with this practice, experimenting with strategies of personal storytelling, forging a collective identity, and at times instructing others with a collective call to action.[3] Students who are not in the center of the circle are also playing a performative role in the act of respectful listening, applause, and occasional shared responses. I have seen this exchange before, on the makeshift stages in the capital streets, where women speak into muffled microphones, reminding crowds that women's rights are human rights; in the pueblos during local ceremonies, where villagers call for support to clean and repaint a town wall; and in national gatherings organized to register public complaints to United Nations rapporteurs on their visits to Guatemala. The students are learning the skills they need to participate in everything from small gatherings to national movements, notably how to move and motivate an audience by taking an emphatic, deliberative stance. Alfredo reminds me that "a lot of people here want to be leaders, but then they don't talk. This is essential. . . . The first thing you need to do as a leader is talk."

Valeria closes by reminding the students of the importance of learning this history. "There are many stories to tell. . . . If we don't know our nation's history, we could see another war. And I'm sure that no one here would want to participate in that." She instructs everyone to join hands and share a minute of silence to commemorate the lives lost during the conflict. A few of the younger boys unlatch their hands to slap mosquitos on their legs, but for the most part the boys bow their heads and keep their eyes closed. Even the dog lying in the center is still.

Denial and Depoliticization

On the kayak ride back to the camp, Valeria tells me how she has self-identified as indigenous since learning about her father's disappearance during the Conflicto Armado and her family's exile to Ecuador. Despite that her family is fair-skinned and calls themselves ladino, she maintains that it is important for her to identify as indigenous to help gain respect for Maya culture. Doing so, however, is not easy, not even with the relative privilege of a ladino surname. She is teased as the "defender of the indigenous" in her family, and her brother and friends say things like, "Don't be an Indian." Her friends freely use words that she finds hurtful, like *shumo* and Talishte, a resilient brand of plastic to denote the stereotype of the "stubborn Indian." Flirting with the margins, Valeria often provokes her friends with questions that reveal the constructed nature of ethnicity. "For most people, indigenous just means clothing and language. So I ask them, 'if you learn an indigenous language and put on traje, will you be indigenous?' And 'if they learn Spanish and take off their traje, are they ladino?'" Invariably, their answer to both questions is *no*. Although these questions risk positioning indigeneity as an essential identifier, for Valeria it serves as a demonstration that Maya need to assert their cultural difference even as they are under pressure to become a "modern indigenous people" (Bastos, 2012, p. 164).

Valeria volunteered at Tzolok Ochoch as part of her interest in psychology and child development, not to teach about the armed conflict. She decided to organize the film event because she feels that schools do a disservice to young people by promoting historical silence "as if it [silence] were a true form of commemoration." Growing up, her grandmother and mother told stories about taking part in the urban resistance movement, and Valeria could not understand why her schoolbooks would overlook such a long and important part of the country's past. "And when you think how the pueblos have the same curriculum that we have in the capital, it makes even less sense. . . . The pueblos *need* to know what happened, because it affected mostly them." Increasingly aware of this curricular gap in historical coverage and the unequal accessibility of educational resources, Valeria decided it was important to talk about the Conflicto Armado with the students. "I am young like them, so I think maybe they will appreciate hearing it from me." At the same time, Valeria's youth does not preclude her capacity to teach members of the survivor generation about the history of the

Conflicto Armado. For example, as she prepared the film activity, she realized that the female counselors—most of whom never completed secondary school—lacked in-depth knowledge of the conflict, and she decided to screen the film for them in private. During the credits Telma rested her hand on Valeria's and said, "I heard fighting like this when I was young, but I never knew what it was. It was war."

Young people like Valeria who have gone to great lengths to educate themselves about their country's Conflicto Armado often practice enormous restraint when they confront their fellow citizens' ignorance of the violent past. She does not blame the students or their parents for their lack of awareness; rather, she accounts for the lack of "public consciousness" of the Conflicto Armado by referencing the political project of terror and its ubiquitous partner, silence. As Stanley Cohen (2001) explains, "The social conditions that give rise to atrocities merge into the official techniques for denying these realities—not just to observers, but even to the perpetrators themselves" (p. 11). When young people employ the two-devils trope, Valeria laments, "this is a discourse that reflects the way the state *wants* us to remember," a narrative frame that Valeria particularly relishes countering. At times she articulates her obligation to educate others about Guatemala's violent past as her civic duty, noticeably as a member of the postgeneration and a daughter of a *desaparecido* (disappeared), but also as a Guatemalan whose education, social privilege, and urban location have granted her access to historical knowledge and awareness of the historical dimensions of contemporary inequality. "Here in the rural areas, you don't see the civic participation that you see in the capital. . . . They don't have books to learn about the past. And they don't have protests they can join, like I do in the city. . . . I feel like I am bringing something to them that they don't have." We stay close to the shore and paddle quickly to beat the evening rain, as I consider how Valeria immediately conjures urban resistance movements as the face of civic participation. I stare off in the dark, thinking about Aurora.

Overnight Aurora went from Tzolok Ochoch's quintessential success story to a tragedy that exposes the inherent risk of the school's mission. Some of the students knew her as an upperclassman, and others as their human rights teacher, but everyone remembers Aurora's kindness, unyielding sense of social justice, and tireless commitment to the lucha. Many students are baffled about why anyone would kill such a caring and committed person, piecing together their understanding of Guatemala's violence with the circumstances of her death. Gloria and Silvia believe that Aurora must have been wearing an elegant *huipil* (traditional blouse) or an expensive necklace that attracted the attention of petty thieves. They theorize that the thieves must have spotted her on the dock and commissioned a private boat to follow her; once far enough from the shore, they attacked and stole her belongings. Even as they craft the story, they remark to each other how clever the thieves must have been to follow her boat in the dark. Others concoct a story that the men she was traveling with were criminals or had "problems with someone." In this scenario Aurora was collateral damage in a premeditated assassination directed at the men with whom she was traveling. These students insist that the crime had nothing to do with Aurora's leadership and that her death was circumstantial and apolitical.

But a handful of students view her murder quite differently, classifying Aurora's identity as a luchadora as a natural liability. Alfredo claims with certainty, "They killed her because she was an activist, because she was one of the leaders. . . . There is no other explanation." He believes that his classmates have been deceiving themselves in order to stay committed to taking on pueblo leadership roles, as if the fear might seep in and expose the flaws in their imagined paths. "People like her—many of them have died. Many, many, many," he says, shaking his head. "Too many in Guatemala, because of the same [reasons], because they won't stay quiet about what they think, because they speak strongly to others what they want for Guatemala. . . . And, unfortunately, there are people who don't like to listen. . . . So they say, 'Oh look, someone wants to wake up the pueblo. We can't let that happen. Let's kill her.'"

Alfredo, Ramiro, and Pancho go on to express the significant "blow" that hits the pueblo each time another leader is murdered. Alfredo explains, "This is why in the majority of villages, the leaders no longer speak, because they are afraid. They are afraid because they know if one says something today, tomorrow he will be threatened."

Ramiro adds, "They are afraid to talk about how we need to overcome [the challenges of exploitation (superar)] . . . afraid to motivate the people. So we are left to stay like this [*quedarse así*]." The loss of a leader becomes the defeat and submission of a pueblo's hope to overcome exploitation, because the threats are not directed solely at individuals but at the collective movements that they stand to motivate.

Even Aurora's brother, an alumnus of the school, admits to this: "If it affected only our family, that would be one thing . . . [but] her death affected the whole community." Aurora's death, like the untimely murder of hundreds of activists, effectively stalled the pueblo's collective gains under her leadership and drove them back into silence.

Ricardo notes that whenever someone is ready to claim their rights, the image of Aurora's body floating in the water haunts them with a singular purpose. It becomes a threatening "spectacle of what happens and can happen to anyone" (Levenson, 2013a, p. 25). Like the written threats Aurora received the weeks before her murder, there remains a nonverbal threat in the memory act: to remember her courageous work also carries with it the tragedy of her death and the unsettling reminder that her killers are free to kill again. Who, under these conditions, has the courage to pick up where she left off?

When the investigators found the bodies, in what they later called a massacre on the river, Aurora's was first, her white *huipil* stained with blood. Each of the bodies was found with personal belongings intact, watches left on wrists, wallets and cell phones tucked into pockets. This was not a robbery. Aurora endured seven bullets fired with a nine-millimeter pistol, several at her head. Her death was not circumstantial. Aurora was a role model for indigenous youth and especially for indigenous women, but in the grand scheme of things she was a *quienquiera* (social nobody) who could be killed with impunity.[4]

Together, the boys concur that they have "not yet" been silenced into fear. Aloud, they share their plans to participate in the lucha until the day they are threatened or their work endangers their family. Their voices are soft as they make this pact, as if inevitably that day will come.

The Sickness

Several days later the girls meet in a small open patio space with uneven picnic tables and no walls. We set up the projector and hang a white sheet from the rafters. Though the image is wrinkled, warping Chava's face, we let the film roll. The girls immediately fall silent, the only sound is hands slapping mosquitos on bare skin. The space is small, and some of the girls sit on the railing or each other's laps. Others lie on the floor where they cannot see the screen but listen with their eyes open, occasionally turning to see what they have missed. During the shooting scenes, some girls cover their mouths with their hands. When Chava's uncle sings "Las casas de cartón," the girls listen quietly.

As the film enters its final sequence, Valeria calls me over to the corner of the patio where Glenda, one of the tenth-grade students, is lying limply on the wooden floor. Many girls lie around during the day and evening, exhausted, falling asleep abruptly in the midst of class. They wake up before sunrise and are in motion until bedtime, cleaning, working, and studying. There is little escape from the extreme heat. It is not hard to see that they are routinely fatigued and dehydrated, so that the sight of Glenda sprawled out on the floor does not surprise me until I see her body tense up, tremor, and release. Valeria strokes Glenda's hair and massages her arm, limp except for her fists, which are pressed into tight knobs. Irma is next to her, her hand wrapped around Glenda's fists. I kneel down, watching Glenda's belly to make sure she is breathing, realizing that she is not resting or fainting but is being "visited" by spirits. I hold out a fan made of palms and wave it frantically. Though I have heard about the "sickness," and I am reassured that Glenda has a constant breath, the sight of a young girl's body, limp and nonresponsive, is alarming all the same. Irma bangs a fist on the wall behind her, six loud thumps. I glance over, remembering that banging the wall is one of the signs that the spirits are here. She does not return my gaze, but quietly places her fist in her lap, as if telling herself to be calm. I tickle Glenda's ankles with my fingernail. Her skin is smooth and cool, not clammy like the rest of us. When she tenses up again, Valeria and I try to uncurl her fingers and hold our palms against hers to flatten her hands. Her eyes are unfocused, and her eyelids, as the girls have described to me, shudder like curtains in an open window.

When the film ends, a small crowd rushes to leave. Valeria pleads with them to stay for the activity, but they insist they are tired and have chores early in the morning. Glenda is still unconscious, her body lying flatly at the top of the stairs and the patio's only exit. A cluster of girls step over her and walk briskly down the path to their dorms. A few of Glenda's classmates notice her on the floor and give me concerned looks that I can only imagine I return with equal parts worry and perplexity. They crouch next to us, pick up Glenda's fist, and snap into action. They pull off a blanket from the clothesline and, in moments, lift Glenda onto the blanket. They have enough experience to know that they cannot wake her in this state and that they will need to carry her down the hill to the clinic. Wobbling their way down the path in the dark, they leave Glenda's shoes behind. One of the girls gently places them in the corner of the patio.

Valeria makes a quick announcement to the remaining students that Glenda is fine and assigns the girls to groups with slips of paper to answer the discussion questions, which she had to rephrase since she did not keep the list from the previous activity. Most stay out of loyalty to Valeria and not genuine interest in the film, one of the girls later explains. As they split into groups, Andrea pulls me into her dorm. Inside, Irma is lying on a bed. Five girls surround her, and others sit on neighboring beds looking on. Irma's hands are clenched in fists, and she kicks up her legs several times, escaping her friends' grasp. They explain that they have to hold her down because she was running in circles. In other instances, girls who "get sick" have run wildly into the woods or the river, and in extreme cases they have tried to drown themselves or grabbed a machete and waved it around. These stories have been passed down among cohorts of students. Andrea presses her hands on Irma's right leg. We call her name gently, "Irma, Irmita, where are you? Open your eyes, you are in the dorm with us; we are here, all your friends are here." Irma breathes heavily, her stomach hollow and then arched, her chest lifting off the bed. One girl rubs her belly, and Irma's body lowers heavily.

Tina, a thin girl with long braids, turns to me with urgency. "Can you please . . . tell Valeria to stop this activity right now, because if she doesn't, Irma is only going to get worse." Pleading, she says, "She is not going to come back." I race to find Valeria, fearing the worst, that the girls are experiencing repressed memories of violence triggered by the film. Earlier in the week Valeria confided that several girls expressed concern over viewing violent content. Suddenly I think Valeria was right to worry and that I have been naive that children born into war could separate their bodies from its suffering. When Valeria arrives Tina says nothing about the film causing the sickness. Together they stroke Irma's arms and tell her not to worry, that she is safe. Periodically, Irma's body relaxes, and the girls continue their attempt to reach her with words. "Irma, what is it, what do you see? Who is calling you?" The dorm counselor comes in and is startled to see Irma writhing on the bed. Her message not to worry about Glenda is less reassuring now, though she repeats several times that Glenda simply has gastritis and is awake in the clinic. Andrea looks at me and shakes her head, explaining that the counselors lie "because no one wants to admit what is happening."

Meanwhile, the girls who stay for the activity present their summaries. Before they begin, Valeria assures them that they don't need to stand if they prefer to sit for their presentations. Sonia is the first volunteer and remains kneeling on the floor. She holds the paper with both hands and reads, "'What is the result of immigration?' The result of immigration is that people leave and go to a different country. And I think immigration is good. Why do I think it is good? Well, I think it is good, because for example this boy was able to leave from this, this, this situation, and maybe he was able to support his family this way." Valeria nods and encourages the girls to applaud. They do, but most of them look distracted. Sonia smiles proudly.

The next girl holds the paper up to her face, so close that her warm breath flutters its edges. Her group members look over her shoulder with interest as she speaks. "'What type of violence did you see in the film?' Physical violence, violence against children, and also mental violence. 'Give us three examples.' For example, the hitting, the assassinations, and the massacres that we saw." Valeria thanks her, somewhat mechanically, and the girls applaud.

Another begins. "'Do you think that the conflict could happen again in Guatemala?' Yes, because it depends on the government." To this, Valeria responds with her first call for more information, "What do you mean?" Smiling, the girl comments that the government changes every four years. Valeria presses on, asking about the kind of government that would need to be in power to allow another conflict of this scale to take place. The girl looks baffled and then overwhelmed before she gives up.

Across the patio Diana offers to help. "I have heard that there could be another war if we had a government that was military." Valeria seems satisfied with this response. The point has been made that military regimes and dictatorships are linked to the country's history of violence.

Rubi nearly interrupts the incipient applause to add, "What is Otto Pérez, but an ex-soldier, an ex-general." She pauses, as if unsure how to connect her thought to the conversation. "So, there are possibilities." She says this with a grin, masking the reality of her words and her private fear of remilitarization. The girls applaud, and several nod at Rubi for her voluntary addition.

Rubi's family is from Petén, and though she was away at school when the massacre of almost thirty campesinos took place, she returned home during the subsequent state of siege, to find rows of soldiers lining the streets. She recalls her parents' worry. "It was difficult for them to see soldiers again . . . after all that they had done." But Rubi's own fear lies not in memories of what the soldiers did, but what they might do now. The recent presidential election was a reminder of the enduring power of the state military and the popular divisions that their reemergence evokes. Rubi's family, along with a faction of community members, campaigned against Otto Pérez Molina, based on his affiliation with the military during the Conflicto Armado. Dialogue first began among village leaders, then spread to neighboring villages, culminating with the production of a video with footage of Pérez Molina serving as an officer, which went viral on the Internet. The message was clear: vote for anyone *but* him—he cannot be trusted. In Rubi's words, "although he has washed his hands of it, he has been stained with blood." She laments that their organizing was successful on the local level but did not prevent his presidency: "The majority of the people voted for him, so what can we do? Because they don't know about him. . . . Those living in the capital, they didn't live the Conflicto Armado, and that's where the majority of the population lives, so that's where the vote counted more. But he won, so what can we do? We only hope that what they say is true, that what happened cannot happen again . . . that we will not fall again."

Gabriela is the last to present and the only student who opts to stand when she talks. As she stands, she adjusts her headband, pulling back her wavy hair. She faces Valeria and folds the paper until it is a small square. "'Why did war take place in Guatemala?' Well the truth is I don't know, but I imagine there was a conflict between two sides. The war lasted thirty-six years. We don't know what year it began, but we know it lasted thirty-six years. And this caused many people to flee the country. I know many people who left, and they abandoned everything so they could flee. And we can see this today in delinquency and poverty, because many people fled to other countries to avoid death, and they left all their things and returned with nothing." The girls nod solemnly. Many of them were born outside Guatemala's borders, and their families returned to the promise of postwar peace that shattered like a teacup.

Valeria later admits to feeling surprised at some of the girls' responses. She anticipated a lack of direct knowledge about the past but hoped that the girls would think more deeply about their reactions to violence and injustice. She imagined they would integrate the film with the stories they have heard from their families, the way the boys did. After the group presentations, she gives an impromptu overview of the Conflicto Armado, feeling that the girls needed to leave more aware of "our history." Leaning against one of the beams in the center of the patio, Valeria begins. "Well, let me tell you a little about the Conflicto Armado." Valeria goes into a fair amount of detail about the decade of socialist democracy and the agrarian reforms and international wrath they evoked, the unjust involvement of the United States on behalf of a business venture that profited on the exploitation of indigenous labor, the sudden opportunities for poor children to attend school, and the precious land granted to campesinos one day and taken away the next. She emphasizes that dissatisfaction with the status quo and indiscriminate repression took place in both rural and urban areas—a point of great personal importance to her. She speaks of the youth component of the guerrilla organizations and the ongoing turmoil of disappeared family members whose relatives are still left with unanswered questions today. Her voice does not quiver. Though the story is personal for her, one might never know.

As she closes, she emphasizes the value of learning about a painful history but moves beyond the explanation that merely knowing the past will prevent its repetition:

> It is part of our story and part of what we have to change, moving forward. When we see someone with a weapon, we shouldn't say, "Oh, look how powerful they are." Right? We need to try to reduce the number of arms in our country and to bring more justice for the people. . . . And like your classmate says, we can see that all of this could happen again with a military government, and this is something that we should not allow, because after this war they signed the Peace Accords. In the Peace Accords they tried to make it so that this could not happen again. So we need to look for what the accords mean and to put them into practice and to demand from our government that we don't fall again into what happened.

As Valeria recounts this history, students listen attentively.

Valeria instructs us to make a circle and hold hands to honor the dead and disappeared and to "send positive energy to the victims." One student says it was this act that thrust open the border between this world and the world of the ancestors and that this is why so many visited that night.

The sickness becomes a principal disruption during Valeria's film event and probably impacts the quality of discussion as well as the dwindling number of students and the distracted state of those who remain. The evening is a sharp contrast to the boys' eager participation and serious practice with orating. Valeria did not have the help of a cofacilitator, nor did any of the counselors attend the film viewing. Though she is preoccupied with the girls' sudden sickness and the challenge of facilitating on her own, she seems to convey lower expectations for the participation of female students. The group of volunteers are invited to remain seated and offer no more than a few sentences, many of which consist of the text framing the questions offered by Valeria. Yet the triumph for the female student presenters has less to do with the content they present than the practice of public speaking. Each one is openly bashful about participating, concentrating intently on Valeria as she speaks. Though the school clearly nurtures community loyalty and participation for all students, the adults do not anticipate equal outcomes for the female and male students. Rarely, a female student emerges as a gifted orator and a passionate, independent thinker. Aurora was one of the most noteworthy of Tzolok Ochoch's female students, and even in death her reputation for inspiring the most challenging and unlikely causes remains a strong model.

Spirits of the Once and Future Guatemala

It happened this year, and last year, and the year before last. After the film we sit in the dark, and students share what little they know about the sickness and its seeming inevitable return. "The first time we know about was when our teacher was a student, but she says it happened before that. Maybe it happened when her teachers were students. . . . And maybe it happened all the way back to our ancestors, but if it happened to them, they knew what to do. They respected the Maya spirituality, but we don't know anymore how to appease the spirits."

No one knows for sure what it is or why it happens. Even the ones who are "called" do not understand why. There are many stories, but there are shaky explanations as to why the ancestors would make themselves present in the form of threats and violent images. The school's Maya-culture teacher and spiritual guide explains that the violent elements of the sickness symbolize the extent to which humans and nature have fallen out of harmony. But several students believe that this explanation misses the mark, collapsing interpersonal violence into a broader contract that Mayas have brokered with their land. One of the teachers believes its recurrence and violent expression is distinctly linked to the children's experience with violence: "There are kids here who have lived outside of Guatemala because of the Conflicto Armado, and they have seen violence, either here or there. They have seen people get shot. They have seen their mothers raped. They have watched soldiers commit mass murders. Maybe they were babies when these things happened, but it stays with them. They remember in some way, but they don't know what they remember. It is there, but it is also not there."

In the dorm Irma is still under the control of the spirits. They are "calling her," and what little she communicates makes clear that there is a man in the room who wants to kill her. We take turns unrolling her fists, holding down her kicking legs, and fanning her. A few girls show one another their palms, red from pressing so hard. After nearly an hour Irma comes to, rolls to her side, and covers her face, bursting into tears. Tina leans over and hugs Irma, and Irma's fingers grip Tina's back, pinching the fabric of her T-shirt. Irma then begins shivering, her face wet with tears. Abruptly, she pulls away. In Q'eqchi' she tells Tina to leave her alone and explains that she just wants to sleep. Tina looks hurt as Irma crawls into bed, unhooks the mosquito net, and almost immediately falls asleep. The girls climb off the mattress and start changing into their pajamas as if nothing has happened. The lights go out, and the girls click on their flashlights and sit up in their beds. They explain, "We want to talk about it, but we don't know what to say, because we don't know what it is." They talk about being scared, about how the girls who are *called* become someone else, taking on another's physical strength and seeing things they have never seen. They do not believe it is the ancestors calling on them to reassert their spirituality and restore balance between humans and nature. Some say it is ghosts of people who have suffered that remain close, like the spirits that wandered the mountains after the war or the girl who died in the river last year or the forbidden abortions that take place in the woods.[5] One of them compares the experience to the film, saying that it is hard to watch someone suffer when you don't know what you can do to help. Another agrees that she felt "so badly for the children who had to live that war." After a moment Tina says with a note of sarcasm, "Those children were our parents."

Altered states of consciousness have been theorized as modes of accessing embodied memories and simultaneously acts of countering and altering those memories (Bacigalupo, 2016; Connerton, 1989; Stoller, 1995). Paul Stoller (1995) argues that "the sentient body is culturally consumed by a world filled with forces, smells, textures, sights, sounds, and tastes, all of which trigger social memories" (p. 7). Although the film depicts war in El Salvador, the sensory and emotional experience of witnessing violence through a visual medium triggers embodied memories, constructed through both real and imagined accounts. In Marianne Hirsch's (2008) work among second-generation Holocaust survivors, photographs are a powerful medium for constructing "postmemories," which are "transmitted . . . [intergenerationally] so deeply and affectively so as to *seem* to constitute memories in their own right" (pp. 106–107).

Glenda remains in the clinic for several hours until she comes out of the sickness, disoriented and unable to walk. Her friends do not leave her side throughout the ordeal, unfolding her fists, stroking her arms, and stuffing cool compresses under her neck. They reassure her that they will keep her safe and invite her to confide in them if she is pregnant or has been drinking. At certain points Glenda opens her eyes and does not see us. She stares frightfully at the corner of the room, fighting off the man who is trying to take her away. Telma waits outside the examination room with the medic, allowing the girls to care for Glenda, though every once in a while she peeks her head in and warily instructs them to stop talking to Glenda and just wait. The medic, a trained emergency responder, has seen this sickness among the students many times but never outside this community. He calls it "collective hysteria." Though initially worried about the girls' symptoms, once he saw that it was affecting many girls, he realized it was a "collective story." He understood then that it was a consequence of the war, though he could not explain how. Writing about "*males de campo*" in postwar Peru, Kimberly Theidon (2013) describes these illnesses as evidence of "disordered social relations and . . . the spiritual and moral confusion that characterizes a postwar society." In her accounts, survivors of war often describe their afflictions as external agents such as sadness, fear, or evil, "grabbing" them (pp. 45–46). Although being "called" by the spirits is arguably a gentler form of entry, the girls' sickness is nonetheless a bodily intrusion by an external force. Expelling these harmful agents can thus be conceived as a way of guarding against the internalization of fear and violence, sparked not by the film alone—but by the film's convergence with the girls' lived experience with violence and legacies of war. Together these sources activate their postmemory.

One by one, several girls get "called" and fall sick. All the girls who get sick that night share the same image of a crowd hovering over them, with one man who emerges as the principal voice telling her to accompany him into the spirit world. Each girl senses that she is in danger and fights him off with her body.

That night in bed, sharing the top bunk with Andrea, I cannot stop conjuring my own flashing images of the Conflicto Armado, textually mediated images from testimonies and accounts of Maya women with babies pinned across their bodies, running, running. As Tina reminded her friends, these girls are those babies. Long after the doors are locked and the girls are sleeping, Andrea whispers to me, "Do you hear? It is happening to another." I listen and hear pounding, walls rattling with the erratic percussion of a girl's body. And all at once it hits me that the *girl who died in the river* is Aurora.

In the morning Irma, Glenda, and the other girls who got sick claim to remember nothing. They complain of headaches and sore hands.

We Are Poor Because They Have Impoverished Us

The cafeteria has been converted into an auditorium, lined with rows of folding chairs and decorated with freshly picked flowers. The entrance is draped with a floral garland, and the cement steps dusted with pine needles. A sign on the wall reads, "Welcome to the action research presentation of the senior class." Though Tzolok Ochoch does not usually host a school-wide assembly for *seminario* projects, this year two representatives from the Ministry of Education have traveled to the school to attend the students' presentations.[6] Two student hosts, one male and one female, grip an oversized microphone, and the remaining seniors stand attentively to the side. As the hosts speak, they look from the audience to the long table of school administrators and ministry officials. Gesturing to the Maya calendar painted on the cement wall, the hosts describe the significance of the calendar day, one that holds great promise for meeting challenges. They offer a blessing in Spanish and then Q'eqchi'. As they finish, a boy steps from the crowd and blows a conch shell. On cue, three boys in the back of the room begin playing marimba.

The student presentations last several hours, covering topics from climate change to education, violence, and poverty. Each group of students presents an overview of their issue, the research they carried out, and its implications for Guatemalan society. Though it is mostly boys leading the presentations, all group members stand at the front of the room, looking out at more than one hundred faces. Students from the ninth, tenth, and eleventh grades fill the chairs, along with every teacher in the school. One family, dressed in their most vibrant traje, have traveled from a nearby village to see their son present.

Throughout, there are casual references to the Conflicto Armado and the Peace Accords, remarking on the unfulfilled promise of bilingual education and the legacy of violence that today's youth has inherited. One boy says, "Our elders suffered much violence, and we, the new generation, are now suffering the consequences." There are bold claims about the shared challenges and duties of their generation and almost constant mentions of the specific plight of indigenous communities. The students are armed with statistics to support their positions: alarming disparities among rates of literacy and completion of elementary school, the infamous framing of more than 70 percent of Guatemala's land in the hands of only 2 percent of its people. The consensus message across groups is that youth have an essential role to play in interrupting current trends of inequality and social suffering, so that they can change the trajectory of Guatemala—if not for themselves, then for the next generation. Poor and indigenous Guatemalans cannot sit by idly as their country continues along a path that was paved for them centuries ago, by outsiders.

Students attend this school, in part, to gain the skills to become community leaders, so that they can better themselves (superarse), creating an alternative future for themselves, their family members, and their communities. The vision hinges on individual actions contributing to a collective goal of Guatemala becoming a "true democracy," where indigenous populations have an authentic voice. But there is no romanticism about what everyone in the room instinctively knows entails a collective sacrifice—possibly one whose results will become evident only in the next generation. For example, Arturo leads his group presentation on violence, describing a constellation of conflict whose legacy will span generations unless disturbed by asking hard questions that move backward and forward in time. He says, "One of our goals is to identify how to minimize violence for the new generations. . . . If we want to overcome [these obstacles (superar)], we need to understand this violence . . . that many of us have lived."

Sergio's group, presenting on poverty, wants to move beyond reporting well-known statistics that indigenous populations suffer conditions of extreme poverty. They focus on identifying the factors that they feel most influence poverty: ignorance, sickness, apathy, corruption, and dependence. As they close, they make an effort to connect to the audience, justifying and provoking an active stance through the familiar logic that the rural poor must act together because they have been left to act alone. "We are the ones who suffer poverty, so we are the ones who have to work to get out of it."

Students at Tzolok Ochoch are acutely aware of the challenges they face as youth on the margins. Andrea describes her distress at seeing the conditions of extreme poverty that her grandparents endure. "It gives me pain to see how they live. . . . And their children can't help them, even if they *are* working. They have no time to study, just work, work. . . . Many times one thinks that working is to become prosperous or to advance, but no, things always stay the same." Education plays a critical role in this cycle of poverty. "If you need an education to get a good job, and the poor people can't get educated, how are they supposed to overcome [these oppressive conditions (superar)]? . . . They [the government] limit us." Other students share in the irony that the Guatemalan government is invested in developing the country, but their policies simultaneously hold back indigenous peoples, leaving many to believe that "the government doesn't allow us to get ahead [superar]."

When students finish, one by one the adults at the long table move to the center of the room. Each responds to the important themes encompassed in the presentations, the power of community participation, and the value of education in the collective struggle. The vice principal promises his students, "Together, we will continue in this lucha," and one of the teachers identifies today's youth as playing an essential role in the struggle for justice and rural development, "Believe me, young people, with your strength we will move ahead."

When the principal takes the stage, he begins in Q'eqchi' and then proceeds in Spanish, echoing a tradition in indigenous protests and commemorations wherein speakers begin with a formal greeting in their native language, apologize for their use of Spanish to communicate their message, and then continue in Spanish. With pride, he announces that the students' completion of their projects marks their capacity to take "responsibility for their pueblos." He goes on to position education as both an individual and community resource: "This is about self-development but also about taking care of others, taking care of our people." Particularly moved by the theme of poverty, he deviates from what sounds like a sincere, but practiced, speech: "I want to tell you, the indigenous population is not poor.

They have impoverished *us*—we *have been impoverished.*" Later, he positions the younger generation as capable of changing Guatemala's path: "You young people have become educated, and you will keep learning, and this is how we will change . . . by each of us [contributing] a grain of sand." The *seminario* teacher comments on his pride that when students set out to design their projects, they thought of issues impacting their own communities before they thought of the urban centers. He too makes clear that the responsibility to change Guatemala's story lies with the young people in the room. Change will begin with civic action and not at the level of public policy: "We need a mature, critical reflection on the question, *What can I do?* . . . Because if we don't change for one another, no one will change for us." These words are dear to many of Tzolok Ochoch's committed students, who believe that they need to want change "more than others want Guatemala to stay the same."

The ministry representatives are the last to take the floor. Notably, one is a fair-skinned woman and the other a lanky Garifuna man who speaks with fluid hand gestures. They are representatives of a state institution with a long history of "schooling" rather than "educating" indigenous youth, but they are not ladino males who sailed easily through an unjust system.[7] The woman's comments are brief, as she thanks Jesus Christ for the students' capacity to succeed in their education. Her words stand apart from the messages of the other speakers, but that she is a woman means a great deal to the female students, who accept that gender struggles cut across ethnicity and social class in complex ways. The man moves comfortably to the front of the room, acknowledging the challenge for most students to express themselves in Spanish, a language that "is not our own." On the subject of bilingual education, he surprises many in the room by supporting the message that strong and committed civic action must precede state policy reforms if they are ever to fulfill the promises of sector-wide transformation.

While some indigenous communities vehemently demand the cultural right to learn in their mother tongue and view bilingual education policies as a necessary form of decolonization (Cortina, 2014), others worry that indigenous languages will always be linked to "backwardness" and will not translate into opportunities for social mobility or modernization (Bastos, 2012; Jiménez Estrada, 2012). Though socioeconomic advancement is not the foremost goal undergirding the educational philosophy at Tzolok Ochoch, the school enforces a strict language policy to speak only Spanish and English. While this is incongruous with other institutional goals to instill pride in Maya culture and commit students to rural community development, Tzolok Ochoch does not have the autonomy or the resources to implement a bilingual curriculum, as they are bound to national policies. Yet while enforcing the school's language rules, teachers and leaders offhandedly remind their students that all-Spanish instruction is a violation of their cultural rights and the promises made to indigenous peoples in the Peace Accords. Privately, teachers share concerns that students do not participate as actively as they could in class activities due to language barriers, noting that EIB could transform the students' academic performance. The school's policy against speaking indigenous languages in classrooms, set alongside efforts to make students aware that EIB is an unfulfilled right, together illuminate another democratic disjuncture in students' lives. This message is clearly delivered at the assembly, as EIB is highlighted as both a democratic disjuncture and a marker of historical injustice—a legacy of war and the transitional justice process that failed to restructure opportunities for indigenous populations. The principal says, "Since the Peace Accords, we have been promised the right to bilingual education, but who is going to give life to these promises? *Us*. We will. It is in *our* hands." His closing statements powerfully convey that the work of transitional justice has been sidelined, deemed resolved, criminalized, and relegated by the state to private spaces but that active civic engagement can push the issue back into the public consciousness.

The principal completes his remarks with yet another reminder that the students have the power to continue the struggle, but that it will indeed be a struggle: "Your challenge is that today you have to develop more.... You have to raise the consciousness of others." Graduating students are only approaching the beginning of these challenges, not celebrating their resolution.

Tzolok Ochoch's Civic Mission and Its Inherent Risks

Tzolok Ochoch places a strong emphasis on acquisition of the skills and cultural capital required for students to effectively participate in a ladino world, a political landscape that values articulate Spanish and meticulous appearance. Indigenous actors who wish to be heard will not only require fluency in the language of power, but they will need to be confident and persuasive at conveying their message. Speakers should make eye contact and use their bodies to express themselves. Equally important, they will have to present themselves for the part. Clothing should be clean and pressed. In the spotlight, they can wear traditional dress, but they cannot look poor. Poverty risks unraveling the message. Mastering these skills is essential for a disempowered group struggling for a legitimate political voice, and this commitment is ingrained in the school culture at Tzolok Ochoch.

Students are almost constantly called on to participate in the lucha, and there is an implication that these lessons, so clearly crafted for protest and community organizing, can be adjusted for participation in wider civic contexts within a polarized state. Yet the consensus is that opportunities for mainstream civic participation do not exist for these groups, whose rhetorical inclusion in nation-building projects mocks their perpetual location at the fringes.

At the core of everything students do at Tzolok Ochoch, there is an ethical and civic obligation to the pueblo, through the lens of a shared plight of poverty and exclusion from the polity. Though there is an ethnic dimension to the history of exclusion, there is also a sense of community forged with others on the margins, immaterial of their ethnic background. This shared identity is relatively uncontested and often replicated among students themselves, with the exception of Maya spirituality posed as an explanation and resolution for problems such as the "sickness" affecting students. There is almost constant use of first-person plural pronouns as if the school community composed a single group, unified in both their history of shared suffering and their desire to change the country through the act of overcoming and transforming exploitative conditions (superar).

At the heart of the philosophy lies a deep concern for others and an inclination to decenter the polity by committing to the pueblo over the state. As Ramiro says, being a leader requires anticipating resistance, willingness to endure risk and suffering, and a readiness for a solitary journey even when one's intentions are collective: "We have to think about our preparation, so I prepare myself, prepare myself, so that I will work hard, hard . . . and we have to think about doing it all alone, to leave the government outside, not to think of the government, to think of the pueblo above all. To help the people who have nothing." Ramiro and Alfredo identify two approaches to advancement: an individual pursuit of success and a collective pursuit of justice. This distinction resonates with the sentiment that a poor Guatemalan who breaks from a life of deprivation has abandoned something essential in his aspiration to move ahead. If he does not stand on the same plane "with the people," he stands apart from them.

Although the school does not place extensive curricular emphasis on the Conflicto Armado, its legacy pulses just below the surface of their social-justice goals. The war is widely (and somewhat erroneously) assumed to comprise a shared historical memory and a foundation to the students' call to justice, not solely in acknowledgment of collective suffering, but as recognition of the unfulfilled promises rooted in the postwar transition. But, importantly, the struggles that began in the context of armed conflict have taken on new forms. The struggle in the present is like the struggle of the past in that one contends with popular indifference and a neglectful state but also encounters new sets of actors whose power mobilizes in the face of a "waking" indigenous consciousness. Students at Tzolok Ochoch, equipped with the leadership skills they gain in school, are expected to contribute to this formation of consciousness and hold the state accountable for its obligations to citizens. Though they are warned that the struggle will be arduous and ongoing, there is little discussion of the inherent dangers in these civic actions. There is little discussion of events like Aurora's eerie murder along the school's border or her potential return as a violent spirit.

Even apart from the decision to embrace risk through community leadership, youth empowerment comes with pressures of its own. Students speak about their desire to prove through example that Guatemalan youth are not "lost." This entails carving paths that deviate from delinquency, but also paths that are not "light." Graduating from Tzolok Ochoch signifies that students have earned the right to lead their communities, but they are also indebted to them. The common dream of overcoming exploitative conditions (superar) works against the seeming inertia of things staying the same (quedarse así). Doing nothing is yet another risk; that is, the threat of changelessness is an implicit call to action. Even in the face of palpable threats, to do nothing—when one is educated to do something—is a betrayal to the pueblo. In this sense, the capacity for this generation of poor youth to return to their communities as empowered leaders serves as hope that Guatemala can change. Alfredo says, "What this school wants is that we serve something, that we contribute something, so that we are not just sitting in the house with a [diploma] and doing nothing, contributing nothing. So this school wants us to become leaders to make the first step, to become examples. We can return to our pueblos and say, *'This is what we need to do.'* With the will, we can do it. We need to be the first, to be the examples, so that we don't lose hope."

7

What Stands in the Way

At first glance there appears to be little shared across these four communities. These young people are born into dramatically diverse worlds, with their future paths largely laid out for them, and the rigidity of these paths is further ensured by their isolation from one another. But one visible thread weaves across these spaces. Teachers in all schools actively communicate that Guatemala is in dire need of change, and that youth have a role to play—from Profe Castillo's supplication that his students return to Guatemala to put their economic power to good use, to Beti's cautions for students to resist the lure of Guate-psychosis, to César's distracted encouragement that his students escape the pueblo in search of a better life, to Lisandro's urgency that his students stick together at all costs. In many ways, the thread seems to fray here, for one's social location, access to material resources, vulnerabilities as a victim, relationship with the state, levels of structural inclusion, and interpretations of justice and injustice mediate the sense of possibility, obligation, and expectations for citizens' potential contributions to this imagined future.

Constructing a vision of Guatemala's improved future harkens back to the unfinished work of its postwar transition, posing big questions about how to forge a coherent national identity, rebuild the civil contract, and ensure a just peace. The role of citizens in this delicate political arrangement remains unclear—particularly the rights and responsibilities of postgenera-tion citizens, who are taught more often through silence than stories how to interpret the legacy of the war that they inherit. That is, good citizenship today is variously constructed around expressions of patience, loyalty, and faith in the rule of law and, at the other extreme, exasperation and cynicism that the state will change on its own without organized resistance. The legacy of the Conflicto Armado offers the moral justification for adopt-ing either of these civic stances. Meanwhile, perceptions of civic responsi-bilities intersect with contemporary fragility, pivoting around impressions of Guatemala as a weak state in need of a robust civil society, a repressive state distrustful of civil society, or a corrupt state inattentive to civil soci-ety. Ideas about what good citizens *ought* to do cannot be shaped without simultaneously reflecting on what citizens *can* do. In this sense, "hope is circumscribed by the metrics of the possible" (Appadurai, 2007, p. 30).

Historical interpretations of the relationship between past and pres-ent violence, past and present repression, and past and present resistance movements reverberate through the spectrum of civic stances that young people create for themselves, along with their willingness to take on the associated risks. Whether the events of the Conflicto Armado, its transi-tion, or the weak postwar state individually or collectively triggered the set of current challenges facing Guatemala has become less relevant than the ways that individuals and groups interpret these historical relationships. If there is continuity in historical injustice, then the popular struggle is also ongoing, creating an opening for civic participation in the postwar. Yet continuity also implies that the risks of involvement remain high. If the war ended, today's challenges are linked to different accountable agents in what must be the *post*-postwar. Young people's daily experiences with dem-ocratic disjunctures (Holston, 2008; Holston & Caldeira, 1998; Rubin, 2007, 2012) overlay the "authenticity gaps" of peacetime (Lederach, 2005, p. 49), revealing both historical continuity and rupture. How adolescents construct these gaps and their historical antecedents influences the choices that they make, mediating their sense of social trust, belonging, and effi-cacy. Although history is not at the forefront of every civic decision, there are moments when its evocation is formative, alternating as a call to action, a bid for compliance, or a rationale for retreat.

For some young people the recent history of the Conflicto Armado stands in the way of their ability to take action, recognizing the high price paid for so few gains. The failure of the collective movement serves as a warning against future attempts to shift the status quo. For others the collective movement was little more than a gathering of criminals whose power to deceive innocent people into joining their misguided struggle caused great harm. The loss is borne by the nation, a reminder that political involvement, especially when forged in opposition to the legitimate state, carries the inevitable cost of suffering. And then there are those who see valor and value in the popular struggle to make Guatemala a more just place, inserting themselves as the new protagonists of the ongoing struggle. Their social location and identification as members of "historically oppressed groups," subject to systematic oppression "over long periods of time, over generations" (Bashir, 2008, p. 52), dictates their position in this unfinished struggle, as well as their shared obligation to carry it forward. Yet young people make meaning of their identities as "historically oppressed" peoples in contrary ways.

The themes highlighted in this chapter are intended as an entry point for understanding the ways that young people's construction of the past, that is, their historical consciousness, functions as a mediator in their civic development in Guatemala's postwar present. I comparatively examine the role of formal and informal education in shaping young people's civic identities, orientations, and expectations for themselves, fellow citizens, and their collective futures. These manifest through (1) the preservation of divisive memory communities, (2) distinct strategies for interpreting injustice, and (3) perceptions of Guatemala's legitimacy as a democracy.

Memory

Two principal memory communities contribute to Guatemala's social and political divisions: one working to make the history of the Conflicto Armado present and the other working to erase it—whether through acts of violence or on the grounds that contemporary violence renders past violence irrelevant. Schools play a significant role in reproducing these distinct memory communities and their particular civic attachments. Young people in each of these schools learn less about the history of the Conflicto Armado than about adults' interpretations of memory's public contest during the country's transition. Moreover, the central role of memory in contemporary politics necessitates its acknowledgment as a civic dimension of postwar life, as a past that demands either tribute or rejection.

Within each classroom there is a striking amount of identity construction centering around an ambiguous, flexible "us" and an ambiguous, flexible "them." For the most part, these classrooms and the spaces in which they are situated comprise largely homogeneous communities. With few exceptions, students at each school hail from the same social class, a reality that goes hand in hand with the privatization of secondary education and the identity politics historically transposed onto physical spaces, often cutting across ethnicity. Moreover, schools readily expand their identity constructions to accommodate their student body. This relative within-school homogenization results in the de facto segregation of existing social categories, so that these four schools essentially cater exclusively to the urban elite, the urban working class, the rural indigenous, and the rural poor. Yet the collective constructed in each of these spaces is defined more by its historical experience with privilege, injustice, or invisibility vis-à-vis the state than by any fixed social or spatial category. In this sense, schools comprise distinct "memory communities" (Booth, 2006), and by nature of their isolation from one another, schools play a key role in their preservation (Bellino, 2014b, 2016).

With few opportunities for diverse memory communities to interact with one another and little space to bridge multiple perspectives through dialogue, students not only increasingly inhabit different Guatemalas in the present but also inherit distinct pasts and imagine distinct futures. These multiple paths for civic development, and their intricate links to historical injustice, help explain why the boundaries between *us* and *them* seem variously affixed to ethnicity, space, and social class. In effect, these memory communities comprise distinct civic communities, giving voice to a particular impression of what it means to be Guatemalan and what good citizenship requires in the postwar moment. These expressions of "linked fate" serve to connect like communities, at the risk of increasing division between unlike communities. The risk here is that young people learning in segregated settings "lose contact with one another, learn different things in different ways, and come out different kinds of people with little or nothing in common" (Swift, 2003, p. 36).

On the subject of the Conflicto Armado, most adolescent students lack extensive historical knowledge but, with the explicit guidance of their teacher, find relative consensus in its historical interpretation. Though Guillermo openly rejects Profe Castillo's emphasis on two devils, even backing the legitimacy of his position with reference to its location in a "book I read," his classmates talk over him, reframe the narratives of suffering as collateral damage during war, and the teacher invalidates his contributions by instructing students to think "like a state," while rendering all historical evidence on the subject of war "biased."

In spite of the truisms circulating the classroom that history is "written by the victors" and that learning history ensures against "repeating the past," Profe Castillo's emphasis that historical analysis be objective guides students toward a zero-accountability interpretation of the Conflicto Armado. This not only nullifies state accountability for past wrongs but actively negates struggles to bring the past to justice in the present day as "misuses" of historical memory. On this subject Profe positions historical memory as a force of division in a country struggling to reinvent itself as pluricultural, warning students about the potential dangers of history's capacity to promote rancor. In this sense, he advocates that the past be acknowledged as a significant historical event but not be internalized as an anchor for one's selfhood. What Profe fears is what Bashir Bashir (2008) formulates as essential to the identity of historically oppressed groups, who "shap[e] the very sense of self in terms of conflict" (p. 54). Students build on this perceived threat of historical memory by critiquing indigenous rights movements as making illegitimate claims on the state. There are also collective efforts to create temporal markers between wartime violence and post-postwar violence as two distinct sets of parenthesis (Booth, 1999), both of which comprise extreme conditions and therefore demand extreme measures. Again the message is vocalized as a shared narrative: today's violence is worse than that of the past. Ellen Moodie's (2010) theory of "unknowing" is fitting here, in that the ethnic and class components of the civil war become "actively unknown, converted into non-knowledge" (p. 196) to cope in the violent present and justify one's privilege in a classed society.

Set apart from his peers, Alejandro is firm in his beliefs that his classmates need to face their parents' "dark pasts" and that the country cannot move forward without collectively scrutinizing its self-inflicted wounds. The letter he brings to school articulates the ongoing nature of historical injustice, even at the risk of sparking conflict among students who view the campaign as a "misuse" of historical memory and an attempt to grant privileges, rather than rights, to indigenous communities.

Though Beti arguably offers more interpretive space for Paulo Freire students, she too makes clear delineations about the "spiral" of historical injustice and its central place in Guatemala's identity. The Conflicto

Armado does not comprise a "parenthesis" within Guatemala's past but rather "ellipses" (Booth, 1999, p. 250) that denotes an ongoing struggle. To Beti's delight, students share in this counternarrative when they assert that Guatemala is "still" living the counterrevolution. The Conflicto Armado remains so unresolved for this population that students cannot identify an appropriate image with which to close their visual timeline. Ultimately, their fitful chronology funnels into the reality of ongoing inequality rather than pay tribute to the "fictions" of peaceful coexistence. Constructing contemporary violence as both an extension and an outcome of past exploitation positions students as enduring struggles that have historically defined Guatemala's divisions.

At International Academy the memory of the war is positioned as an impediment to Guatemala's prospects for peace, whereas at Paulo Freire it is the absence of this memory that impedes Guatemala's future, situating peace as contingent on justice, and justice as contingent on public memory. In direct contrast to Profe Castillo's presentation of historical memory as a source of intergroup division that should be interpreted with caution, Beti presents historical memory as a critical civic obligation. These divergent orientations hinge on the construction of historical injustice as either continuous or discontinuous. Countering public discourses such as the assertion that "history promotes rancor," Beti demonstrates how silencing historical memory effectively signals historical continuity and, in turn, a civic duty to dismantle ongoing patterns of injustice. Meanwhile, recognition of historical continuity is what uniquely positions this group of young people as the next generation of urban intellectuals, poised to instill a social conscience that acknowledges historical dimensions of inequality and exploitation. Their future is set against the inevitable resistance they will encounter in citizens, whom Beti routinely faults for "lacking" a civic education and a historical consciousness.

Whereas in other classrooms historical injustice plays a central role in the construction of civic identity, César maintains that the Conflicto Armado is not relevant to the lives of his students at Sun and Moon, who are tasked with adapting to a changing modern world. The struggles facing the community today are distinct and profound: new violent factions, corrupt police, threats of mob violence, dispossession of land, and a severe lack of employment opportunities.

Student accounts of the Conflicto Armado at Sun and Moon rely heavily on the "systematic vagueness" (Edwards & Potter, 1992, p. 162) of historical agents. In moments of uncertainty about which of the two forces were more powerful, more legitimate, or more ruthless in their acts of violence, students make efforts to remind one another that ultimately these questions are less relevant than the experience of manipulation and mistreatment of those caught between, the space their families inhabited. This "schematic narrative template" (Wertsch, 2002, p. 60) proves such a resilient frame that even the film's portrayal of state brutality serves not to subvert, but to widen, their stories to account for this (alleged) counterevidence. At times César's contention that both groups were responsible, based on his own experience of dual recruitment, effectively guides students back to their original claims of entrapment, even as they grow increasingly frustrated at their impression of the guerrillas' intentional deception. As their narrative shifts between two devils and one, the enduring lesson of the past is that "we" are the innocent victims, alternately ignored or exploited by the repressive state, the meddling of activists and rights groups, and now the agenda of international corporations. In this way, the ambiguity of their narrative accounts for a range of experiences with injustice, while linking the pueblo's identity as indigenous, rural, and poor to a state of permanent victimhood. Yet who is accountable for their oppression is not made entirely clear.

Like many pueblos "affected" by the war, Río Verde remains divided, with multiple memory communities living alongside one another in relative distrust. Even Leonardo and María Carmen shape distinct memory groups within the family, based on which sons can claim status as guerrilliños, an identity that comes with particular pride and accountability to abide by the rule of law at all costs. Community knowledge of the roles that people played during the war remains a source of distrust and justification for high levels of vigilance, yet these identities are also redefined within the context of new justice issues. Though at times there seems a willingness to relinquish a divided past for the shared uncertainty of their future, the periodic eruptions of mob violence also provoke a collective turn inward, further unraveling the community fabric. In some cases, expressions of agency splinter along perceptions of the war's legacy and whether the unjust conditions of the present necessitate illegal resistance or a retreat from the public sphere. The lack of strong community ties is further reflected in the sentiment expressed by teachers that the only way forward is to escape, not through collective action but through economic development and individual advancement (salir).

At Tzolok Ochoch, the ongoing lucha and its historical connections to the Conflicto Armado are referenced almost incessantly, framed as an intergenerational memory and a call to collective action. During a school assembly school leaders ceremonially pass the lucha to the senior class, positioning them as the next generation of luchadores and community leaders. The war is more than a historical anchor; it is a call "to 'do justice'" (Booth, 2009, p. 364) and, in this sense, a civic obligation that spans generations. Simultaneously, the lucha functions to unify interethnic solidarity among the rural poor, a struggle poised against the state, the military, the oligarchy, foreign businesses, *finqueros*, and anyone who contributes to their collective marginalization. Like accounts at Sun and Moon, ambiguity of past and present actors often functions toward greater inclusion, so that the suffering of "our people" alternates between the rural, the rural poor, and the (principally rural, poor) indigenous. As the *us* expands and retracts, so does the *they*, of which there are many.

Presumably the Conflicto Armado is one of the cornerstones of the lucha, despite that the school makes little effort to formally include this history in the curriculum. Its legacy is present in the near-constant reflection on social injustice at Tzolok Ochoch, yet some students know little about this history of war. Adults in each of these communities struggle with how much interpretive agency to grant young people in constructing and deriving meaning from the violent past. While some, like Alfredo, are able to narrate their parents' lived experience of suffering and survival, historical facts are frequently rendered irrelevant in constructing the consensus story of how "they impoverished us" though exclusion, exploitation, and extermination. Despite their lack of historical details, these students carry war legacies in their bodies in a variety of ways, through visceral fears of helicopters, acute anxiety over soldiers, and ancestral spirit possession. In these ways, they embody "postmemories" (Hirsch, 2008) as "knowledge in the blood" (Jansen, 2009), even as they make efforts to distinguish between the trauma their parents lived and the legacy of historical injustice that they inherit in the postwar.

Rooted in diverse pasts and presents, each of these communities projects distinct pathways for young people, implying that student youth have a shared future. Constructing a sense of a shared fate is one of the goals for societies in transition, so that previously divided populations are able to imagine a future that will unite them under the banner of a new national identity, shared commitment to democracy, and a collective obligation to shape a society at peace (Cole & Murphy, 2009; Davies, 2004b; Lederach, 2005). In particular, "linked fate" implies interdependence and recognition that "the welfare of my community is directly related to the welfare of your community" (Lederach, 2005, p. 62). Yet the clear divergence of these young people's orientation to the issues afflicting their country—to say nothing of the differential quality of education, range of postgraduation opportunities, or disparate social locations—suggests that they will remain divided in their imagined futures. More worrisome, there is an encoded message that the welfare of one community depends on the exploitation of another. The hardening of these social divisions demonstrates why "just any education is not enough to prevent conflict" (King, 2014, p. 136). Though the future trajectories of Paulo Freire and Sun and Moon students do not work against each other and at times forge tenuous connections, young people studying at the International Academy and those at Tzolok Ochoch stand to come into direct conflict. These schools are by no means promoting violence—but in many ways they shape trajectories intentionally designed to confront one another and in this sense risk reproducing the boundaries of the past. The fates of these young people are bound to cross but not merge.

Injustice

Across these four school-community sites, young people shape their civic attitudes through experiences with democratic convergence and disjuncture (Rubin, 2007, 2012). Markers of Guatemala's instability are everywhere, and even elites are not impervious. But to what do these young citizens attribute these contemporary challenges? Do they regard them as the legacy of historical injustice and an aborted transition or as markers of enduring authoritarianism, or is this a state that means well but is held captive, weakened by old groups, corrupted by new groups, and destabilized by justice struggles for the past amid a host of contemporary problems? In diagnosing these societal challenges, how do educated youth imagine the role and responsibilities of the state and citizens in resolving them?

At the International Academy students routinely articulate individual and cultural deficit explanations for violence and poverty. Their refrains commonly scapegoat indigenous populations for contributing to Guatemala's escalating violence and lack of global status. Indigenous desires to maintain cultural distinctiveness has been a "dead weight" on the country since its colonial origins. Even their teacher employs this discourse in (a rather misleading) attempt to provoke them, inviting a series of emphatic denials that indigenous subjugation is the reason their families have accumulated such extreme wealth. Students argue that their wealth was not built on the backs of indigenous laborers but in spite of the strain this population has placed on the country's weak economy. Students turn this history of colonial exploitation on its head, faulting enduring cultural traits such as indigenous stubbornness and laziness as the reasons that the country remains undeveloped. Moreover, perceptions that indigenous cling to victim status through requests for privileges rather than equal rights serves as a reminder that the history of the Conflicto Armado must be filed away if Guatemala is to progress. If the state concedes more cultural rights to indigenous populations, students reason, the country will only be held further back. Cultural rights, such as the right to be educated in one's mother tongue, are evaluated on the basis of their value in the global market. Collectively, these perceptions lead to frustration that government handouts and accommodations teach people to receive rather than work to join the modern, global world.

When Profe Castillo asks his students to reflect on what they "promise to do to make Guatemala a better country," student responses center almost exclusively on individual civic duties such as their promises to "abide by laws" and vote "for the president who will make Guatemala succeed." While a fair amount of responses make vague claims to "help others improve the situation in the country," many reflect the prevailing belief at International Academy, ingrained in the school mission to shape future business leaders: "to start my own company and create jobs." Most of these young people express confidence in their futures and the role that economic development will play in resolving Guatemala's problems. In addition to jobs, students express a striking amount of concern over the lack of indigenous education, by which they mean an absence of moral values, and a readiness to turn to violence because they "cannot take care of themselves."

The connections that students draw between economic development and peace are made more visible by the exception of Alejandro's frustration that Guatemala's "development depends on exploitation." As he circulates the letter opposing the expansion of the hydroelectric company in Ixil communities, his classmates distance themselves from the issue and position indigenous communities in resistance as impediments to the country's progress and, by extension, disturbers of the peace. Despite Alejandro's commitment to indigenous justice struggles, the failure of his letter campaign to engage his classmates serves as a reminder of the obstacles, such as social distancing and stereotyping, facing the collective action to which his parents have dedicated themselves. Anastela and Rodolfo explain the long haul of collective struggle, warning against measuring success immediately after action and reminding Alejandro that they are not solely motivated by the pragmatic outcomes of their participation. But this does little to persuade Alejandro that their struggle is worth the effort. His perception that these tactics lack effectiveness stands in the way of his own efforts to take action. One piece of evidence that he draws on is the past itself—if collective struggle had the power to make a difference, the Conflicto Armado would have turned out differently.

Students at Paulo Freire readily vocalize their concern for Guatemala's future. They believe the state needs to adjust its relationship with its citizens, investing in basic services such as health and education. Awareness of structural inequalities is fundamental to the political and historical consciousness that these students construct, though their most visceral desire is a resolution for the injustice they experience in their daily lives, so that they may "walk freely in the streets." The relationship they perceive between state fragility, poverty, and violence stems from personal experience as victims of assaults and their resentment toward the inverted civil contract, realities that Beti emphasizes she "cannot hide" from her students.

Students' desire for change is stifled by their lack of trust in state actors and institutions. These students claim, based on firsthand experiences, that the police are their enemies. In some cases, they view police as inept, but more often they cast police officers as menacing. Given these inversions and the gaps they create in the civil contract, adolescents develop sharply contrasting perceptions of what citizens enduring these conditions can do to change the course of their lives. Though they tend to place more emphasis on the need for state accountability and structural change (through both reallocating resources and dismantling impunity) than individual capacities to bring about change through civic action, they do identify openings for individual and collective participation. One opportunity centers on the role of civil-society organizations, such as Rodrigo's interest in "joining organizations that work for peace and living to help others and not just myself." On this subject, students reference working with organizations that promote human rights as well as denouncing corrupt government practices, emphasizing the monitoring role that civil society can play in transitioning democracies, as well as the potential for "parastate" agents to fill the gaps in weak states. Impressions that the state is weak can generate openings for action, so that individuals become more capable agents of change.

In contrast, perceptions of the state as corrupt facilitate reflections on the limits of civic power in a state that willfully allows injustice to plague the lives of particular groups of citizens. The urban working class is positioned as an increasingly dispensable population of *quienquieras*, possessing just enough resources to make them viable victims but lacking sufficient means to become visible in death. Recognizing the limits of power for people "like them" prompts students to remove themselves from the public sphere, believing that they can help by "*avoiding* violence."

The tension between what citizens can do and what the state will allow them to do resurfaces in students' voluntary involvement in the neighborhood project to reclaim public space by scratching off gang graffiti. Their impression that the municipality is employing the activity as a publicity stunt and that the activity does not address the underlying causes of delinquency stirs them from an "empowered" stance to one of "discouragement" (Rubin, 2007, p. 470), suggesting that direct confrontation with the forces that repress and neutralize everyday participation serves to guide civic action away from public spaces and into the private realm. Their stance shifts more dramatically from active to passive when the day ends with several assaults. When these individuals become victims, they are directly confronted with their stopping points, both external and self-imposed limits on their civic agency. Yet even amid these daily experiences with the deepest disjunctures of Guatemala's democracy, these young people do not jump to conclusions about delinquents' lack of humanity, nor do they unanimously retreat from the public sphere. They continue to see a complex picture of violence as a social problem with roots in the country's history of inequality. At times this critical orientation sufficiently counteracts their daily experience with injustice.

In Río Verde injustice is pervasive, inescapable, and constant, especially for poor, rural, and indigenous populations such as the students who attend Sun and Moon. Like adolescents in urban areas, these young people face choices about whether and under what conditions good citizenship requires becoming involved (*involucrarse*) or removing oneself (*apartarse*).

For example, students initially sympathize with the largely urban nor-malista protest movement, including their illegal tactics such as roadblocks to draw attention to their cause. Their affinity is grounded in the shared experience of struggle to claim rights and the reality that illegal protests are often the only ones that are visible, amid countless "invisible struggles." Yet when David points out that the state has both responded with force and announced that they will not change the educational policy, the students promptly lose faith in the movement. This knowledge deems the protest counterproductive, shifting the perception of activism from a mechanism poised to seek justice to one tragically entangled in social disruption. Students do not see value in dialogue that they expect will be one-sided and inevitably cause more repression. Their certainty seems to persuade César himself, who acknowledges Guatemala's persistent gap between democratic promises and the lived reality. While Sun and Moon students view both possibilities and flaws in the turn to illegal protests, what begins as a rationalization for extreme measures in extreme times culminates in a fatalistic disavowal of civic agency and a call to retreat when it is in the interest of maintaining peace.

The anxiety over whether to participate or withdraw is further complicated by the legacy of the Conflicto Armado in this village, where many survivors describe their experience as one of entrapment "between two armies" (Stoll, 1994). Involvement is inherently dangerous but also inflammatory and confrontational. To take action, even through legal channels, can be regarded as a hostile, disruptive, and even self-serving act, given that consequences are often collective.

The people of Río Verde continually find themselves positioned between structures of power. Students crave openings for collective action but view these spaces as tentative and often futile. They desire support from adults in their community and their government to take action, in hopes of escaping oppressive conditions (salir), but the legacy of suffering clings to the safety of noninvolvement. Learned helplessness prevails as a solution through avoidance, perpetuating the self-fulfilling prophecy that attempts to take action will inevitably lead to failure. Rather than resist the forces that stand in the way, there is a sense of duty (to fellow citizens, not the state) in accepting and adapting to injustice as a way of life and, accordingly, searching for private escapes. On issues ranging from vigilante justice to negotiating with the mine to be a "good neighbor," their frustration wavers between a neglectful, repressive, and corrupt state to irresponsible citizens whose turn to illicit measures weakens the rule of law and the validity of protest as a civic expression. Young people sense the wall enclosing around them, leaving little opening for civic action—should they create a *salida* through revolution, as Álvaro proposes, or accept the enclosure and turn inward, toward individual betterment and moral growth, as Rosa suggests?

Students at Tzolok Ochoch share many of the same challenges to exercising their civic voice, when so much in their lives demands struggle. Teachers at Tzolok Ochoch work to promote civic knowledge and values particular to the rural poor, emphasizing structural violence and historical drivers of inequality, while working against individual and cultural explanations for Guatemala's past and present fragility. For example, Lisandro's forceful reframing of his students' individual and cultural explanations for high rates of uneducated and unemployed indigenous women illustrates the profound injustice of a structural arrangement that privatizes secondary education. In a similar vein, the principal makes a point to publicly clarify that the "indigenous population is not poor. *They* have impoverished *us*," emphasizing the historical and structural explanations for contemporary inequality. These discursive reframings shift accountable agents from citizens, who allegedly do not value education, hard work, or the contributions of women, to the structural conditions created and upheld by those in power, which impede the development of selective groups. Simultaneously, these structural critiques work against students' internalization of persistent stereotypes that they will likely confront—stereotypes alive and well at the International Academy—and which might otherwise impede their perceptions of what they are capable of achieving in and out of school.

Yet the path to change is not only structural but also in the hands of citizens, as long as they find ways to work together. As students remind one another, "We are the ones who suffer poverty, so we are the ones who have to work to get out of it." Keenly aware that the state will not act on their behalf, students note that it falls to them to "give life" to the unfulfilled promises of the Peace Accords. Like in Sun and Moon, students here feel that the history of exploitation, particularly for indigenous groups, is ongoing. Ongoing injustice functions not toward a narrowing of civic opportunities but rather an intensification of the collective struggle and the role of postwar generation youth in advancing that struggle. There is widespread recognition among students that joining the lucha will require ongoing, risky, and selfless work, a resolve to bring about change set against the will of all those who benefit from the status quo. But their commitment to collective action is also grounded in the knowledge that the struggle is vital to their survival—the only path to a just future.

Democracy

Although President Otto Pérez Molina is a retired military general and was democratically elected, his term was widely cast as Guatemala's return to the "military governments" of the past. Whether this was an ominous or auspicious return depends on one's interpretation of the military's role in Guatemala's past, frequently divided between stories of military repression or protection.

Pérez Molina's rise to power and his unapologetic remilitarization campaign as the new face of national security forged a knot in time. On the one hand, a "military president" marks a return to the authoritarian past, visible proof of the connections between past and present injustice. Historical continuity is not merely symbolic; Pérez Molina has been implicated in human rights violations, including massacres in the Highlands. For some populations, their president is literally the face of their past oppressor. Additionally, his reemployment of elite military forces such as the Kaibiles suggest that his leadership strategies, like those of prior presidents, are heavily informed by repressive military tactics of the past (Doyle, 2012; J. López, 2010). Across Latin America, the military functions as a real and symbolic "'carrier' of authoritarian legacies" (Agüero, 2004, p. 233). On the other hand, Pérez Molina's presidency marks a departure from the past and an indication of the collective readiness to redefine the role of the military. In many ways, desire for military intervention is rooted in, and reflective of, nostalgia for the predictable order of the past. But it has also been fueled by the notion that current violence in the country demands a state of exception, even if increased militarization disregards aspects of the Peace Accords and risks repeating some of the forbidden lessons of the past.

During the election period and since his term began, political graffiti spread across the bare cement walls of the capital city, along with social media campaigns to clarify Pérez Molina's links to the past and what his presidency means for Guatemala's "transition." This political shift lends support for Edelberto Torres-Rivas's (1999) concern that Guatemala will continue along the "oscillating path between democracy and dictatorship" rather than pledge an "irreversible" commitment to democracy (p. 285). But many students fear that Pérez Molina's increased support for remilitarization implies something more menacing than the shortcomings of democracy. In the rows of soldiers lined along capital streets, in the rising instances of states of siege in the rural pueblos, in the visible investment and infrastructure of military barracks and checkpoints across the country, and even in the murals that pronounce the military as the people's "brother" and the "protector" of peace, these young people fear the possibility of a new war.

At the International Academy Profe Castillo emphasizes that Pérez Molina is a civilian president. Working against an external critique of the current president's legitimacy, the teacher builds solidarity with the children of the conservative Right. In direct opposition to claims that this presidency signifies a dangerous step backward for Guatemala, Profe Castillo instead casts this as a demonstration that Guatemala has resolved the legacy of the Conflicto Armado. In this way, he instructs students to reinterpret public dialogue and debate, wary of the misuses of historical memory.

Students concur that the country was ironically safer during the war, given that violence then was justified and predictable, while the violence now can affect anyone at any time, for any reason. Again, the process of "unknowing" (Moodie, 2010, p. 172) is fitting: unknowing the political and structural elements of historical injustice leaves the impression of the "new era's risk as something to manage individually" (p. 171). Profe Castillo, too, upholds this hierarchy of suffering on the grounds that there is more violence today during the time of alleged peace. Students largely trust in the military as an institution, significantly more than they trust the police force. Laura and Isabella express confidence that the military intervention in Barillas was a necessary measure, and Isabella believes that military presence ensured her safety from the townspeople during her stay. When the state of siege in Barillas is lifted, Laura interprets this as an irresponsible decision on the part of the state, predicting that the townspeople will soon return to violence without military supervision.

In the safety of their home, Alejandro and his parents make references to the military's integral and ongoing role in polarizing the Left and Right. Their nightly news rituals encompass critiques that the expansion of military power and the use of martial law are authoritarian acts, highlighting the threads of historical continuity. Driving past military checkpoints as they exit the capital, the whole family holds its breath. Alejandro views the people in power as "bad guys" and considers mounting military presence akin to the rumbling of war drums.

At Paulo Freire the message is unequivocal that the country once again has a "military government." Students easily offer support that the military's privileged status marks an ongoing legacy of injustice, while military impunity signifies a lack of equal rights. Pedro links the return of a military leader to Guatemala's lack of "cultural memory" and unwillingness to face the past. Yet the most problematic historical connection they see is Pérez Molina's rise to power through democratic elections. This "paradox" is reinforced by Beti's assessment that citizens voted for a former general because they lack civic education and historical consciousness.

Students at Paulo Freire have developed strong critiques of their current government, not solely on the basis of its growing militarism, but also through keen awareness of social-justice issues and their lived experience with democratic disjunctures. They sense that the urban working class is only one of many groups intentionally excluded from state decisions, which are not guided by the moral principle of the common good. At times these young people construct affinity with their assailants based on their mutual neglect by the state. They live, work, and travel among delinquents and sometimes are mistaken for them. Rather than hold perpetrators individually accountable, they redirect their frustration toward the shortcomings of the postwar democracy. Similarly, when their everyday life is impeded by strikes and protests, these students express more frustration toward the state for necessitating disruptive struggles than the protesters for causing disruption.

The fluidity of their civic stances rotates around their constructions of the state as weak and repressive. Students' essays and everyday conversations reiterate the idea that the civil contract is inverted, noting a state too weak to guarantee basic rights and the unjust irony of a government intimidated by criminals, rather than criminals being held in check by the rule of law. While many Guatemalans position democracy's failings as a rationale for reinstituting authoritarian security mechanisms, students at Paulo Freire apply their frustrations to a critique of Guatemala's weak commitments to democracy. Meanwhile, their utmost desire to "walk freely in the streets" is increasingly entwined with Guatemala's capacity to democratize, not remilitarize.

At Sun and Moon, students similarly experience democracy almost exclusively through its disjunctures. Like Beti, César acknowledges the fissures that lie between constitutional laws and the constraints on exercising civil rights, especially because, as he freely admits, the "government right now is military." But students' skepticism of the current leadership is not focused on Pérez Molina's dark past or what his election implies about the country's deficient historical memory of their parents' suffering. Sun and Moon students are more concerned with the president's application of mano dura and the potential for military intervention in their village. Authoritarian legacies operate in today's land and natural resource conflicts, threatening village security and autonomy, as well as the very homes these students inhabit. Though in many cases the law is on the side of the people, the state is not. The state appears to routinely defend the rights of corporations over the rights of its citizens, a message made more audible with each military intervention. The army returns to the Highlands when indigenous communities do not consent to development projects, when community leaders make visible corporate repression and environmental negligence, and most assuredly when the people come together in resistance.

The possibility that Río Verde could be overtaken by the army functions as a renewable source of fear at the forefront of every young person's mind when they consider public action. While many adolescents express their longing to resist the power of the mines or simply to engage in a dialogue about their long-term intentions, they conjure dark images of what might happen if the military were to become involved. The power of this threat is so great that it effectively drives townspeople into a position of neutrality as a mode of self-protection. Rather than risk sparking conflict through resistance, they actively withdraw. Most of the students at Sun and Moon do not fear a return to full-scale war, in part because they willfully abstain from conflict, seeking refuge in the self-assurance that they will be spared as long as they do not become "involved." Although they lament that the pueblo has no voice, on this matter they would rather not risk being heard.

The refrain that the pueblo has no voice also resonates for students at Tzolok Ochoch. For both rural populations, the recurrent experiences of exclusion and invisibility contradict the promise of pluricultural democracy. Students at Tzolok Ochoch are well versed in the constitutional laws and social, economic, and cultural rights guaranteed to them that habitually go unfulfilled. School lessons highlight the importance of identifying these rights, as well as the civic obligations students have to search for collective, legal means to claim these rights, even while acknowledging that knowing the law and claiming rights are not one and the same. As Andrea says, people are aware of their rights but afraid to claim them.

There is a strong perception at Tzolok Ochoch that the military never relinquished power, and that this authoritarian continuity is an ongoing challenge to democracy. The intersection of historical knowledge, present experience, and future anticipation of the military's role bring to the surface anxieties about whether Guatemala might relapse into a full-scale war. Male students fear being drafted against their will into military service, a possibility that would shatter their future goals. Students reflect on the discriminatory nature of military checkpoints, serving as legal forms of harassment with the veneer of national security. Valeria makes an effort to frame the possibility of a future war as connected to the lessons of the Conflicto Armado, noting the links between repression and authoritarian political arrangements. And students' fears of soldiers are both vicariously inherited and renewed through firsthand experiences such as states of siege in their hometown. Rubi captures this tension when she struggles to balance her distrust of the current presidency with the rhetorical knowledge that what "they" promise about history not repeating itself will prove true, implying a risk of faith.

Interrupting Legacies

There is growing consensus among scholars, practitioners, and advocates working in transitional justice contexts that legacies of violence, division, and authoritarianism require active disruption in educational spaces to dismantle their power, whether through historical critique or peace-building strategies, such as the making of alternative value systems (Davies, 2007; Jansen, 2009; Weldon, 2010a, 2010b). But in postwar Guatemala the violent past and the violent present crisscross like tension wires supporting a bridge. Confronting historical legacies is confounded by postwar violence, not only because tracing the origins of authoritarian practices becomes entangled in historical processes of continuity and change, but also because linking past and present entails risk. Philippe Bourgois (2001) exhorts ethnographers to engage in the important work of untangling these historical processes, in part by examining their interaction and the way violence refracts and regenerates over time, across space, and in various forms: "The challenge of ethnography . . . [is] to clarify the chains of causality that link structural, political, and symbolic violence in the production of an every-day violence that buttresses unequal power relations and distorts efforts at resistance" (pp. 29–30).

In this book I have traced young people's understanding of historical injustice and examined how histories of violence, the legacies they produce, and the legacies sparked through the transitional processes shape youth subjectivity in profound and lasting ways. In tracing these linkages we see how legacies travel uneven paths through narrative and silence, across generations and disparate social spaces, interacting with postwar conditions that manifest locally, regionally, and globally. We also see that young people interpret and navigate past and present justice issues in distinct ways, while developing a sense of their civic identities and their capacity for meaningful and secure participation. At the conflict's end, the CEH wrote into their report, "Fear, silence, apathy, and the lack of interest in participating in the political sphere are among the most important consequences of having criminalized victims and comprise an obstacle for the active participation of all citizens in building democracy" (1999, p. 33). Indeed, fear, silence, apathy, and distrust manifest today as legacies of the war and obstacles to democracy. But they are also, at times, effective precautions in the context of pervasive insecurity and continued repression of popular movements. In other words, what is presumably a legacy of civic passivity is also actively appropriated as an adaptive strategy in a high-risk setting, at times with the active encouragement of educators, parents, and community members. Legacies circle back on themselves here, as the present context becomes increasingly similar to the past, where lines between violent actors, strategies, and repressive structures become blurred.

Caught between old and new systems of oppression and the unfulfilled promises of democratic transition, postwar youth are positioned as citizens-in-waiting. If a better future is attainable, there seem to be two paths: one of renewed struggle and resistance, and all the loss it risks; and one of cautious noninvolvement, and all the patience it demands. I turn now to the ways that young people's interpretations of historical injustice serves to underscore, and in some cases undermine, dimensions of the contemporary risk structure.

8

The Hopes and Risks of Waiting

Strategies for Managing Wait Citizenship

As seen throughout this book, state fragility conveys to young people that the state is unwilling or unable to protect and provide for them or uphold their basic rights. Conventional expressions of democratic citizenship such as voting in elections, volunteering and participating in collective-action projects, reporting crimes to law enforcement, intervening in local disputes, and advocating for rights and inclusion are widely perceived to be constrained by inept and corrupt structures. There is hesitance across classrooms and homes to cast Guatemala as a democratic state, labeling the government "military" but rhetorically insisting on the political structure of a democracy. The continuation of conflict structures within government and uninterrupted legacies of authoritarianism, including those embedded in the educational opportunity structure, render Guatemala no longer authoritarian, but not yet democratic. The discursive construction of these contradictions—often for the purpose of cautioning young people about the limits on civic action—signifies teachers' and parents' own positioning as wait citizens, caught between democratic ideals and disjunctures. As Javier explains, the nature of Guatemala's democracy is hard to define: "We are not at peace. Some say we are still at war. . . . We are not democratic. Our state is repressive. I don't know what we are. I guess we are something in the middle. Maybe we are both?" Alfredo similarly refuses to recognize Guatemala as a democracy: "The Constitution says there is democracy. The Peace Accords say there is democracy. There is democracy. . . . But it is not being fulfilled, because the indigenous people have no voice. So how can we speak of democracy in Guatemala?" With Guatemalan society as both repressive and democratic, "in the middle" of war and postwar, citizens are caught in between. While waiting for security, structural inclusion, and voice, citizens are forced to "[create] new geographies of political intervention and citizenship" (Honwana, 2013, p. 18).

Here in this final chapter, I revisit some of the questions posed in the opening chapters and articulate a framework for how citizens-in-waiting approach civic choices. It is important to reiterate that the state of waithood is a consequence of the structural context and not an inherently passive or apathetic state. It does not denote youth "inactively 'waiting' for their situation to change" (Honwana, 2013, p. 4), although that is sometimes how young people respond to the structural constraints and exclusion they experience. As Javier Auyero (2012) makes clear, emphasizing the waiting of subordinated groups in relation to the state is not meant as a deprivation of citizens' agency but rather a way of capturing one's agency vis-à-vis the state: "True, they are agents; but *in their interactions with the state*, their sense of agency is minimal to nonexistent" (p. 154).

In listening to youth voices, we hear much caution and careful consideration about whether and when to take public action, concerns over being silenced or discredited, and the central role of hope embedded in the civic act of waiting. As we have seen, some young people are empowered to participate as individuals or join civil-society organizations, whereas others retreat on the grounds that personal security demands withdrawal from the public sphere. Deliberating about how and when to participate in an undemocratic democracy invokes an implicit calculation between present and potential risk. For some, living at the margins or living in isolation and fear is the high cost paid for safety, whereas for others these conditions present such a fundamental denial of rights that the risks of taking action outweigh the risks of inaction. In these cases, the prospect of things "staying the same" serves as a point of departure, while other times it serves as a stopping point and an appeal to resign to current circumstances. Similarly, some children of activists or guerrilleros gravitate toward social-justice issues, readily picking up where their parents left off, while others receive clear messages to abstain from political involvement, willfully constructing an alternative path, unburdened by risk. Accordingly, the Conflicto Armado comprises a call to action for some, while for others the legacy of its failure to transform society serves as a reason to withhold.

In a number of anthropological studies, "risk taking, whether calculated, intentional, or rebelliously reckless, has been assumed to be part of everyday life . . . as something to be minimized" (Cole & Durham, 2008, pp. 14–15). Guatemalan youth demonstrate awareness of the risk structure that permeates their lives and constrains their capacity for secure and efficacious action, especially when civic participation takes the form of resistance. In making choices about how to exercise their citizenship, youth weigh risks against one another, considering the potential costs and benefits of action and inaction. In the process, they illustrate that risk is relational and context-specific. As one risk is minimized, another becomes heightened. Doing nothing in the face of oppression, for instance, minimizes risks of physical harm but maximizes risks that come with isolation, silence, and invisibility. Calculating risk is a strategy that young people use to manage the politics of wait citizenship. The schema of a civic risk calculus is not meant to signify a rational decision-making process, nor is it meant to identify individuals as risk-averse or risk-embracing types of people. Rather, it is a heuristic designed to reflect the precarious openings young people detect in the spaces between dangerous actions and coercive structures. Youth "bids for citizenship" (Abu El-Haj, 2015), everyday "ways of making claims for belonging" (p. 35), thus traverse along calculations of risk and their willingness, capacity, and sense of obligation to mediate those risks, informed by their encounters with historical injustice in and outside of schools.

Risk

Across the four school communities highlighted in this study, three salient risks to civic action emerge: (1) the criminalization of involvement as socially disruptive, ranging from accusations of meddling to alleged terrorism; (2) risks of physical harm, often through repression by those wishing to silence justice-oriented movements and their spokespeople; and (3) the risk of futility, that individual sacrifice and struggle will ultimately prove useless. Given the diverse geographies of past and present violence, young actors in each space interpret and manage these risks in a variety of ways.

Yet there is also commonality functioning across cases. Young people at each school speak about the dangers of standing out, of being too visible, and the protective strategies of blending in, staying quiet, and gauging how others view them. Further complicating matters, invisibility functions both as a mode of protection and a risk, in that *quienquieras* are anonymous, but they can be killed without turning heads. Material wealth alternates as protection, so that one can purchase private security, and a risk, in that it attracts criminals. The normalcy of risks reconfigures criteria for what constitutes secure, effective, and socially acceptable participation. To mediate the risk of ineffectiveness, one can turn to illegal strategies for taking civic action, but this in turn heightens the risk of criminalization and provokes a greater risk of repressive response. To protect against criminalization and physical harm, one can withdraw from the civic sphere, sacrificing effectiveness for security. And to subvert criminalization, one might turn to illegal strategies to educate the public about the legal right to protest, at the risk of being cast as delinquent. At the heart of these risks and the adaptive strategies they demand lies a tradeoff between the risks one endures in the present and the risks one is willing to undertake to change that present.

For most students at the International Academy, their family's wealth comes with an inherent risk, one that requires vigilance and investment in the form of private security, armored cars, and gated communities. These young people claim to live without fear, but they also are in the constant company of armed bodyguards and have normalized their strategies for self-protection. Their economic capacity to employ these protective measures enables them to move freely and draw lines between safe and unsafe spaces. Yet despite their ability to move freely in "safe" spaces, these students long for freedoms they cannot access, such as the opportunity to drive in an unarmored car or with the windows open.

At times students speak of their need to "make a show" by having a bodyguard, so that the symbolic display becomes a form of prevention, guaranteed protection that rarely requires demonstration. Unlike students of poor or working-class families, many of whom locate security in anonymity, most students at International Academy claim that the show is a necessary device, because elites cannot easily blend in. Meanwhile, Alejandro contends that the show is merely a status symbol among fellow elites, yet another right that can be purchased rather than claimed.

In contrast to the relative security of his classmates, Alejandro's landscape of risks and his approach to their calculus is starkly different. Given his parents' commitment to activism, Alejandro inherits the risk of political repression for giving voice to injustice. Like many activists, Anastela and Rodolfo are highly vigilant of their surroundings and distrustful of anyone outside their most trusted networks, dispositions they have acquired through difficult lessons learned during the Conflicto Armado, whose value has transcended the wartime era. They have intentionally imparted their social-justice orientation to Alejandro, along with its necessary precautions. Alejandro applies these lessons seriously, identifying his own need to know with whom he is speaking at all times and adjusting his discourse to fall within the bounds of the person's inevitably dark past or present, as if the moral universe he invokes has to be reconfigured for each interaction. This skill has proven important, given that his classmates are part of the country's elite. Over the years Alejandro has sought balance in his desire to make friends and his parents' perpetual need for caution.

Anastela's initial elation that Alejandro took the initiative to circulate the "Open Letter" is later negated by her concern that his interest might be construed as meddling and risk repercussions. At times it is uncertain whose actions carry risks to whom; for example, does Alejandro's letter risk harm to his parents for their involvement, the indigenous populations it aims to protect, or Alejandro himself? Ultimately, the risk is not individual but collective, and the willingness for one to take action regularly imposes risks on the other. For the most part, Alejandro understands his parents' willingness to risk their safety for the greater good. But despite his strong personal commitment to social justice, his desire to eventually work on behalf of global indigenous rights, and his moral superiority at living with his "eyes open," he does not see usefulness in civic action. In this way, the subjective fear attached to risk is not the same for Alejandro and his parents. Anastela and Rodolfo acutely fear repression, concerned that they have been named terrorists, are under surveillance, and may "bring danger" to those they are trying to help. Anastela never doubts the importance or usefulness of their work, though Alejandro does so almost constantly, reminding her of the sacrifices they make as a family for the slim possibility that their participation will make a difference.

At times Alejandro makes efforts to protect his parents from the risks of their work, on the grounds that it is both dangerous and ineffective. In these instances Alejandro's fatalism becomes a coping mechanism (see

Monroe, 2014), in that it allows him to distance himself from his parents' high-risk involvement, as well as mitigate his own everyday risks. He claims to undertake the letter project as a self-demonstration that civic action is ineffective. And he regularly acknowledges the inevitability of death, often with morbid austerity. According to Alejandro, the sprawling power of those who repress means that they can reach anyone, even the most cautious and protected.

Although Alejandro cannot achieve invisibility or neutrality, given his parents' visibility as public figures, he is able to evade risk through escape, by studying abroad. As Anastela and Rodolfo continue to root themselves deeper in the struggle to fight for a better Guatemala, they have wholeheartedly committed to supporting this form of protection as exit—not for themselves but for their son.[1]

At Paulo Freire Beti casts the current state of affairs in Guatemala as a collective state of psychosis, suggesting the toll of constant risk calculation and describing how fears of violence breed new threats, sometimes masked as precautions, such as carrying arms to ride the bus. This classification resonates with student experience, in that their lives have come to be increasingly defined by the risks they are willing to take and the precautions they apply to mediate those risks.

Though their education at a left-leaning institution is intended to prepare them to take on the risks of intellectual critique and various liberal forms of participation, these students also exhibit strategies of risk avoidance. They have internalized the recurring message from adults to "see nothing, say nothing, and do nothing," echoing survival strategies adopted during the war. With a long list of *don'ts*, adults have guided young people toward inaction as a responsible mode of engagement: don't fight back when a delinquent assaults you, don't draw attention when a stranger harasses you, don't ask questions when dead bodies turn up in the street, don't interact with people who look like gang members, don't interfere when you hear a belt unbuckling on the street, and don't call the police when you are the victim of a violent crime. These warnings translate into a need for self-awareness of one's physical appearance, such as Pedro's realization that wearing a ski mask caused others to see him as a gang member, Javier's mother's forbidding his use of a bandana for fear that he would be mistaken for a delinquent, and Cristal's desire for a tattoo that she knows would allow authorities to cast her as a prostitute. These risks also demand constant vigilance of one's surroundings, generating both suspicion and caution in everyday exchanges. Students like Paulina have achieved a level of normalcy, such as her relative mobility within the capital on the condition that she is accompanied by her mother, father, or brother and her frequent social engagements with the neighborhood church. Her family has instituted a set of precautions and social boundaries to ensure her relative safety. For other students, the list of precautions grows so long and fraught that they reportedly refuse to leave the house, as in Luisa's case, where she describes her neighborhood as characteristically unsafe. Still others identify their socioeconomic status as a perpetual risk, making people "like them" attractive targets for petty crime, irrelevant of the precautions they take.

Recognizing the limits, at times self-imposed, on one's ability to take action shapes the subjectivity of these young people's experience as civic actors, at times in profoundly disempowering ways. As Cristal explains, "safety" requires "let[ting] yourself be a victim and accept[ing] that you can't do anything about it." The realization that the state's fragility has fundamentally shifted basic security assurances from the duty of the state to the citizen incites a deep resentment toward the state for tolerating this inversion of the civil contract. Young people revise their expectations of the state and fellow citizens, noting the risks of nonconformity, whether thinking differently, expressing dissent, or physically standing out. All forms of deviance risk one becoming more noticeable, memorable, and thereby more targetable. Students speak frequently about the need to remain safe coming at the cost of "be[ing] yourself." In these moments youth contemplate the ways adults have instructed them to wait and withhold, to restrain from reacting too quickly, as a measure of safety.

Despite all precautions, however, there is a sense of inevitability about one's eventual victimization, evidenced in Luisa's assurance that Pedro will both become a victim and change his civic stance once he has endured the existential experience of powerlessness. Pedro maintains that his deliberately broad "social trust" (Flanagan et al., 2010; Flanagan & Stout, 2010) serves to offset his fears, while Luisa "sees only the bad" in people. Luisa subverts this character judgment with an appraisal of the casualties that befell those who naively believed that others were inherently good. Her words reveal how the state of "Guate-psychosis" fundamentally alters social trust, so that trust is a risk rather than a protective factor. In her view, wait citizenship implies inevitable submission, knowing that violence will touch one's life, that no one in Guatemala escapes the experience of victimization.

Victimization yields a strong sense of powerlessness, but it does not uniformly lead to withdrawal. Both Luisa and Cristal are angry at their recurrent experiences as victims, but their anger manifests in different ways. As Luisa further removes herself from public and social interactions, Cristal becomes emboldened. Cristal openly resents the message that she is expected to succumb to whatever she is forced to endure, whereas Luisa resolves to consent to life in cautious isolation, the only recourse to security amid pervasive *violentaciones*. One notable difference between Luisa and Cristal is their level of perceived mobility in their home neighborhoods, but these contrasting stances also speak to the tension between students whose lives have been marked by extreme physical violence and those who have experienced "only" common violence.

At Sun and Moon similar messages abound regarding the protective strategies of risk aversion and particularly the construction of neutrality and withdrawal as civic virtues in the shared commitment to avoid conflict. Youth in this community routinely speak about wanting to change their lives but feel powerless to act, given the lack of support and the lack of viable choices available to them. Consequently, they explain that the "only thing you can do" is search for ways to withdraw from issues that risk sparking conflict, even if avoidance ensures their own continued subordination. In the fragile present moment where mob violence is an increasingly regular occurrence, nearly anything can incite violence, even Gregorio's peppers.

Like the students at Paulo Freire, these young people carry long lists of what *not* to do: not to meddle in private affairs, not to critique the mines, not to speak about the roles of their families during the Conflicto Armado. While they are instructed not to walk after dark and not to travel to the pueblo's borders, for the most part the precautions in Río Verde center on avoiding conflict through noninvolvement. The legacy of the Conflicto Armado speaks volumes through the endurance of popular concerns that collective action is a form of social disruption, and those who get involved are agitators risking harm not only to themselves but to all those around them. Given the array of risks and the lessons of the Conflicto Armado in this village, the "good citizen" is an exceedingly insulated version of Joel Westheimer and Joseph Kahne's (2004) "personally responsible citizen" (p. 241), in that he or she abides by laws, abstains from conflict, and minds his or her own business. In this context, the orientation to oneself as a singular civic unit might be more aptly named the *privately* responsible citizen.

Although students struggle with the notion that withdrawal is their most promising adaptive strategy, sympathizing with the normalista movement and recalling ambitious efforts of other pueblos to organize against mines and hydroelectric corporations leads them full circle to where they began: acknowledging their powerlessness to change the course of their lives when caught within repressive and exclusionary structures. The risks of civic involvement are stacked against the narrow possibility that action will lead to change. For example, when Amílcar recounts his father reporting his neighbors to the human rights office, his classmates knowingly recognize his inability to penetrate an unjust system, along with the potential repercussions of his neighbors for "meddling," as the price he paid for doing what he believed was right. The school's emphasis on structural impediments is further enforced by the circulation of stories like this one, reminding others that actions carry tangible risks and often yield little in return. While change is unlikely, risk is almost certain.

The inevitability of risk creates an unlikely opening for expressing agency through inaction and retreat. Recognizing the limits of one's power requires adjusting where one invests energy. At times perceptions of the futility of civic action and high levels of social distrust facilitate a redrawing of borders around communities of accountability to more intimate groups, where young people can be effective actors and ensure their relative safety. Ricardo almost exclusively interacts with his church group, though even they are not sufficiently trustworthy to leave the family house in their care for a weekend. As Leonardo and María Carmen illustrate, the only trust that exists in the pueblo lies within the bonds of family.

Alongside the risk of taking action lies its implicit counterpoint: the risk of things staying the same. While at Tzolok Ochoch the present risk structure urges a call to action, at Sun and Moon the conviction that active citizens "invite" conflict operates as a strong deterrent to participate in any action that carries risk. In this way, inaction, withdrawal from the public sphere, and neutrality on issues of civic significance emerge as choices unburdened with the moral accountability of becoming "involved." Not acting implies an active choice to be apolitical. Though inaction in the face of ongoing injustice implies remaining a victim of current conditions of racial inequality and injustice, it comes with a guarantee that one cannot be cast as a criminal. If one is neutral and apolitical, then he or she is an authentic victim. Again, the legacy of the Conflicto Armado emerges as a significant force in the constellation of available civic choices. If the movement fails, as the guerrilla movement failed, the real victims will not be those who fought injustice and suffered but those who suffered unjust conditions in abstention. The only mechanism for change is to forge an apolitical pathway, not through the risks of collective resistance but through individual escape (salir).

For many students at Tzolok Ochoch, their home villages are increasingly marred by drug-related violence, vigilante justice, and military securitization. The boarding school environment allows students to temporarily put aside everyday risks, yet the school mission to forge the next generation of community leaders introduces a new set of risks for young people to contemplate. In contrast to their peers at Sun and Moon, students at Tzolok Ochoch do not view the guerrilla movement as a failure but rather an incomplete struggle, one that their generation is capable of continuing. Though not all students at Tzolok Ochoch enthusiastically embrace their roles as agents of social change, there is a strong sentiment that the rural poor needs to act in solidarity against the multitude of forces working against their advancement. The lucha is their path to a better future, but it is also their present reality—they are born into the lucha, where merely surviving is a struggle. Andrea speaks to the unrelenting challenges the rural poor face simply to remain in place. While other groups struggle and move ahead, they struggle and continue to suffer. Accordingly, struggle implies both the present state of suffering and a path to a different future: the first a condition of their lives, the second a means for changing them. In this sense, the current conditions constitute a greater risk than those presented by taking action. The unsustainability of the present, coupled with the possibility of change, sufficiently tips the balance in favor of action, along with a readiness for the risk that this path demands. Again, school discourse plays a distinctive role in shaping this path, emphasizing the risks of inaction and the benefits of collective action.

Despite recognition that survival at the margins implies a struggle, this student population unwaveringly constructs civic action around a fundamental shift in Guatemala's current power arrangements. Within this reconfiguration of the civil contract, loyalty is directed to the pueblo over the state. Accordingly, if action is authentically civic, it is collective, and if it is authentically collective, it aims to challenge the status quo—and any attempt to shift power relations in Guatemala inherently carries risk. Whereas at Sun and Moon, the call to pull oneself out of poverty, secure employment, and support one's family fall under the rubric of responsible citizenship, for students at Tzolok Ochoch, these are construed as self-centered actions that place the individual over the common well-being. The law-abiding citizen does more harm than good by upholding rather than resisting the unjust civil contract. Moreover, exits are safe pathways that do not entail risk. Importantly for students at Tzolok Ochoch, there is an implicit belief that one has to take on risk to become a legitimate civic actor. While at Sun and Moon, good citizens are encouraged to avoid risk, at Tzolok Ochoch risk is a prerequisite to authentic citizenship.

Keeping one's eyes open to injustice at times demands the need to close one's eyes to the threat of political violence. This yearning to remain empowered, while intentionally deleting embedded elements of the reality that one is trying to change, is illustrated through the school's silencing of Aurora's murder. Even when Aurora's death is acknowledged among students, there is almost a consensus avoidance of the political dimension of the crime. Aurora's murder profoundly echoes frames of meaning from the past conflict, reinforcing the idea that she can be remembered as an innocent victim only if her political agency is erased. The alternative is that she was a political agitator who got what she deserved for meddling, *por algo será*. Interpreting murder in Guatemala is a complex political act with collective implications for hope and despair. In this way, unknowing is enmeshed in the risk structure. Aurora's family, too, has worked to depoliticize her death, refusing a state-issued bodyguard on the grounds that others might think they were "involved in something" or "looking for trouble." By maintaining that Aurora's death was circumstantial, she is remembered as a victim and does not serve as a warning against political involvement, nor can she be cast as a criminal agitator. Yet, privately, she is a martyr. Alfredo, Ramiro, and Pancho gravely accept that one day, they too will suffer threats and face the decision to continue the lucha or to withdraw and protect themselves and their families. For them this future path, bound to risk, is guaranteed.

Hope

Young people carve out tenuous paths, at times engaging in acts of self-deceit to sustain their hopes that Guatemala can change and that individuals and communities possess the agency to shape this imagined future. In some cases, survival depends on ironic reversals of agency and hope. Kristen Monroe (2014) describes the central role of fatalism and hopelessness in survivors' testimonies, and John Paul Lederach (2005) identifies the "ethos of pessimism" (p. 54) that functions as a protective strategy in long-term peace building. According to Lederach, "hope coupled with indifference" is analogous to not cynicism or passivity but a "grounded realism" (p. 55) integral to survival. Recognizing the adaptive value of strategic pessimism, many young Guatemalans see the dangers of hopes that are relegated to permanent waithood. In some instances, young people call on one another to disarticulate hope and expectations, to accept the limits of civic agency in the face of structures that constrain, and to resign to the reality that Guatemala has not, and will not, change. Hope and fatalism are thus tied together, intensified by risk structures that encourage patience as a long-term adaptive strategy.

For many students at the International Academy, hope for Guatemala's future depends on letting go of the past. Recognizing insecurity as a deterrent to economic investment, Guatemala's capacity to develop and modernize demands addressing security threats in the present, a commitment that, in turn, demands forgoing justice struggles for past losses. Profe Castillo upholds this logic in his warning that historical memory "guarantee[s] the delay of Guatemala's development." Though the teacher's critique of historical memory leads to his justification that Guatemala's future depends on a unified national imaginary, students interpret ethnic heterogeneity as the persistent cause of the country's delayed modernization. Ethnic divisions and the application of cultural rights to uphold them are considered an obstacle to Guatemala's development.

Alejandro's decision to pass around the "Open Letter" is both a defiant act, poised to garner support for the indigenous struggle among the children of their repressors, and a defeatist act, a self-fulfilling prophecy that his peers will not embrace the issue. A window into the country's elite, Alejandro's classmates confirm for him that repression embedded in development projects unfolding across the country remains invisible for them. Although Alejandro admits disappointment—but not surprise—that his friends have their "eyes closed" to the system of injustice on which their fortunes rely, he mediates his resentment with a rationale that they do not want to admit that Guatemala is "going to hell." He reasons that their willful denial is a coping mechanism, permitting them to continue inhabiting their narrow, elite worlds. This notion is echoed by the principal, who articulates the limits of what the school can do to promote social awareness when students' hopes for reforming Guatemala jeopardizes their own privilege.

Yet Alejandro's letter also functions to confirm his skepticism of civic action when positioned against the rigid walls of power. Describing his parents as periodically "delusional" romantics, Alejandro views himself as a realist who has stared into the eyes of power, facing what his parents refuse to see: that their position in society is fixed. The arbitrary nature of victories credited to popular movements reaffirms Alejandro's belief that "they" are controlling the outcomes in ways designed to intentionally take away hope. For Alejandro, hoping that Guatemala will change is as useless as his parents' commitment to the protest marches and the naive optimism they type into their solidarity e-mail blasts. Even when the state of siege in Barillas is lifted, Alejandro is skeptical that protests or open letters made any difference, concluding that it must have been a political strategy for the state to remove it when they did. His suspicion serves multiple purposes, so that arbitrariness reinforces the fraught relationship between collective action and social change. On the one hand, Alejandro is able to renounce his own obligation to participate on the grounds that citizens are powerless to the impulses of a state so clearly orchestrated by criminals. Meanwhile, his pessimism intensifies his desire for his parents to confront their own powerlessness to change the country and to narrow their civic accountability to a more intimate circle—the family—rather than the pueblo.

At Paulo Freire students fluctuate between their desire to take on active roles in civil society and their recognition that the inversion of the civil contract has placed severe limits on their ability to participate in civic spaces. For example, when students gather to clean the park graffiti, Javier talks about the power of collective action and the need for local togetherness to overcome division and indifference. Though dismayed by the lack of community engagement among neighbors, he does not resort to fatalistic explanations until several hours later when he is assaulted on the street, confessing that violence is "just the way it is here." Exceptionalizing Guatemala as a place where violence is an everyday fact of life does not denote a surrender of Javier's agency but his recognition of the limits on civic action. In retrospect, Javier recasts the park project as a facade where citizens—not just state actors—fall short on their promises. Moreover, what use is there in repeatedly clearing gang graffiti, when the state is unwilling to protect citizens from gangs?

Even Beti supports this need to adapt to Guatemala's "normal," noting that "Guate-psicosis" demands vigilance of oneself and others. While Beti hopes that her students will find inspiration in the history of the urban working-class struggles, Paulo Freire students appear genuinely empowered until they are reminded of the life-and-death choices inherent in calling the police to a crime scene, speaking up on a bus, or walking along their neighborhood street. Their hopes for the future sink when confronted with the scale and nature of the forces that stand in the way of change, forces that remind them of the safety that resides in nonparticipation.

In several instances, hope and hopelessness come head-to-head. Luisa openly tries to persuade both Pedro and Xila to submit to the idea that Guatemala is beyond hope. Xila struggles to maintain pride in her country while working against strong perceptions that Guatemala is "bad," a reputation she perceives is generated by those who pass judgment without taking action. In these moments young people struggle to cast Guatemala's unfulfilled promises as either hopeful potential, demanding patience; or as disillusionment, requiring withdrawal. Waiting is essential, though hope is optional. Luisa rationalizes her fatalism through predictions of perpetual victimhood, describing how the order operating within Guatemala's "disorder" has inverted the civil contract. In contrast, Xila constructs hopelessness as the risk, noting that as long as there is hope that Guatemala can change, there will be Guatemalans working to make it so. These conversations about whether Guatemala is "beyond hope" are among the most visible conflicts I witnessed among young people in this community. In several cases these conflicts were intentionally directed at me, as students looked to me and wondered about the book I promised to write about their lives. They asked, "What do you think, Michelle? Can we change? How will you tell people we are?"

At Sun and Moon hopelessness is captured in the refrain that young people "don't have a chance to get out [salir]." Any extrication from adversity risks martyrdom, which will not instill hope but rather contribute to collective despair that nothing can change and that anyone who resists will not live to see the proof that it is so. Young people draw on the distant, recent, and ongoing history of harm suffered by those who have spoken out, noting that Guatemala has already undergone too much loss to risk taking action for a better future. The past serves as a heavy reminder that accepting the unjust present, avoiding politics, and "staying in the middle" are the only ways to ensure any future at all. There is life in passively waiting.

María Carmen and Leonardo are the exception in their ability to draw hope from the past, emphasizing how much has changed since the Conflicto Armado, thanks to the dedication and courage of the guerrillas. They argue that young Guatemalans need to understand how much the country has gained over time, that many of today's taken-for-granted rights were earned with their ancestors' blood. But their children resist this story of historical progress, pointing out how much has remained the same. María Carmen struggles to maintain her demarcations around the geography of safe and violent times and places, but with Martín's insistence she too accedes that violence continues to affect their lives today, constricting their ability to keep doors open for fresh air and leave the house unattended. For most Guatemalans the victories that both the guerrillas and the urban working class claim "have either been destroyed . . . stand in permanent disrepair . . . are continually falling apart . . . or exist in name only" (Levenson, 2013a, p. 12). After much waiting for the state to offer the pueblo a voice, the mine has become the new site onto which hopes and expectations for a better future are imagined. Today the people wait for the mine to offer them employment, a way to feed their families, a private *salida*. Together they wait.

Surrendering hope and retreating from the public sphere creates a narrow opening for private escape. Finding an exit is unlikely, as their teacher's presence in the village reminds them. Though César encourages his students to get out (*salir*), there is shared recognition that they are all "stuck." At best, Río Verde will become a boomtown whose rapid development will spark improvements like jobs and infrastructure and long-term consequences such as pollution, prostitution, delinquency, and alcoholism, followed by eventual joblessness at the mine's inevitable exit.

The people of Río Verde are repeatedly positioned as "waiting clients" (Auyero, 2011, p. 6) rather than active citizens, in the promises made by the powerful institutions in their lives. Hope that the future will be different requires patience, but their patience is growing as thin as the arms of the town's malnourished children. Civic action is ineffective, as actions repeatedly collide with walls of power only to spring back at the people themselves. Young people report feeling so unsupported in their efforts that they have been instructed to relinquish their agency almost entirely. Even Gregorio's peppers will fail, and the reasons why are endless—if they are not destroyed by individual spite, the agency of fate itself will spoil them. Rather than take action and risk disappointment, students at Sun and Moon have learned that it is better to retreat to intimate communities such as family, and sometimes even further inward, into the private self. If there are no expectations, there are no disappointments.

Students at Tzolok Ochoch believe that they need to take on the risks of the lucha to provide the pueblo with hope. Among the various pressures placed upon them, young people risk falling short of others' expectations, taking on the task of "becom[ing] examples," and employing their bodies as sources of hope, as well as the hosts for collective despair. To be an authentic civic actor, the lucha requires commitment to a selfless, perilous, and collective struggle. Many who came before them have promised to commit to the pueblo, only to later fail and abandon them in search of private gains. Like Rigoberta Menchú's alleged profits from her Nobel Peace Prize and pharmaceutical chain, like former guerrilleros who supposedly received better settlements during peace negotiations than victims' groups, like the community leaders who are rumored to have "joined the oligarchy," it appears all too common for those who gain access to power to fall into corruption. Forgetting their promises to the people, the lure of material wealth offers a private escape. Young people struggle to identify positive civic models who have not eventually disappointed or else been disappeared before they were able to disappoint. In their construction of recurrent abandonment, young people create an expectation that civic leaders must remain poor, marginalized, and at-risk to be construed as authentic advocates. If civic agents accrue too much power, they appear corrupt and have fallen into the system they were supposedly struggling against. If their actions are effective and appear too easily accepted or if they are not physically repressed along the way, they must have been corrupt all along. These severe constraints on authenticity imply that only those who remain at the margins or die trying are the true luchadores. Underlying these beliefs is the notion that politics in Guatemala is inherently corrupt and individuals inherently corruptible. Yet these students firmly believe they are different. Their commitment to the pueblo will ensure that they adhere to the true lucha, a path that their ancestors shaped long before the Conflicto Armado.

Though not all students who commit to the struggle regard their choices in existential terms, there is no denying that the struggle carries the possibility of violent harm. In this sense, there is an unavoidable, though not necessarily conscious, confrontation with death in the choice to pursue a life path where risks at times appear suicidal. Contributing to the lucha offers something larger than a political sacrifice to the *now*. In taking action, there is a sense of civic purpose and collective obligation to disrupt the pattern of historical injustice. Struggling for a better Guatemala implies acting toward a better future, even if one will not live to experience it. Rather than occupy a state of perpetual anticipation or avoidance of the political repression they will inevitably encounter, young people at Tzolok Ochoch orient their lives toward the legacies they will leave behind, even if doing so carries the risk of death. Like the legacies they have inherited, the next generation will undergo the ultimate subversive act and find inspiration in the enormity of the losses endured and the astonishing resilience of those who walked knowingly into harm's way to dream a better life into being. Amid a generation of youth cast as wait citizens, the lucha will continue.

This book is filled with instances in which young people are exposed to the historical dimensions of injustice, while simultaneously shielded from them. In and out of school, young people are routinely called on to know, trust, and act on what adults tell them about the past, without opportunities to analyze it for themselves. Even the most critical orientations toward injustice unfold in classrooms where youth have limited interpretive agency, and nearly homogenous student populations make it difficult to counter dominant narratives. Educators at Tzolok Ochoch and Paulo Freire, for example, radical in their self-identifications, resort to authoritarian pedagogy to dismiss counterperspectives and move students toward conscientious consensus. Authoritarian classrooms contradict citizenship educational goals, so that grappling with injustice is made more challenging for students who are developing their own sense of "what happened . . . why, and why it was wrong" (Davies, in press b, p. 6).[2] Elizabeth Jelin's (2003) reminder that postgenerations inevitably judge the actions of previous generations sits in tension with teachers' and parents' frequent reluctance to grant young people the moral autonomy to scrutinize the past. Accordingly, young people's lack of historical understanding and their reliance on emotive connections to particular interpretations has more to do with the silences and partial narratives they encounter than their disinterest in the past. For every young person conveying an attitude of not-knowing, there are adults not-*telling*. Not-knowing is a consequence of an "education system [that] *deprives* youth of the past" (Giracca, 2009, para. 3).

In their schools young people are not oblivious to the moral complexity of addressing the divided past. Some students like Alejandro fault their teachers for silencing a significant historical period that continues to impact their lives, while students like Rosa contribute to their teacher's efforts to circumvent the war in favor of ostensibly more useful and relevant lessons. And some, like Álvaro, are attuned to the reality that schools are "part of a larger framework of social relations that are structurally exploitative" (Apple, 1995, p. 9), recognizing the limits on what can be said and done within school walls. Yet it is problematic that teachers conceive no formal curricular structure for addressing the armed conflict and its consequences, no set of agreed-on facts other than dates, and that moral and ethical questions about freedom, dissent, and egregious human rights violations are routinely sidestepped in favor of promoting vague promises of "never again," which is taken to mean anything from avoidance of war to not intervening with a neighbor's garden. The narrative of this past has become reduced to a mere phrase.

Schools are often looked to as buffers from insecurity and risk that students experience in their daily lives and an unequivocal social good, where messages of peace and youth empowerment circulate unproblematically. Less frequently, school culture, opportunity structures, curricula, and pedagogy are recognized as contributors to unequal power relations and intergroup tensions (Burde, 2014; Davies, 2004b, 2007; King, 2014). The same history, narrated differently, both unites and divides: it forges collective identity and a sense of solidarity among historically oppressed groups and spurs youth into action to defend their sense of right and wrong; it also serves to justify discrimination and exclusion, rationalize current social hierarchies, dismiss rights movements, and enforce boundaries between identity groups. Teachers' decisions about how to engage with the past—if at all—are motivated by genuine concerns about what Guatemala needs. They do not want students burdened by a morally troubling past, distracted by it in the face of more pressing concerns, confused by it as they encounter widespread misinformation, or endangered by it in the landscape of current risks. Each of the social studies teachers in these schools believes their instructional choices help individual students and society at large in reconciling with historical injustice—whether through purposeful memory or purposeful silence, through pointed recognition of the state's role or through deliberate erasure of accountability. At the very least, teachers believe they are doing no harm. But if the education sector is expected to contribute to transitional justice efforts, schools need to take an ethical stand against histories of injustice. In the context of transition, "conflict sensitive" education's central ethic of *do no harm* is not enough; what is needed is "justice-sensitive" education (Davies, in press a).

However we view educational responsibility in the aftermath of conflict, one question we cannot evade is the effect on young people's civic development when the complexity of a history whose judgment is ruminating in courts is routinely withheld. As I have shown, young people coming of age in a profoundly unequal, high-risk society do not navigate or adapt to these conditions without asking questions about how they came to be. In other words, youth civic development entails questioning the "historical dimension" of injustice and oppression (Bashir, 2008, p. 49), even when emotive connections preclude the complex work of historical inquiry and the disentanglement of legacies from causes and outcomes. On one hand, the distinction between historical continuity and rupture seems to be an issue of historiographic concern, irrelevant to the civic opportunities that young people face today. Whether the conditions of chronic violence and deep structural inequality are direct outgrowths of, or more discretely connected to, the Conflicto Armado does not change the prevalence of criminal networks, the violent repression targeting popular movements, the limits on one's social and spatial mobility, and the unequal quality of schools serving distinct identity groups. But young people's perceptions of historical continuity and change profoundly shift how they interact with these structures and orient themselves as civic agents in a still fragile democracy. Varying constructions of historical injustice generate different imagined possibilities for the long-awaited future, and the role of people *like them* in shaping that future. In this sense, whether youth envision themselves as subject to their circumstances, subjects of them, or creative agents who actively shape and define them may determine the thin wall between perceptions of an inevitable past and an irreversible future or the conviction that the future, like the past, can be shaped through conscious and reflective decision making.

Afterword

In the months preceding Efraín Ríos Montt's 2013 trial, transitional justice in Guatemala once again made global headlines. *Justice delayed, justice for genocide*. Young people who knew about the decades of struggle to forge a legal space for justice watched the blank pages of history become public debate. Others stood by and learned that Ríos Montt was not a thief but a *génocidaire*; the civil war was not "no one's" fault, nor could it be blamed on the Guatemalan people for their violent culture. The world was watching Guatemala—and for once, it seemed, the concern was not its terrifying escalation of crime or the tattooed male bodies whose transgressions know no borders but the political will to deliver on promises of postwar democracy and historical justice. The Ixil Maya community, the human rights organizations they collaborated with, their legal representatives, and the attorney general took on great risk for a chance to be heard, and the world was listening. Justice would be done.

Inside Guatemala there was optimism in the accomplishment of penetrating national courts, raising public awareness, and defaming war criminals. But these hopes for overdue justice were set against the strategic value of pessimism in a society where young people understood that "abnormal is the normal." In every promise lurks potential despair, a flash-forward to the disappointment of yet another change unmet. This is the waiting demanded of postwar citizens. This trial would be a true test—was

Guatemala capable of achieving justice, or was it beyond hope? Young people in each of these four communities predicted that the case would wither in court like the others, dragging on until Ríos Montt died a peaceful death. They teased that house arrest in Guatemala was tantamount to living in a gated colonia, privileged and protected. With sarcasm they noted, "He is safer than we are."

When Ríos Montt was found guilty, students shared their disbelief that justice, though severely delayed, had been done. There was no more denying genocide, not when Ríos Montt was sentenced to eighty years in prison, not when the whole world knew what happened. The verdict opened a world of opportunity for a functioning justice system and social justice as a long-awaited outcome of the transition. It revealed the way democracy and historical memory were coiled together. It also pried open a space in schools to participate in "historical dialogue" (Barkan, 2009). Some of the International Academy students lamented this as a setback and joined the conservative Right, demanding that guerrillas also be brought to justice— that one devil's demise warranted equal judgment of the other's actions. But ten days later, when the guilty verdict was annulled, life returned to normal. Cristal from Paulo Freire wrote to me, "This is why it is better not to care so much . . . because one never knows what will happen in Guatemala." Others worried that the trial was a step backward, that it would now be more difficult to procure justice or garner international support. Alfredo from Tzolok Ochoch wrote, "Now everyone knows how we are. They know . . . we have no justice here." In Michael Jackson's (2007) view, fatalism can be "one way of avoiding the judgmentalism that so often perpetuates violence, one way of accepting the forces over which one cannot prevail, one way of enabling life to be reborn from the ashes of history" (p. 39). Young people's predictions that the trial would dwindle allowed them to focus on the immediate decisions in their lives over which they had some say—college, work, seeking a livelihood that would support their families.

Two years after Ríos Montt's overturned conviction, Guatemalans organized and strategized on social media, commanding that Guatemala "wake up." I watched these same young people type in messages demanding that their current president resign, announcing that the people were tired of waiting and sleeping, that they would no longer tolerate criminals in both "state offices and the streets." *Guatemala has awoken!* Global media again spotlighted Guatemala. For months citizens gathered in the streets in protest, and the world celebrated a vibrant civil society that united in its discontent and demands for change, important signs of democratic gains and solidarity across generations and ethnic and class lines, a "Guatemalan Spring." In many ways, Guatemala accomplished the impossible in September 2015: the pressure of civil society managed to unseat their president, forcing him to resign with the knowledge that he would be sent to prison for his involvement in a multimillion-dollar customs scandal. On the morning Guatemalans woke up with no president, Alejandro from the International Academy wrote to me, as if he knew what the world was thinking and wanted to set me straight, "I do not think this is a victory of the people. . . . The will of the populace is nothing but screams of anger and frustration at closed doors, windows, and walls. Slowly people are starting to become an active part of society, but many do not realize yet that we do not hold the power to lead our country toward what we want." Meanwhile, Gregorio from Sun and Moon wrote to tell me that nothing had changed in Río Verde. Everything was calm in the village, and the people were continuing to search for ways to escape poverty (salir). The scandal in the presidency remained largely irrelevant to their everyday struggles.

Placing these recent political changes in historical and global context is important. Guatemala is the first country to prosecute a former head of state for genocide in a national court. The conviction, although overturned, demonstrates the possibilities for justice and public acknowledgement in transitional democracies. Following this trial, which has since been suspended indefinitely, eighteen former military leaders were arrested for crimes against humanity, spanning massacres and disappearances, linked to evidence from exhumations of a mass grave found in a former military base. Q'eqchi' women who were systematically raped and held in sexual slavery have also brought their perpetrators into Guatemalan courts. Indigenous communities have come together to physically blockade entrances to mines, utilizing popular media to document and spread knowledge of rights abuses committed by extractive industries, and some have filed cases in international courts, challenging corporate development practices. These advances speak to the persistence of grassroots struggles, even in one of the most dangerous settings for human rights advocates, demonstrating that civil society does not have to wait for structures to change; rather, collective action can upend unjust structures through committed and persistent struggle. Former president Otto Pérez Molina's resignation and subsequent trial is also noteworthy. In court Pérez Molina voiced concern that "[if] this can happen to someone who resigned the presidency, what can happen to an ordinary citizen?" (Malkin, 2015, p. A18). This statement reflects the distorted logic of a society where impunity has served to protect elites at the expense of ordinary citizens. In fact, what is remarkable is precisely that a member of the political and military elite is not evading punishment. What is remarkable is that Pérez Molina has been held subject to the same justice proceedings that apply to any ordinary citizen.

What initially surprised me is how easily the successes of these recent transformations appear to be reinterpreted by the young people in this book. In their understanding, these changes are artificial, irrelevant, and orchestrated by powerful forces rather than a consequence of civil-society pressure. Pérez Molina was brought down to protect other elites, who have maintained their power in the shadows. More important, his downfall was not a revelation of his sinister links to historical injustice but a corruption scandal, an economic wrongdoing rather than outrage that he crossed a moral or ethical line by assigning differential value to human life. The current president has little political experience and is backed by military hard-liners, a sign that the conflict structure remains intact. In other words, these changes are not without significance, but nor are they revolutionary.

The gap between how these moments are regarded at home and abroad evokes questions about whether Guatemalans themselves—or any social group for that matter—are in a position to see change when they are immersed in it. Is incremental change visible without the passage of time? Yet if we ignore their frustrated, skeptical, and at times disinterested reactions, we miss something essential in how young people experience their lives as wait citizens. We miss the ways young people regard high-level gains as symbolic, in the absence of a redistribution of resources and opportunities. We miss the ways that citizenship and one's prospects for civic efficacy and inclusion are shaped through everyday encounters with injustice and democratic disjuncture. We miss the important links between young people's evolving civic attitudes and their interpretations of power relations, past and present. We miss the ways that youth look to their government for signals that their actions will be seen and heard. Despite global praise, these young people reminded me that these steps forward have been entangled with ongoing repression toward women, young men, lawyers, judges, journalists, activists, and community leaders. Progress toward justice, however conceived, sits uneasily alongside ongoing violations and repression. In Guatemala, violence and democracy cannot be viewed as distinct processes, because they have never been distinct processes. Their skepticism is a reminder that in societies undergoing transition, judging whether change is authentic and sustainable requires a "wait-and-see approach" (Lederach, 2005, p. 57), set against the "continuous and immediate" (p. 58) suspicion that changes are superficial. True, there are more people living with their "eyes open" to the inequities and injustices that permeate their society, but there are also more orejas and more structures to fear and distrust.

Over the years I have held out newspaper clippings and e-mailed articles to young people when Guatemala seems on the cusp of change or in the thick of it: "Look, a new law against femicide. Look, they captured narcos in the state police. Look, they sent Ríos Montt to prison." Although some youth draw a measure of hope from state-level reforms or news of a criminal's capture, others express doubt that the impact will be significant or long lasting, resenting that in Guatemala one is expected to celebrate their state's ability to uphold a basic law. Both a remnant of the past and a condition of the "postwar" present, this doubt functions paradoxically as fatalism and hopeful anticipation, promoting patience and impatience as civic virtues. What is "normal in every country" is exceptional in Guatemala. In these moments the refusal to praise small victories is one way of looking forward and saying, *We expect more. This is not enough.* Guatemalan youth continue to wait.

Acknowledgments

Mayra tells me that the large tree in front of her family home saved her life. She spreads her fingers across the thick base and tells me what that she remembers most clearly from her childhood, growing up during Guatemala's Conflicto Armado. Every night the local patrol marched past the house on their route through the village. She gestures to a narrow dirt road along a steep hill. Her father had been taken early, so it was just Mayra, her mother, and sisters to keep safe. And the tree kept them safe. When the patrol did their rounds, they climbed and hid in the branches. I study the tree's tenuous arms, wondering how they cradled six people. Remembering trees in my own backyard, that I climbed for the thrill of it, put into sharp relief the distance between our childhoods, our transitions to adulthood, and the futures available to us. But our lives became knotted together, again and again: me and Mayra, Alejandro, Natalia, Luis Fernando.

This work is dedicated to my Guatemalan families and friends, who invited me into their homes, communities, and classrooms and took the time to contemplate what makes historical injustice visible, even when unspoken; who sat with me on blistering afternoons and cool evenings, sorting through photographs and newspapers, patiently navigating my steady stream of questions and teaching me how to see what they saw; who shared secrets of things that happened and things that didn't, but might. Thank you for sharing your lives with me, for trusting me with your stories and struggles. Though I cannot list you by name, I hope you hear your voices in this work. Thank you for trusting me to carry your stories across borders, to narrate and translate them, to tell and retell them, to ask deep questions of them, and to place them alongside others in an effort to find the threads that connect and divide. I hope this book became what you hoped it would.

Throughout the research and writing process, I benefited from the generous and critical listening of Sara Lawrence-Lightfoot, Meira Levinson, and Karen Murphy, who taught me to braid together the empirical and aesthetic, the educational and political, and the scholarship and advocacy that undergird this work. Without you, I would not have found the voice (or the stamina) to tell this story. I am also grateful to Sarah Dryden-Peterson, who has helped me explore how young people imagine a better future through education, and to Lili Cole, for advocating for education's "place at the table" of transitional justice, and to the many committed individuals at Facing History and Ourselves, who supported me in my earliest stages of thinking about historical legacies and the fragility of democracy.

I have also benefited from the advice and wisdom of many scholars, practitioners, and advocates. Gastón Gordillo, Judith Maxwell, Klaus Neumann, Elizabeth Oglesby, Timothy Smith, Felisa Tibbitts, Judith Torney-Purta, and the many wonderful teachers I have found in the Council of Anthropology and Education, particularly Thea Abu El-Haj, Andrea Dyrness, Emma Fuentes, Marki LeCompte, Bradley Levinson, and Gregory Tanaka, inspired this work and contributed valuable feedback at various stages. A special thanks to Marjorie Faulstich Orellana, several anonymous readers, editors Kimberly Guinta and Marlie Wasserman, and Rutgers University Press for their careful reading of this manuscript and excellent recommendations. Everything in this book improved with your help. Dana Burde and Elisabeth King generously shared resources and insight into the publication process. Mariella Bacigalupo, Elizabeth Moje, Julia Paulson, Jim Williams, and Lizzie Worden—dear mentors and friends—sent notes of inspiration reminding me that this was an important book to write. Your words hang on my walls and mean more than I can say. I am also indebted to Deborah Levenson, Daniel Rothenberg, and especially Victoria Sanford, who guided me—cautiously and patiently—through this seemingly implausible, inverted world. Your commitments to historical justice continually inspire me. And thanks to the unflagging dedication of individuals such as Amílcar Méndez, Byron Titus, and Jorge Velasquez, and organizations such as the Comalapa Youth Group and HIJOS, who continue to struggle for a just Guatemala and who allowed me to research with and alongside them.

I owe a special debt of gratitude to Harvard University's David Rockefeller Center for Latin American Studies and June Erlick, for consistently and enthusiastically supporting this work and for creating a community where dialogue about memory and democracy in Latin America holds a central place. This work was generously supported by the United States Institute of Peace's Jennings Randolph Peace Scholarship and Harvard University's John H. Coatsworth Fellowship. Thank you for believing in this work and the power of education to contribute to creating a more just and peaceful world. Thanks also to *Harvard Educational Review* and *Comparative Education Review* for permission to revise and reprint text that first appeared in these journals.

Last, none of this would be possible without the love and support of my family and especially my parents, Lydia and Anthony, who accepted all paths I chose to travel and taught me to always, always trust in the power of good writing and good friends. And to my partner, Nate, who left tiny notes in the margins of early drafts, who gave me the space to listen for the right story to tell, and who listened with me for the right way to tell it. Thank you all. *Mil gracias.*

Notes

Chapter 1   Citizen, Interrupted

1 Names of individuals and rural villages have been changed to pseudonyms to protect the identity of participants. Data drawn from outside the principal research settings are attributed to actual place names.

2 Transitional justice refers to a context or set of processes initiated in the aftermath of authoritarian governance, armed conflict, or human rights violations. The transition implied is often toward a democratic system of governance and encompasses a set of "transitional" processes that address past injustices to stabilize society. These processes range across contexts and may include truth commissions, trials, reparations, memorialization, and other institutionalized expressions of historical justice. See de Greiff (2009) and Fletcher, Weinstein, & Rowen (2009).

3 The civil war was termed the "Armed Conflict" by the truth commission (CEH, 1999), a discourse utilized in school curricula and frequently adopted by youth.

4 The WHO considers a homicide rate of 10/100,000 inhabitants "epidemic." Guatemala's homicide rate in recent years hovers in the low 40s/100,000. See Cruz (2011); UNDP (2012); and UNODC (2010).

5 Policy documents define the category of youth in Guatemala with various age ranges, spanning from thirteen to thirty, though Guatemalan youth become legal citizens at age eighteen. See UNDP (2012, pp. 5, 12). See also Levenson (2013a, pp. 11–16), for a discussion of historical, legal, and social definitions of childhood and youth in Guatemala.

6 "Fragility" is a contested term. See Barakat, Zuki, & Paulson (2008) and Miller-Grandvaux (2009).

7 Personal communication, April 10, 2012, Somerville, MA.

8 While most primary schools in Guatemala are public and tuition-free, only one

third of Guatemalan high schools are public, and most of these institutions are located in urban areas (Poppema, 2009).

Chapter 2   Education and Conflict in Guatemala

1 While *mara* refers to gangs presumably affiliated with transnational criminal networks, *pandilla* implies locally organized youth networks engaged in petty crime. See Burrell (2009, pp. 100–101) for how these categories are (mis)applied.
2 At the time there was already growing dissatisfaction with President Árbenz among conservative elites and a consolidating oligarchy, so the coup may have "served 'as a catalyst' in an already polarized political environment" (Coatsworth, 2005, p. xiv).
3 The CEH (1999) describes this divergent "carrot and stick" approach, though scholars have described "model villages" as prison camps rather than genuine efforts to reintegrate displaced populations. See M. Mack, 2011; Manz, 1988.
4 See Bourgois (2001) and Scheper-Hughes & Bourgois (2004) for theories of structural, symbolic, and physical violence as normative and reproductive.
5 During my interviews with teachers, only one mentioned this day as a monthly (not weekly) requirement from the Ministry of Education.
6 See Sanford (2008) for further discussion.

Chapter 3   International Academy

1 For example, see Azpuru (2011) and Azpuru & Zachmeister (2015).
2 KONY 2012 began as an Internet video campaign produced by the nonprofit group Invisible Children. The video raised global awareness of war criminal Joseph Kony and the extreme violence carried out by members of the Lord's Resistance Army.
3 Following the war, Ríos Montt and his political party (Frente Republicano Guatemalteco [FRG; Guatemalan Republican Front]) remained powerful fixtures in Guatemalan politics. Ríos Montt served in Congress for nearly a decade, a position that granted him immunity from his crimes. Since the recent end of his term, he has been indicted for genocide, tried, and found guilty. At the time of this fieldwork, Ríos Montt was indicted on charges of genocide, but had not yet stood trial. Most of the students at International Academy knew very little about the case, which was making international headlines. Several students hypothesized that he was on trial for economic misdoings.
4 *Shumo* is a racialized term referring to the "stigmatized plebeian mongrel" (González Ponciano, 2013, p. 312). González Ponciano interprets anti-*shumo* discourse as a reaction against the "social climbing and 'new money' ... [of] those who attempt to leave their assigned slot in local and global hierarchies" (p. 310).
5 See Novelli (2011) on the multiple interpretations of peace education. Although transformative liberation is a form of peace education, pacification is as well. Similarly, see B. Levinson (2011) on ways in which citizenship education wavers between fostering critical agents and socializing passive subjects of the state.

6 Swartz et al. (2012) describe the "quiet violence of dreams" as a "double-edged sword, of high aspiration coupled with slim chances of success" (p. 32).

Chapter 4   Paulo Freire Institute

1 At the close of the academic year several students had not received satisfactory grades to graduate from Paulo Freire Institute and were repeating their senior year. In all, nearly one quarter of the class that initially signed up for the USAC entrance exam ultimately did not pass and was ineligible to enroll. With no opportunity to continue their studies, they instead pursued (mostly retail) jobs in the capital and plan to delay college.

Chapter 5   Sun and Moon

1 In an effort to foreground the verisimilitude of youth discourse and the analytic import of participants' chosen terms for self-presentation, I have preserved a number of Spanish words and phrases in the text. In particular, young people distinguished between goals such as *salir* (to exit, leave, get out of), *superar* (to overcome an obstacle), and *superarse* (to better oneself). *Salir* often referred to escaping poverty or getting ahead as an individual without shifting the status quo. In contrast, *superar* and *superarse* (notably, *superarnos*, to better ourselves) often conveyed collective and transformative goals in the interest of contributing to the common good.

2 In general, youth found violent acts more justifiable when they served to help or protect families.

3 Guatemalan youth are "more than 10 percentage points below [the] Latin American ICCS average" for this item (Schultz et al., 2011, p. 66).

4 César admitted to assigning the project partly for my benefit, though he reasoned that it would be a valuable cultural exercise for his students.

5 See Jackson (1998) on subjectivities shaped around concurrent dimensions of past and present, material and spiritual, worlds. María Carmen has the linguistic capacity to conjugate the past tense.

6 In 2011 the Ministry of Agriculture estimated close to 1,400 land disputes. See Isaacs (2010a).

7 Parastate agents refer to actors or networks acting alongside or in cooperation with the state. See Adams (2011) and Peacock & Beltrán (2003).

8 See Jelin (2003) for further discussion of passivity as implied in human rights discourse.

Chapter 6   Tzolok Ochoch

1   The Q'eqchi' pseudonym "Tzolok Ochoch" translates to "House of Learning."
2   *Nahuals* are animal-like spirits associated with the Maya calendar.
3   These rhetorical actions evoke elements of testimonial narrative (see Beverley, 2004), as well as the discourse of storytelling in community organizing (see Ganz, 2009; see also Jackson, 2006).
4   See O'Connor & Portenier (2007) and Sanford (2008) for further discussion.
5   See Wilson (1995) for more on Q'eqchi' beliefs about *tzuultaq'a'*, mountain spirits of those who suffered death, displacement, and *susto* (fright) during the war.
6   A *seminario* is a course with a service education component.
7   See Apple (1995) and Gramsci (1971) on the distinction between schooling and educating and on schooling's role in maintaining the status quo.

Chapter 8   The Hopes and Risks of Waiting

1   After one semester of college abroad, Alejandro encountered a number of bureaucratic challenges with his student visa. He and his family believe that Anastela and Rodolfo's activism against international mining companies effectively compromised his ability to study abroad. The risks of involvement, in this sense, transcended Guatemala's borders.
2   B. Levinson (2007) describes civic education teachers in Mexico who recognized similar tensions between a history of authoritarian governance and the tradition of authoritarian pedagogy. Based on the International Association for the Evaluation of Educational Achievement's cross-national civic education studies, Torney-Purta (2002) has found that open classroom climates, which promote respect, dialogue, and shared problem solving, are positively linked to civic learning outcomes.

References

Abu El-Haj, T. (2007). "I was born here but my home it's not here": Educating for democratic citizenship in an era of transnational migration and global conflict. *Harvard Educational Review, 77*(3), 285–316.

Abu El-Haj, T. (2015). *Unsettled belonging: Educating Palestinian American youth after 9/11.* Chicago, IL: University of Chicago Press.

Adams, T. M. (2011). *Chronic violence and its reproduction: Perverse trends in social relations, citizenship, and democracy in Latin America.* Washington, DC: Woodrow Wilson International Center for Scholars.

Agamben, G. (1998). *Homo sacer: Sovereign power and bare life.* Stanford, CA: Stanford University Press.

Agüero, F. (2004). Authoritarian legacies: The military's role. In K. Hite & P. Cesarini (Eds.), *Authoritarian legacies and democracy in Latin America and Southern Europe* (pp. 233–262). Notre Dame, IN: University of Notre Dame Press.

Ahonen, S. (2005). Historical consciousness: A viable paradigm for history education? *Journal of Curriculum Studies, 37*(6), 697–707.

Alston, P. (2007) *Civil and political rights, including the questions of disappearances and summary executions* (Report of the Special Rapporteur on extrajudicial, summary, or arbitrary executions, Mission to Guatemala, August 2006). New York, NY: Human Rights Council, United Nations.

Anderson, B. (1983). *Imagined communities: Reflections on the origin and spread of nationalism.* London, UK: Verso.

Angvik, M., & von Borries, B. (1997). *Youth and history: A comparative European survey on historical consciousness and political attitudes among adolescents.* Hamburg, Germany: Körber-Stiftung.

Appadurai, A. (2007). Hope and democracy. *Public Culture, 19*(1), 29–34.

Apple, M. W. (1995). *Education and power.* New York, NY: Routledge.

Auyero, J. (2011). Patients of the state: An ethnographic account of poor people's waiting. *Latin American Research Review, 46*(1), 5–29.

Auyero, J. (2012). *Patients of the state: The politics of waiting in Argentina.* Durham, NC: Duke University Press.

Auyero, J. (2013). Children at toxic risk. In M. Hashemi & M. Sánchez-Jankowski (Eds.), *Children in crisis: Ethnographic studies in international contexts* (pp. 82–99). New York, NY: Routledge.

Azpuru, D. (2011). *Political culture of democracy in Guatemala, 2010: Democratic consolidation in the Americas in hard times.* Washington, DC: United States Agency for International Development.

Azpuru, D., and Zachmeister, E. J. (2015). *Cultura política de la democracia en Guatemala y en las Américas, 2014: Gobernabilidad democrática a través de 10 años del Barómetro de las Américas.* Washington, DC: United States Agency for International Development.

Bacigalupo, A. M. (2016). *Thunder shaman: Making history with Mapuche spirits in Chile and Patagonia.* Austin, TX: University of Texas Press.

Barakat, B., Zuki, K., & Paulson, J. (2008). *Desk study: Education and fragility.* Retrieved from http://toolkit.ineesite.org/toolkit/INEEcms/uploads/1150/Desk_Study_Education_and_Fragility.pdf.

Barkan, E. (2009). Historians and historical reconciliation. *American Historical Review, 114*(4), 899–913.

Bartlett, L., & Vavrus, F. (2014). Transversing the vertical case study: A methodological approach to studies of educational policy as practice. *Anthropology and Education Quarterly, 45*(2), 131–147.

Barton, K. C., & Levstik, L. S. (2004). *Teaching history for the common good.* Mahwah, NJ: Erlbaum.

Barton, K. C., & McCully, A. (2010). "You can form your own point of view": Internally persuasive discourse in Northern Ireland students' encounters with history. *Teachers College Record, 112*(1), 142–181.

Bashir, B. (2008). Accommodating historically oppressed social groups: Deliberative democracy and the politics of reconciliation. In W. Kymlicka & B. Bashir (Eds.), *The politics of reconciliation in multicultural societies* (pp. 48–69). Oxford, UK: Oxford University Press.

Bastos, S. (2012). Multicultural projects in Guatemala: Identity tensions and everyday ideologies. *Latin American and Caribbean Ethnic Studies, 7*(2), 155–172.

Bellino, M. J. (2014a). Educating for human rights consciousness. *Listening: A Journal of Communication Ethics, Religion, and Culture.* Special Issue, *The social construction of human rights,* Fall, 136–157.

Bellino, M. J. (2014b). Whose past, whose present? Historical memory among the "postwar" generation in Guatemala. In J. H. Williams (Ed.), *(Re)constructing memory: School textbooks and the imagination of the nation* (pp. 131–152). Rotterdam, Netherlands: Sense.

Bellino, M. J. (2015a). Civic engagement in extreme times: The remaking of justice among Guatemala's "postwar" generation. *Education, Citizenship, and Social Justice 10*(2), 118–132.

Bellino, M. J. (2015b). The risks we are willing to take: Youth civic development in "postwar" Guatemala. *Harvard Educational Review, 85*(4), 537–561.

Bellino, M. J. (2016). So that we do not fall again: History education and citizenship in "postwar" Guatemala. *Comparative Education Review, 60*(1), 58–79.

Benson, P., Thomas, K., & Fischer, E. F. (2011). Guatemala's new violence as structural violence: Notes from the Highlands. In K. Lewis O'Neill & K. Thomas (Eds.), *Securing the city: Neoliberalism, space, and insecurity in postwar Guatemala* (pp. 127–146). Durham, NC: Duke University Press.

Beverley, J. (2004). *Testimonio: On the politics of truth.* Minneapolis, MN: University of Minnesota Press.

Bocarejo, D. (2013, February). *Longing for the state: Moral economy, legal subjects, and the war on drugs*. Paper presented at David Rockefeller Center for Latin American Studies, Harvard University, Cambridge, MA.

Boix-Mansilla, V. (2000). Historical understanding: Beyond the past and into the present. In P. N. Stearns, P. Seixas, & S. Wineburg (Eds.), *Knowing, teaching, and learning history: National and international perspectives* (pp. 390–418). New York, NY: New York University Press.

Booth, W. J. (1999). Communities of memory: On identity, memory and debt. *American Political Science Review, 93*(2), 249–263.

Booth, W. J. (2006). *Communities of memory: On witness, identity, and justice*. Ithaca, NY: Cornell University Press.

Booth, W. J. (2009). Kashmir Road: Reflections on memory and violence. *Millennium: Journal of International Studies, 38*(2), 361–377.

Bourdieu, P., & Passerson, J. C. (1990). *Reproduction in education, society, and culture* (2nd ed.). London, UK: Sage.

Bourgois, P. (2001). The power of violence in war and peace: Post–Cold War lessons from El Salvador. *Ethnography, 2*(1), 5–34.

Buckland, P. (2005). *Reshaping the future: Education and post-conflict reconstruction*. Washington, DC: World Bank.

Burde, D. (2014). *Schools for conflict or for peace in Afghanistan*. New York, NY: Columbia University Press.

Burrell, J. L. (2009). Intergenerational conflict in the postwar era. In W. E. Little & T. J. Smith (Eds.), *Mayas in postwar Guatemala: Harvest of violence revisited* (pp. 96–109). Tuscaloosa, AL: University of Alabama Press.

Burrell, J. L. (2013). *Maya after war: Conflict, power, and politics in Guatemala*. Austin, TX: University of Texas Press.

Bush, K. D., & Saltarelli, D. (2000). *The two faces of education in ethnic conflict: Towards a peacebuilding education for children*. Florence, Italy: Innocenti Research Centre, United Nations Children's Fund.

Caldeira, T.P.R., & Holston, J. (1996). Democracy and violence in Brazil. *Society for Comparative Study of Society and History, 40*(4), 691–729.

Carretero, M. (2011). *Constructing patriotism: Teaching history and memories in global worlds*. Charlotte, NC: Information Age.

Carretero, M., & Bermudez, A. (2012). Constructing histories. In J. Valsiner (Ed.), *Oxford handbook of culture and psychology* (pp. 625–646). Oxford, UK: Oxford University Press.

Cesarini, P., & Hite, K. (2004). Introducing the concept of authoritarian legacies. In K. Hite & P. Cesarini (Eds.), *Authoritarian legacies and democracy in Latin America and Southern Europe* (pp. 1–24). Notre Dame, IN: University of Notre Dame Press.

Coatsworth, J. H. (2005). Introduction. In S. Schlesinger & S. Kinzer (Eds.), *Bitter fruit: The story of the American coup in Guatemala* (2nd ed., pp. ix–xix). Cambridge, MA: David Rockefeller Center for Latin American Studies, Harvard University.

Cohen, S. (2001). *States of denial: Knowing about atrocities and suffering*. Malden, MA: Blackwell.

Cole, E. (2007a). Introduction: Reconciliation and history education. In E. Cole (Ed.), *Teaching the violent past: History education and reconciliation* (pp. 1–28). Lanham, MD: Rowman & Littlefield.

Cole, E. (2007b). Transitional justice and the reform of history education. *International Journal of Transitional Justice, 1*, 115–137.

Cole, E., & Murphy, K. (2009). History education reform, transitional justice, and the transformation of identities. *International Center for Transitional Justice*, 1–4.

Cole, J. (2005). The Jaombilo of Tamatave (Madagascar), 1992–2004: Reflections on youth and globalization. *Journal of Social History 38*(4), 891–914.

Cole, J., & Durham, D. (2008). Introduction: Globalization and the temporality of children and youth In J. Cole & D. Durham (Eds.), *Figuring the future: Globalization and the temporalities of children and youth* (pp. 3–23). Santa Fe, NM: School for Advanced Research Press.

Comisión para el Esclarecimiento Histórico (CEH). (1999). *Guatemala: Memoria del silencio* [Guatemala: Memory of silence]. Guatemala City, Guatemala: Comisión para el Esclarecimiento Histórico.

Connerton, P. (1989). *How societies remember*. Cambridge, UK: Cambridge University Press.

Cortina, R. (2014). Introduction. In R. Cortina (Ed.), *The education of indigenous citizens in Latin America* (pp. 1–18). Bristol, UK: Multilingual Matters.

Cruz, J. M. (2008). The impact of violent crime on the political culture of Latin America: The special case of Central America. In M. A. Selgison (Ed.), *Challenges to democracy in Latin America and the Caribbean: Evidence from the Americas Barometer, 2006–2007* (pp. 219–249). Nashville, TN: Vanderbilt University Press.

Cruz, J. M. (2011) Criminal violence and democratization in Central America: The survival of the violent state. *Latin American Politics and Society, 53*(4), 1–33.

Cullather, N. (1999). *Secret history: The CIA's classified account of its operations in Guatemala, 1952–1954*. Stanford, CA: Stanford University Press.

Davies, L. (2004a). Building a civic culture post-conflict. *London Review of Education, 2*(3), 229–244.

Davies, L. (2004b). *Education and conflict: Complexity and chaos*. London, UK: Routledge.

Davies, L. (2007). Can education interrupt fragility? Toward the resilient citizen and the adaptable state. In K. Mundy & S. Dryden-Peterson (Eds.), *Educating children in conflict zones: Research, policy, and practice for systemic change* (pp. 33–48). New York, NY: Teachers College Press.

Davies, L. (In press a). Justice-sensitive education: The implications of transitional justice mechanisms for teaching and learning. *Comparative Education*.

Davies, L. (In press b). *Post-conflict education reconstruction and transitional justice*. Internal study. New York, NY: International Center for Transitional Justice.

De Greiff, P. (2009). Articulating the links between transitional justice and development: Justice and social integration. In P. de Greiff & R. Duthie (Eds.), *Transitional justice and development: Making connections* (pp. 28–75). New York, NY: Social Science Research Council.

Doyle, K. (2012). *The pursuit of justice in Guatemala* (Electronic Briefing Book 373). Washington, DC: George Washington University/National Security Archive.

Dryden-Peterson, S., Bellino, M. J., & Chopra, V. (2015). Conflict: Education and youth. In J. D. Wright (Ed.), *International encyclopedia of the social and behavioral sciences* (2nd ed., Vol. 4, pp. 632–638). Oxford, UK: Elsevier.

Dyrness, A. (2012). Contra viento y marea (Against wind and tide): Building civic identity among children of emigration in El Salvador. *Anthropology & Education Quarterly, 43*(1), 41–60.

Edberg, M., & Bourgois, M. P. (2013). Street markets, adolescent identity and violence: A generative dynamic. In R. Rosenfeld, M. Edberg, X. Fang, & C. Florence (Eds.), *Economics and youth violence: Crime, disadvantage, and community* (pp. 181–206). New York, NY: New York University Press.

Edwards, D., & Potter, J. (1992). *Discursive psychology*. London, UK: Sage.

Fabian, J. (1983). *Time and the other: How anthropology makes its object.* New York, NY: Columbia University Press.

Fine, M., & Weis, L. (2010). Writing the "wrongs" of fieldwork: Confronting our own research/writing dilemmas in urban ethnographies. In W. Luttrell (Ed.), *Qualitative educational research: Readings in reflexive methodology and transformative practice* (pp. 448–466). New York, NY: Routledge.

Flanagan, C. (2004). Volunteerism, leadership, political socialization, and civic engagement. In R. M. Lerner & L. Steinberg (Eds.), *Handbook of adolescent psychology* (pp. 721–746). New York, NY: John Wiley and Sons.

Flanagan, C., & Levine, P. (2010). Civic engagement and the transition to adulthood. *Future of Children, 20*(1), 159–179.

Flanagan, C., Stoppa, T., Syvertsen, A., & Stout, M. (2010). Schools and social trust. In L. Sherrod, J. Torney-Purta, & C. Flanagan (Eds.), *Handbook of research on civic engagement in youth* (pp. 307–329). Hoboken, NJ: John Wiley and Sons.

Flanagan, C., & Stout, M. (2010). Developmental patterns of social trust between early and late adolescence: Age and school climate effects. *Journal of Research on Adolescence, 20*(3), 748–773.

Fletcher, L. E., Weinstein, H. W., & Rowen, J. (2009). Context, timing and the dynamics of transitional justice: A historical perspective. *Human Rights Quarterly, 31*(1), 163–220.

Freedman, S. W., Weinstein, H., Murphy, K., & Longman, T. (2008). Teaching history after identity-based conflicts: The Rwanda experience. *Comparative Education Review, 52*(4), 663–690.

Funkenstein, A. (1993). *Perceptions of Jewish history.* Berkeley, CA: University of California Press.

Ganz, M. (2009). Why stories matter: The art and craft of social change. *Sojourners, 38*(3), 16–21.

Giracca, A. (2009, March 4). ¿Merecen los jóvenes de nuestro país saber sobre el pasado? [Do our country's youth deserve to know about the past?]. *El Periódico* (Guatemala.)

Goldman, F. (2007). *The art of political murder: Who killed the bishop?* New York, NY: Grove.

González Ponciano, J. R. (2013). The *shumo* challenge: White class privilege and the post-race, post-genocide alliances of cosmopolitanism from below. In C. McAllister & D. M. Nelson (Eds.), *War by other means: Aftermath in post-genocide Guatemala* (pp. 307–329). Durham, NC: Duke University Press.

Gramsci, A. (1971). *Selections from the prison notebooks of Antonio Gramsci.* New York, NY: International.

Grandin, G. (2000). *The blood of Guatemala: A history of race and nation.* Durham, NC: Duke University Press.

Grandin, G. (2004). *The last colonial massacre: Latin America in the Cold War.* Chicago, IL: University of Chicago Press.

Grandin, G. (2005). The instruction of great catastrophe: Truth commissions, national history, and state formation in Argentina, Chile, and Guatemala. *American Historical Review, 110*(1), 46–67.

Grandin, G., Levenson, D. T., & Oglesby, E. (2011a). Intent to destroy. In G. Grandin, D. T. Levenson, & E. Oglesby (Eds.), *The Guatemala reader* (pp. 361–365). Durham, NC: Duke University Press.

Grandin, G., Levenson, D. T., & Oglesby, E. (2011b). An unsettled peace. In In G. Grandin, D. T. Levenson, & E. Oglesby (Eds.), *The Guatemala reader* (pp. 441–444). Durham, NC: Duke University Press.

Guatemalan Army High Command. (2011). Inverting Clausewitz. In G. Grandin, D. T. Levenson, & E. Oglesby (Eds.), *The Guatemala reader* (pp. 417–420). Durham, NC: Duke University Press.

Gupta, A., & Ferguson, J. (1992). Beyond "culture": Space, identity, and the politics of difference. *Cultural Anthropology, 7*(1), 6–23.

Hale, C. R. (2002). Does multiculturalism menace? Governance, cultural rights and the politics of identity in Guatemala. *Journal of Latin American Studies, 34*(3), 485–524.

Heater, D. (2004). *A history of education for citizenship*. London, UK: Routledge Falmer.

Heymann, P. B. (2012). Organized crime in Latin America. *ReVista, 11*(2), 2–4.

Hirsch, M. (2008). The generation of postmemory. *Poetics Today, 29*(1), 103–128.

Holston, J. (2008). *Insurgent citizenship: Disjunctions of democracy and modernity in Brazil*. Princeton, NJ: Princeton University Press.

Holston, J., & Caldeira, T.P.R. (1998). Democracy, law, and violence: Disjunctions of Brazilian citizenship. In F. Agüero & J. Stark (Eds.), *Fault lines of democracy in post-transition Latin America* (pp. 263–296). Miami, FL: North-South Center.

Honwana, A. (2013). *The time of youth: Work, social change, and politics in Africa*. Boulder, CO: Kumarian.

Husseyn, A. (2005). Resistance to memory: The uses and abuses of public forgetting. In M. Pensky (Ed.), *Globalizing critical theory* (pp. 165–184). Lanham, MD: Rowman & Littlefield.

Ibarra, C. F. (2011). *El recurso del miedo: Estado y terror en Guatemala* [The recourse of fear: State and terror in Guatemala] (2nd ed.). Guatemala City, Guatemala: FyG.

Instituto Interamericano de Derechos Humanos [Inter-American Institute of Human Rights]. (2007). *Inter-American report on human rights education* (No. 4). San José, Costa Rica: Instituto Interamericano de Derechos Humanos.

Inter-American Dialogue and Organization of American States. (2007). *National dialogue on democracy: Ten years after the Agreement on a Firm and Lasting Peace*. Washington, DC: Inter-American Dialogue.

Isaacs, A. (2010a). Guatemala. In J. Dizard (Ed.), *Countries at the crossroads: A Survey of democratic governance* (pp. 211–232). New York, NY: Freedom House/Rowman & Littlefield.

Isaacs, A. (2010b). Guatemala on the brink. *Journal of Democracy, 21*(2), 108–122.

Jackson, M. (1998). *Minima ethnographica: Intersubjectivity and the anthropological project*. Chicago, IL: University of Chicago Press.

Jackson, M. (2006). *The politics of storytelling: Violence, transgression, and intersubjectivity*. Copenhagen, Denmark: Museum Tusculanum.

Jackson, M. (2007). *Excursions*. Durham, NC: Duke University Press.

Jansen, J. D. (2009). *Knowledge in the blood: Confronting race and the apartheid past*. Stanford, CA: Stanford University Press.

Jelin, E. (2003). *State repression and the labors of memory*. Minneapolis, MN: University of Minnesota Press.

Jiménez Estrada, V. M. (2012). Education in Ixim Ulew (Guatemala): Maya indigenous knowledge and building new citizens. *Canadian Journal of Native Education, 35*(1), 61–78.

Kaiser, S. (2005). *Postmemories of terror: A new generation copes with the legacy of the "dirty war."* New York, NY: Palgrave.

Kassimir, R., & Flanagan, C. (2010). Youth civic engagement in the developing world: Challenges and opportunities. In L. R. Sherrod, J. Torney-Purta, and C. A. Flanagan (Eds.), *Handbook of research on civic engagement in youth* (pp. 91–113). Hoboken, NJ: John Wiley and Sons.

Katz, C. (2004). *Growing up global: Economic restructuring and children's everyday lives*. Minneapolis, MN: University of Minnesota Press.

King, E. (2014). *From classrooms to conflict in Rwanda*. New York, NY: Cambridge University Press.

Lawrence-Lightfoot, S., & Hoffman Davis, J. (Eds.). (1997). *The art and science of portraiture*. San Francisco, CA: Jossey-Bass.

Lederach, J. P. (2005). *The moral imagination: The art and soul of building peace*. Oxford, UK: Oxford University Press.

Levenson, D. T. (2013a). *Adiós Niño: The gangs of Guatemala City and the politics of death*. Durham, NC: Duke University Press.

Levenson, D. T. (2013b). What happened to the revolution? Guatemala City's *maras* from life to death. In C. McAllister & D. M. Nelson (Eds.), *War by other means: Aftermath in post-genocide Guatemala* (pp. 195–217). Durham, NC: Duke University Press.

Levinson, B.A.U. (2007). Forming and implementing a new secondary civic education program in Mexico: Toward a democratic citizen without adjectives. In E. D. Stevick & B.A.U. Levinson (Eds.), *Reimagining civic education: How diverse societies form democratic citizens* (pp. 245–270). Lanham, MD: Rowman & Littlefield.

Levinson, B.A.U. (2011). Toward an anthropology of (democratic) citizenship education. In B.A.U. Levinson & M. Pollock (Eds.), *A companion to the anthropology of education* (pp. 279–298). Malden, MA: Wiley-Blackwell.

Levinson, M. (2012). *No citizen left behind*. Cambridge, MA: Harvard University Press.

López, J. (2010). *Guatemala's crossroads: Democratization of violence and second chances* (Working paper series on organized crime in Central America). Washington, DC: Woodrow Wilson Center for International Scholars.

López, L. E. (2014). Indigenous bilingual education in Latin America: Widening gaps between policy and practice. In R. Cortina (Ed.), *The education of indigenous citizens in Latin America* (pp. 19–49). Bristol, UK: Multilingual Matters.

Mack, H. (2011). What is reconciliation? (E. Oglesby, Trans.). In G. Grandin, D. T. Levenson, & E. Oglesby (Eds.), *The Guatemala reader* (pp. 450–453). Durham, NC: Duke University Press.

Mack, M. (2011). Assistance and control. In G. Grandin, D. T. Levenson, & E. Oglesby (Eds.), *The Guatemala reader* (pp. 421–426). Durham, NC: Duke University Press.

Malkin, E. (2015, September 8). Trial ordered for ex-leader of Guatemala. *New York Times*. Retrieved from http://www.nytimes.com/2015/09/09/world/americas/trial-ordered-for-ex-leader-of-guatemala.html?ref=topics.

Mandoki, L. (Director). (2004). *Voces inocentes* [Innocent voices] [Motion picture]. Burbank, CA. Lawrence Bender Productions.

Manz, B. (1988). *Refugees of a hidden war: The aftermath of counterinsurgency in Guatemala*. Albany: State University of New York Press.

Manz, B. (2004). *Paradise in ashes: A Guatemalan journey of courage, terror, and hope*. Berkeley, CA: University of California Press.

Manz, B. (2008). The continuum of violence in post-war Guatemala. *Social Analysis, 52*(2), 151–164.

Marcus, G. E. (1998). *Ethnography through thick and thin*. Princeton, NJ: Princeton University Press.

Marcus, G. E. (1999). What is at stake—and is not—in the idea and practice of multi-sited ethnography. *Canberra Anthropology, 22*(2), 6–14.

Maxwell, J. M. (2009). Bilingual bicultural education: Best intentions across a cultural divide. In W. E. Little & T. J. Smith (Eds.), *Mayas in postwar Guatemala: Harvest of violence revisited* (pp. 84–95), Tuscaloosa, AL: University of Alabama Press.

McCully, A. (2012). History teaching, conflict, and the legacy of the past. *Education, Citizenship, and Social Justice, 7*(2), 145–159. doi:10.1177/1746197912440854.

Menchú, R., & Burgos-Debray, E. (1984). *I, Rigoberta Menchú: An Indian Woman in Guatemala*. London, UK: Verso.

Miller-Grandvaux, Y. (2009). Education and fragility: A new framework. *Journal of Education for International Development, 4*(1), 1–14.

Ministry of Education. (2001). *Estudios sociales* [Social studies]. Guatemala City, Guatemala: Ministry of Education.

Ministry of Education. (2003). *Modulos de aprendizaje* [Models of learning] (Vols. 1–2). Guatemala City, Guatemala: Ministry of Education.

Ministry of Education. (2010). *Interculturalidad en la reforma educativa* [Interculturalism in educational reform]. Guatemala City, Guatemala: Ministry of Education.

Minow, M. (1998). *Between vengeance and forgiveness: Facing history after genocide and mass violence*. Boston, MA: Beacon.

Monroe, K. R. (2014). *A darkling plain: Stories of conflict and humanity during war*. Cambridge, UK: Cambridge University Press.

Moodie, E. (2010). *El Salvador in the aftermath of peace: Crime, uncertainty, and the transition to democracy*. Philadelphia, PA: University of Pennsylvania Press.

Murphy, K. (2013, June 5). *Facing history: Education's role in transitional justice*. USAID Impact blog. Retrieved from http://blog.usaid.gov/2013/06/educations-role-in-transitional-justice/.

Murphy, K. (In press). Education reform through a transitional justice lens: The ambivalent transitions of Bosnia and Northern Ireland. In C. Ramirez-Barat & R. Duthrie (Eds.), *Transitional justice and education: Learning peace* (pp. 65–100). New York, NY: Social Science Research Council.

Murphy, K., & Gallagher, T. (2009). Reconstruction after violence: How teachers and schools can deal with the legacy of the past. *Perspectives in Education: The Pedagogical Transition in Post-Conflict Societies, 27*(2), 158–168.

Murphy, K., Sleeper, M., & Stern Strom, M. (2011). Facing history and ourselves in post-conflict societies. *International Schools Journal, 30*(2), 65–72.

Nash, G. B., Crabtree, C., & Dunn, R. (2000). *History on trial: Culture wars and the teaching of the past*. New York, NY: First Vintage Books.

Nelson, D. M. (1999). *A finger in the wound: Body politics in Quincentennial Guatemala*. Berkeley, CA: University of California Press.

Nordstrom, C. (2004) *Shadows of war: Violence, power, and international profiteering in the twenty-first century*. Berkeley, CA: University of California Press.

Novelli, M. (2011, October). *The role of education in peacebuilding: Case study; Sierra Leone*. New York, NY: United Nations Children's Fund.

O'Connor, K. (Producer), & Portenier, G. (Director). (2007). *Killer's paradise* [Motion picture]. London, UK: BBC.

O'Donnell, G. (1993). On the state, democratization, and some conceptual problems (a Latin American view with glances at some post-Communist countries). Working Paper 192. Notre Dame, IN: Helen Kellogg Institute for International Studies.

Oficina de Derechos Humanos del Arzobispado de Guatemala (ODHAG). (2003). *Eduquémonos para el nunca más: Propuesta pedagógica* [Educating for the never again: Educational proposal]. Guatemala City, Guatemala: ODHAG.

Oglesby, E. (2007a). Educating citizens in postwar Guatemala: Historical memory, genocide, and the culture of peace. *Radical History Review, 97*, 77–98.

Oglesby, E. (2007b). Historical memory and the limits of peace education: Examining Guatemala's memory of silence and the politics of curriculum design. In E. Cole (Ed.), *Teaching the violent past: History education and reconciliation* (pp. 175–202). Lanham, MD: Rowman & Littlefield.

Oglesby, E., & Ross, A. (2009), Guatemala's genocide determination and the spatial politics of justice. *Space and Polity, 13*(1), 21–39.

Palma Murga, G. (2011). Promised the Earth. In G. Grandin, D. T. Levenson, & E. Oglesby (Eds.), *The Guatemala reader* (pp. 454–460). Durham, NC: Duke University Press.

Paulson, J. (2009). *(Re)creating education in postconflict contexts: Transitional justice, education, and human development.* New York, NY: International Center for Transitional Justice.

Paulson, J. (2015). "Whether and how?" History education about recent and ongoing conflict: A review of research. *Journal on Education in Emergencies, 1*(1), 14–47.

Peace Accords. (1996). *Acuerdo de paz firme y duradera* [Agreement on a firm and lasting peace]. Retrieved from http://peacemaker.un.org/sites/peacemaker.un.org/files/GT_961229_AgreementOnFirmAndLastingPeace%28esp%29.pdf.

Peacock, S. C., & Beltrán, A. (2003, September). *Hidden powers in post-conflict Guatemala: Illegal armed groups and the forces behind them.* Washington, DC: Washington Office on Latin America.

Poppema, M. (2009). Guatemala, the Peace Accords, and education: A post-conflict struggle for equal opportunities, cultural recognition, and participation in education. *Globalisation, Societies, and Education, 7*(4), 383–408.

Recovery of Historical Memory Project (REMHI). (1999). *Guatemala never again! The official report of the human rights office.* Maryknoll, NY: Orbis Books.

Reimers, F., & Cardenas, S. (2010). Youth civic engagement in Mexico. In L. R. Sherrod, J. Torney-Purta, & C. A. Flanagan (Eds.), *Handbook of research on civic engagement in youth* (pp. 139–160). Hoboken, NJ: Wiley and Sons.

Ríos-Rojas, A. (2011). Beyond delinquent citizenships: Immigrant youth's (re)visions of citizenship and belonging in a globalized world. *Harvard Educational Review, 81*(1), 64–94.

Rosaldo, R. (1999). Cultural citizenship, inequality, and multiculturalism. In R. Torres, L. Miron, & J. Inda (Eds.), *Race, identity and citizenship: A reader* (pp. 253–261), Malden, MA: Blackwell.

Rothenberg, D. (2012a). Afterword, "No room for despair": The impact of the Guatemalan truth commission. In Daniel Rothenberg (Ed.), *Memory of silence: The Guatemalan truth commission report* (pp. 217–226). New York, NY: Palgrave Macmillan.

Rothenberg, D. (2012b). Introduction, Facing la violencia: The importance of the Guatemalan truth commission. In Daniel Rothenberg (Ed.), *Memory of silence: The Guatemalan truth commission report* (pp. xv–xli). New York, NY: Palgrave Macmillan.

Rubin, B. C. (2007). "There's still not justice": Youth civic identity development amid distinct school and community contexts. *Teachers College Record, 109*(2), 449–481.

Rubin, B. C. (2012). *Making citizens: Transforming civic learning for diverse social studies classrooms.* New York, NY: Routledge.

Rubin, B. C. (2016a). They don't tell it: Indigenous social studies teachers transforming curricula in postconflict Guatemala. *Journal of International Social Studies, 6*(1), 114–127.

Rubin, B. C. (2016b). We come to form ourselves bit by bit: Educating for citizenship in post-conflict Guatemala. *American Educational Research Journal, 53*(3), 639–672.

Ruiz Cabrera, M. C., Veliz Mayen, N. M., Polanco Estrada, J. P., Martínez Aniorte, J. C.,

Arreaga Alonzo, A. Z., Calvo Drago, J. R., . . . de Rosal, C. (2009). *Enlaces: Ciencias sociales [Links: Social Sciences]*. Guatemala City, Guatemala: Santillana.

Rüsen, J. (2004). Historical consciousness: Narrative structure, moral function, and ontogenetic development. In P. Seixas (Ed.), *Theorizing historical consciousness* (pp. 63–85). Toronto, Canada: University of Toronto Press.

Sandoval, M. (2011, January 16). Aquí hubo guerra? [There was war here?]. *El Periódico* (Guatemala).

Sandoval, M. A., & Ramírez, M. R. (2011). Long live the students! (D. T. Levenson, Trans.) In G. Grandin, D. T. Levenson, & E. Oglesby (Eds.), *The Guatemala reader* (pp. 251–255). Durham, NC: Duke University Press.

Sanford, V. (2003a). *Buried secrets: Truth and human rights in Guatemala*. New York, NY: Palgrave.

Sanford, V. (2003b). Learning to kill by proxy: Colombian paramilitaries and the legacy of Central American death squads, contras, and civil patrols. *Social Justice, 30*(3), 63–81.

Sanford, V. (2008). From genocide to feminicide: Impunity and human rights in twenty-first-century Guatemala. *Journal of Human Rights, 7*, 104–122.

Santamaría, G. (2012). Taking justice into their own hands: Insecurity and the lynching of criminals in Latin America. *ReVista, 11*(2), 43–45.

Scheper-Hughes, N., & Bourgois, P. (2004). Introduction: Making sense of violence. In N. Scheper-Hughes & P. Bourgois (Eds.), *Violence in war and peace: An anthology* (pp. 1–31). Malden, MA: Blackwell.

Schlesinger, S., & Kinzer, S. (2005). *Bitter fruit: The story of the American coup in Guatemala* (2nd ed.). Cambridge, MA: David Rockefeller Center for Latin American Studies, Harvard University.

Schultz, W., Ainley, J., Friedman, T., & Lietz, P. (2011). *ICCS* [International Civic and Citizenship Education Study] *2009 Latin American report: Civic knowledge and attitudes among lower-secondary students in six Latin American countries*. Amsterdam, Holland: International Association for the Evaluation of Educational Achievement.

Seixas, P. (2000). Schweigen! die Kinder! or, Does postmodern history have a place in the schools? In P. N. Stearns, P. Seixas, & S. Wineburg (Eds.), *Knowing, teaching, and learning history: National and international perspectives* (pp. 19–37). New York, NY: New York University Press.

Seixas, P. (2004). Introduction. In P. Seixas (Ed.), *Theorizing historical consciousness* (pp. 3–20). Toronto, Canada: University of Toronto Press.

Shaw, R. (2002). *Memories of the slave trade: Ritual and the historical imagination in Sierra Leone*. Chicago, IL: University of Chicago Press.

Sieder, R. (1999). Rethinking democratization and citizenship: Legal pluralism and institutional reform in Guatemala. *Citizenship Studies, 3*(1), 103–118.

Smith, T. J. (2009). Democracy is dissent: Political confrontations and indigenous mobilization in Sololá. In W. E. Little & T. J. Smith (Eds.), *Mayas in postwar Guatemala: Harvest of violence revisited* (pp. 16–29), Tuscaloosa, AL: University of Alabama Press.

Snodgrass Godoy, A. (2002). Lynchings and the democratization of terror in postwar Guatemala: Implications for human rights. *Human Rights Quarterly, 24*(3), 640–661.

Sommers, M. (2012). *Stuck: Rwandan youth and the struggle for adulthood*. Athens, GA: University of Georgia Press.

Stanley, E. (2001). Evaluating the Truth and Reconciliation Commission. *Journal of Modern African Studies, 39*, 525–546.

Stearns, P. N., Seixas, P., & Wineburg, S. (2000). Introduction. In P. N. Stearns, P. Seixas, &

S. Wineburg (Eds.), *Knowing, teaching, and learning history: National and international perspectives* (pp. 1–13). New York, NY: New York University Press.

Steiner-Khamsi, G. (2010). The politics and economics of comparison. *Comparative Education Review, 54*(3), 323–342.

Stoll, D. (1994). *Between two armies: In the Ixil towns of Guatemala*. New York, NY: Columbia University Press.

Stoller, P. (1989). *The taste of ethnographic things: The senses in anthropology*. Philadelphia, PA: University of Pennsylvania Press.

Stoller, P. (1995). *Embodying colonial memories: Spirit Possession, power, and the Hauka in West Africa*. New York, NY: Routledge.

Swartz, S., Hamilton Harding, J., & De Lannoy, A. (2012). Ikasi style and the quiet violence of dreams: A critique of youth belonging in post-Apartheid South Africa. *Comparative Education, 48*(1), 27–40.

Swift, A. (2003). *How to not be a hypocrite: School choice for the morally perplexed parent*. New York, NY: Routledge.

Tawil, S., & Harley, A. (2004). *Education, conflict, and social cohesion*. Geneva: United Nations Educational, Scientific, and Cultural Organization.

Taylor, C. (2013). *Seeds of freedom: Liberating education in Guatemala*. Boulder, CO: Paradigm.

Tedlock, B. (1982). *Time and the highland Maya*. Albuquerque, NM: University of New Mexico Press.

Theidon, K. (2013). *Intimate enemies: Violence and reconciliation in Peru*. Philadelphia, PA: University of Pennsylvania Press.

Torney-Purta, J. (2002). Patterns in the civic knowledge, engagement, and attitudes of European adolescents: The IEA civic education study. *European Journal of Education, 37*(2), 129–141.

Torres-Rivas, E. (1999). Epilogue: Notes on terror, violence, fear, and democracy. In K. Koonings & D. Krujit (Eds.), *Societies of fear: The legacy of civil war, violence, and terror in Latin America* (pp. 285–300). New York, NY: St. Martin's Press.

Turner, V. (1967). *The forest of symbols: Aspects of Ndembu ritual*. Ithaca, NY: Cornell University Press.

Unidad de Protección a Defensoras y Defensores de Derechos Humanos de Guatemala (UDEFEGUA). (2011). *Permitido denunciar*. Guatemala City, Guatemala: UDEFEGUA.

United Nations Development Programme (UNDP). (2012). *Guatemala: Un país de oportunidades para la juventud? Informe nacional de desarollo humano, 2011/2012* [Guatemala: A country with opportunities for youth? National human development report, 2011/2012]. Guatemala City, Guatemala: UNDP.

United Nations Office on Drugs and Crime (UNODC). (2010, February). *Crime and instability: Case studies of transnational threats*. Retrieved from http://www.unodc.org/documents/frontpage/Crime_and_instability_2010_final_low_res.pdf.

Urdal, H. (2012). *A clash of generations? Youth bulges and political violence*. New York, NY: United Nations Department of Economic and Social Affairs.

Vavrus, F., & Bartlett, L. (2006). Comparatively knowing: Making a case for the vertical case study. *Current Issues in Comparative Education, 8*(2), 95–103.

Weinstein, H., Freedman, S., & Hughson, H. (2007). Challenges facing education systems after identity-based conflicts. *Education, Citizenship, and Social Justice, 2*(1), 41–71.

Weld, K. A. (2012). Dignifying the guerrillero, not the assassin: Rewriting a history of criminal subversion in postwar Guatemala. *Radical History Review, 113*, 35–54.

Weld, K. A. (2014). *Paper cadavers: The archives of dictatorship in Guatemala.* Durham, NC: Duke University Press.

Weldon, G. (2010a). *A comparative study of the construction of memory and identity in the curriculum in societies emerging from conflict: Rwanda and South Africa.* Saarbrücken, Germany, Lambert Academic.

Weldon, G. (2010b). Post-conflict teacher development: Facing the past in South Africa. *Journal of Moral Education, 39*(3), 353–364.

Wertsch, J. V. (2000). Is it possible to teach beliefs, as well as knowledge about history? In P. N. Stearns, P. Seixas, & S. Wineburg (Eds.), *Knowing, teaching, and learning history: National and international perspectives* (pp. 38–50). New York, NY: New York University Press.

Wertsch, J. V. (2002). *Voices of collective remembering.* Cambridge, UK: Cambridge University Press.

Westheimer, J., & Kahne, J. (2004). What kind of citizen? The politics of educating for democracy. *American Educational Research Journal, 41*(2), 237–269.

Wilson, R. (1995). *Maya resurgence in Guatemala: Q'eqchi' experiences.* Norman, OK: University of Oklahoma Press.

Wineburg, S. (2001). *Historical thinking and other unnatural acts: Charting the future of teaching the past.* Philadelphia, PA: Temple University Press.

Winton, A. (2005). Youth, gangs, and violence: Analysing the social and spatial mobility of young people in Guatemala City. *Children's Geographies, 3*(2), 167–184.

Youniss, J., Bales, S., Christmas-Best, V., Diversi, M., McLaughlin, M., & Silbereisen, R. (2002). Youth civic engagement in the twenty-first century. *Journal of Research on Adolescence, 12*(1), 121–148.

Index

accountability, 6, 68–69, 78, 195, 213, 217, 222; for Conflicto Armado, 33, 36, 40, 78, 84, 132, 189; zero-accountability interpretations, 132, 189

agency, civic, 11, 21, 196–197, 216

Árbenz, Jacobo, 29, 93, 236n2

Arévalo, Juan José, 29

Argentina, 132–133

authoritarianism, 53, 193, 199–203; contrasted with democracy, 39, 53, 199, 201, 205; in education, 205, 221, 238n2; Guatemalan history of, 8, 12, 85, 199, 202–203, 205; legacy of, 8, 199, 202–203, 205; security and, 53

Auyero, Javier, 206

Barillas. *See* Santa Cruz Barillas

bilingual education, 34, 36, 106, 178, 180–181

Bourgois, Philippe, 203–204

"Las casas de cartón" (Cardboard houses), 158–159, 168

citizenship, 11, 188; classroom discussions of, 74–75; conflict aversion and, 41; indigenous people and, 121; memory and, 86; postwar transition and, 185–186; wait citizenship, 11–12, 21–22, 205–206, 211;

civic action/participation, 19, 41, 60, 79, 97, 119, 166, 180, 182, 196, 206–207; dangers of, 60, 79, 183, 207–209, 238n1; futility of, 207–208, 210, 213, 217, 219; of indigenous people, 227; popular struggle and, 186;

Ríos Montt trial and, 226–227; risks of, 207–215;

civic agency, 11, 21, 196–197, 216

civic development: historical injustice and, 188; of youth, 4, 11–12, 19, 21–22, 187–188, 223

civic efficacy, 16, 79, 228

civic engagement, 10–11, 120, 147, 181

civic responsibility, 17, 26, 143, 186

civil war, Guatemalan. *See* Conflicto Armado

Cohen, Stanley, 28, 166

Cole, Jennifer, 10

collective action, 21, 192, 199, 214, 217, 227; fears about, 5, 212; limits of, 77, 191, 197, 205; youth withdrawal from, 11–12, 57, 195

collective identity, 110, 164, 222

collective memory, 38

colonialism, 5, 29, 76, 94, 114, 194

Comalapa, 24–28

Comisión para el Esclarecimiento Histórico (CEH; Commission for Historical Clarification), 33–36, 39, 42, 67–68

community organizing, 120, 182

Conflicto Armado, 3, 29–31; accountability and, 33, 36, 40, 78, 84, 132, 189; contemporary violence and, 5–6, 44, 48, 94, 134, 154, 187, 190, 200; effect on contemporary youth, 153–154, 186–187; effect on education, 35, 200; films about, 139–141, 157–159; forgetting of, 51, 85–86,

About the Author

MICHELLE J. BELLINO is an assistant professor of educational studies in the School of Education at the University of Michigan in Ann Arbor, where she teaches courses on international education, ethnography, and conflict. Her research, which centers on youth citizenship, historical injustice, postconflict reconstruction, and educational reform, has been featured in *Harvard Educational Review*; *Education, Citizenship, and Social Justice*; and *Comparative Education Review*. She has been recognized as a Peace Scholar by the United States Institute of Peace, a Concha Delgado Gaitan Presidential Fellow by the Council of Anthropology and Education, and a National Academy of Education/Spencer Foundation Postdoctoral Fellow.

Available titles in the Rutgers Series in Childhood Studies

CPSIA information can be obtained
at www.ICGtesting.com
Printed in the USA
LVHW111026280121
677675LV00002B/7

9 780813 587998